DATE DUE FOR

05. FEB

The political economy of modern South Africa

WE DEMAND A LIVING WAGE, NOT LEFTOVERS. Viva Cosatu Viva

Cosatu Viva

WE SHALL FOREVER FIGHT CAPITALISM. WE SHALL FOREVER FIGHT SLAVERY. AWAY WITH DISCRIMINATION FORWARD WITH COSATU

LF STADLER

*The political economy of
modern South Africa*

The political economy of modern South Africa

ALF STADLER

David Philip: Cape Town & Johannesburg
Croom Helm: London

First published 1987 in paperback in southern Africa and Australasia by
David Philip, Publisher (Pty) Ltd, 217 Werdmuller Centre, Claremont 7700,
South Africa

Published 1987 in hardback in the United Kingdom by Croom Helm Ltd,
Provident House, Burrell Row, Beckenham, Kent BR3 1AT

ISBN 0-86486-071-4 (paperback, southern Africa)
ISBN 0-7099-2331-7 (hardback, United Kingdom)

British Library Cataloguing in Publication Data:

Stadler, Alf
  The political economy of modern South Africa.
  1. Apartheid—Economic aspects   2. South Africa—Economic
  conditions—1918–
  I. Title
  323.1'68   DT763
  ISBN 0-7099-2331-7

SECOND IMPRESSION 1989

1000876181

Printed and bound by Creda Press, Solan Road, Cape Town, South Africa

Contents

Acknowledgements

I incurred many debts in writing this book. They are acknowledged in the footnotes. The fact that so many of them refer to work done by colleagues of mine in the University of the Witwatersrand suggests the extraordinary advances which have been made in historical and social studies here during the last decade or so.

Four debts should be explicitly mentioned. One is to Charles van Onselen, whose scintillating work in the social history of the Witwatersrand is matched only by his extraordinary abilities as director of the African Studies Institute in this University. The second is to my departmental colleague Tom Lodge, on whose studies in the history of black politics I have heavily relied. Thirdly, I drew extensively on Douglas Hindson's doctoral thesis for much of the section on influx control. Fourthly, I owe a broad intellectual debt to Dr Phyllis Lewsen, honorary research associate in the Department of History.

Finally, I should like to thank four important people in my life, Jenny, Josie, Catherine and Jonathan, for their forbearance.

1 Revolution, reform and repression in the 1970s and 1980s: the quickening rhythm

I began writing this book in mid-1980, during a period of great political ferment in South Africa and in the southern African region. The decolonisation of Mozambique, Angola and Zimbabwe, and the conflict in Namibia, had changed the regional context of South African politics. Moreover, after nearly twenty years of sustained growth the domestic economy began declining quite dramatically from the mid-1970s. Massive and growing unemployment, together with a radical deterioration of economic conditions and prospects, particularly in the rural areas, portended a radical intensification of the conflicts within the country, which paralleled those in the region as a whole.

With these developments, the contending forces in the region became sharply polarised. The embattled state increased the reach of its coercive, repressive and cooptative powers, while the internal opposition which emerged in the mid-1970s did so in a mood of greater determination and militancy than had been evident since the turbulent days of the early 1960s. These developments produced an increase in the rhythm of political upheaval. Major riots took place in the urban areas in 1976, 1980, 1984 and 1985, punctuating an almost continuously escalating wave of strikes, stay-aways, and boycotts. In the homelands and national states, the ostensibly self-governing territories which the Nationalist government had formed as part of its policy of separate development, there was a marked increase in worker and community action on the one hand, and state repression on the other.

Despite the massive scale of the state repression which they provoked, oppositional activities generated and maintained a momentum entirely at variance with the pattern exhibited during earlier periods of intense conflict. Resistance and protest met by repression had for decades past been a chronic feature in the relations between the state and its black subjects. But previously state repression had produced an abatement of political resistance, which might last for years. After the massacre at Sharpeville, and the banning of the African National Congress and the Pan-Africanist Congress in 1960, a depression lasting for more than a decade settled over African politics.

But since the mid-1970s, the period of recuperation required before people returned to political struggles has shortened. Formerly, repression exercised against one target had a deadening effect on other groups and organisations. In recent times, one form of resistance has fed into another. Thus hundreds, perhaps thousands, of youths who took part in the Soweto rebellion in 1976, or were caught up in the reprisals, went over the border and joined the ANC.

The changing regional context conferred new significance on political organisations. Prior to 1974, the government did not regard the South African Students' Organisation (SASO) as a particularly significant threat. After Mozambique became independent, however, SASO was moved to hold a pro-Frelimo rally, and its leaders were tried and convicted under the Internal Security Act. The changes in the regional context also bestowed on the schoolchildren's rebellion of 1976 a new significance; and thereafter the political behaviour of schoolchildren became the subject of intense interest to the state's repressive agencies. Perhaps the most important development of all was that from the early 1970s the African working class achieved and maintained major advances, after more than a quarter of a century of effective containment by state repression. Significantly, too, conflicts in the workplace spilled over into community struggles. The stay-aways of 1984 were the largest and most sustained in the country's history.

The potentials for a major break in the system were everywhere evident, but it was difficult to foresee the circumstances in which it might take place, or to discern the social and political conjuncture about which it might be hinged. For nearly three decades, white South Africa had lurched from one crisis to another, its rulers guided by the belief that increasing repression, combined with the cooption of and concessions to specific groups, could avert more far-reaching changes. It was difficult to know how different things were during the 1980s or how the decade might develop.

It was no longer possible to be dogmatic about the changes which the state would be prepared to make in order to consolidate the social and economic order. Some commentators believed that the changes initiated since the late 1970s by P. W. Botha's tough and determined yet flexible and adaptable regime constituted the beginnings of a programme of 'reform from above' which could give the system sufficient legitimacy among the non-white underclasses, without jeopardising its legitimacy among whites, to enable it to survive in the middle term.

One intention of these reforms was to replace racial criteria with market principles in determining access to opportunities within the capitalist social order. Such a change would imply fundamental changes in the social and economic opportunities available to different racial groups. There were, however, limits to the extent to which such principles were intended to transform the political and social structures of the society, or, indeed, could meet the needs of more than a tiny fraction of the black community. It might even be argued that some of the reforms introduced by the state themselves precipitated African opposition and resistance on an intensified level. This took place not, as claimed by some government apologists, because they provoked a 'revolution of rising expectations', but because privatisation, notably in housing and transport, inflicted serious injuries on the poorest groups in the African community. In South Africa, as elsewhere, privatisation and deregulation benefit the strong and disadvantage the weak. As elsewhere, the strong are white and the weak are black.

The economy was controlled by corporations with specific grievances with government policy, but they were diametrically opposed to the radical reconstruction of the political economy. For decades the great economic interests have operated successfully and profitably within the parameters of the apartheid state, and there was little to suggest that business would press for its total demolition, without regard for the effects this demolition might have on profits. Notwithstanding its oft-rehearsed statements of opposition to apartheid, business was interested in the modification, not the destruction, of the social and economic order in South Africa which segregation and apartheid policy have helped construct. This does not imply that the business community was racist, but that its calculations in this respect, as in others, were dominated by a pragmatic conservatism.

Business was interested in three kinds of changes. The first would involve dismantling obstacles which apartheid legislation had historically put in the way of the maximum utilisation of labour resources. For instance, the chairmen of several major corporations called for the termination of influx controls as a way of fostering the development of a free labour market. The second was the development of some form of machinery for the settlement of industrial disputes, and, more broadly, the creation of conditions in which a 'responsible' black union movement might flourish. Thirdly, many businessmen demanded the extension of political rights to urban Africans. These demands hinged around the extension of property rights, and were explicitly aimed at achieving some legitimacy for the urban social order. It became a major assumption among the reform-minded elements of the business community that such piecemeal assaults on the apartheid system would in the long run undermine it more successfully than a revolutionary confrontation.

Such demands intersected with, though they were not identical to, the intention of state-induced reforms to preserve the social and economic order through a process of finding support from groups previously excluded from participation in the existing political system. These efforts did not, however, contradict the state's opposition to extending universal adult suffrage in a unified state to all blacks in the country, nor its proscription of radical political organisations. Indeed, many businessmen initially agreed with the government that the state of emergency of 1985 was a regrettable necessity. While the proponents of the strategy of piecemeal and peaceful reform did not necessarily require the preservation of any particular group's privileges within the social order, the 'deracialisation' of certain features of state policy implied the modification and liberalisation, not the elimination, of structural features of the society developed over the past half or three-quarters of a century. During the current period the basic features of this social order were the homelands and national states, which had been instituted during the 1950s and 1960s. The discussion of the development of 'native policy' from the 1920s in Chapters 5 and 6 is intended to show the historical precedents of the current reform move- ment. The state never exhibited any intention to dismantle the homelands states. On the contrary, these structures provided the foundations of the state's reform movement.

An important instance of a reformist project which was intended to modify, rather than to eliminate, the apartheid system was the shift in policy from direct influx controls towards 'controlled urbanisation'. This shift developed out of the policy of regional development which was established during the late 1960s. But it could also be linked to an older strategy in South African 'native policy', which has emerged from time to time as the liberal alternative to the overt coercion of movement and settlement of African labour associated with Nationalist government policy during the premiership of Dr H. F. Verwoerd. Moreover, there was little likelihood that the regime intended seriously to reverse the pattern of segregation in urban areas, though here again many modifications have emerged to the policy established in the Group Areas Act of 1950.

These shifts seem to suggest that the changes initiated by a reformist government during the decade beginning in the mid-1970s were changes in emphasis in policies that had historical precedents in earlier reformist (or liberal) policies, rather than entirely novel departures. In trying to under- stand the direction of the reform movement, it is necessary to understand those precedents.

This book is intended to outline the broad parameters of the political system as it had evolved over the past three-quarters of a century. It was not intended to suggest that those parameters could not be transcended, with or without the consent of the groups which have dominated the social and political order during the twentieth century. It was considered possible that the Nationalist government itself might be a major force in initiating the transformation to a different kind of political order. The possibility was also held out that the government might be overthrown in the effort to resist pressures to move beyond the system's parameters. Rather than make predictions about the outcome of such processes, the purpose of this study was to identify the kinds of constraints that would need to be transcended in order for significant changes to be accomplished. Because it is primarily an exercise in contemporary history, and not of prediction, it is to a lesser extent concerned to identify the forces working for change. The reader of this book will have better knowledge of the outcome of the processes being discussed than the writer did while he was composing it.

The simple argument being made here is that while the efforts the state made to reform the political order during the 1970s were very significant in dictating some of the outcomes of the great transformation which South

Africa is undergoing, they were part of a defensive strategy designed to avert fundamental change, by a process of incremental modifications to the status quo, and were not its leading edge. This argument is necessarily tentative. But if it is not to consist simply of a series of guesses, well-informed or otherwise, it needs to be located in the recent history of the society.

There have been many precedents for the current reconstruction of the state, though none of them achieved the momentum of the efforts of the 1980s, possibly because the crises and contradictions which stimulated those earlier efforts were less intense and the political terrain less vitally contested than during the current period.

My own reading of the precedents set for 'reform from above' in other countries, and in the development of the South African political and social order, suggested that although significant *changes* were possible under the auspices of the present regime, significant *reforms* were unlikely to emerge before a decisive break had been made with the regime, and that even after such a break, reforms would be perilously difficult to introduce or sustain, and might easily be reversed or eviscerated.

The regime, it seemed to me, was capable only of developing elaborations and variations on patterns which have already developed over the past half or three-quarters of a century. These changes have led to greater repression and exploitation, not greater equality and freedom. This reading of the situation was confirmed by the words and actions of members of the government and of the dominant National Party, who saw the purpose of reforms as essentially a strategy of containment and defence of the prevailing social order, and therefore, not surprisingly, taking shape within the framework of independent states, homelands governments, 'orderly urbanisation' and segregated residential areas and services. Reforms that might benefit urban Africans would require the maintenance and possibly the reinforcement of these institutions.

This does not mean that the changes which had been at work for perhaps fifteen years ought to be dismissed as 'cosmetic', nor is it impossible or even unlikely that some of the efforts at cooption and incorporation could generate an institutional base for more radical challenges to the social and political order. The areas in which the state attempted to initiate reforms were, after all, disputed territory, and the results achieved registered the balance of the forces marshalled within it. The labour field since the 1970s provides an important instance of such territory. Very significant changes began to take place within the parameters of the present system.

It is possible that the black labour movement which emerged during the 1970s will turn out to have been the pivotal force in the reconstruction and reform of the political economy, though this is by no means inevitable. But the state's intervention in the labour field was intended to stabilise and preserve as much as possible of the status quo in the face of the labour movement's challenge, and was not a movement towards the transformation of the social and political order.

Reform is one of the more complex and ambiguous terms in the vocabulary of politics. A distinction ought to be made between those kinds of changes intended to preserve the prevailing power structure, including the economic structure, on the one hand, and those which undermine it on the other. The former might involve extensive changes in the positions of particular groups within the political order, including the evisceration of the political rights and powers of whites, the establishment of a fourth House for African representation in addition to the three established for the separate representation of whites, Indians and coloureds, the development of significant forms of representation in local and regional bodies, and a loosening of many of the constraints on inter-racial action, such as the lifting of the ban on inter-racial political organisations and on sexual relations between racial groups. The significance of such changes ought not to be underestimated, and the constitution which was introduced in 1984 will be analysed precisely in order to understand them. All these changes are understood here to signify reforms *in* the social and political order. They ought to be clearly distinguished from reforms which might signify changes *of* that order.

By contrast, the reform *of* the social and political order would require a profound reconstruction of the political society. The requisites for such a transformation might provisionally be defined as those necessary to produce significant changes in the power structures of the society as a whole, including the structures of the economy, such as would bring about material changes in the life chances of the majority of the people of South Africa, including those living in the homelands states, and would not simply involve the ascent of a new elite at the expense of an old one.

The changes which I have in mind are not difficult to understand, but they are enormously difficult to bring about. They would involve reversing the dynamic forces which over the past three-quarters of a century have contributed to the deterioration of the material conditions of a significant and growing proportion of the population, a deterioration manifest in malnutrition on a massive scale, huge and escalating unemployment, and the collapse of peasant production, especially in the homelands.

Moreover, reform of this kind would require the effective participation of the majority of the people in the society in making political decisions. This participation would by no means be secured by institutions such as universal franchise and the removal of the array of repressive controls over political organisation and assembly; but some such arrangements would certainly be the sine qua non of participation.

The reforms which the state introduced during the 1970s and 1980s were concentrated in the major urban industrial areas, where resistance had the most immediate disruptive effect on economic and social relations, and directly tested the state's repressive capacity. These reforms suggest that contrary to the assumptions made by many reform-inclined groups in

South Africa, the liberalisation of government policy is likely to intensify rather than alleviate the problem. But without understating the problems facing the black communities in these areas, it is in the rural areas (the 'white' farming areas as well as the homelands and national states) and the small- to middle-sized urban areas that structural changes, that is to say changes which involve fundamental transformations in the political and economic order, were most urgent. In any case, the crisis of the urban areas was in many ways linked to and exacerbated by the rural crisis. One of the purposes of the state's reform strategy of the 1970s which achieved wide support was to create a privileged stratum of urban 'insiders'. One of the effects of this was for *urban* society to become more stratified, as well as to sharpen the divisions between urban and rural people.

Changes that could meaningfully attack such problems would require an end to the political coercion and repression which was the marked feature of the South African regime and its satellite regimes in the homelands and national states, and the development of participatory and democratic political structures in place of the authoritarian controls exercised by the state and by private powers. Significant change in this direction would also require a massive reconstruction of social services and the economic infrastructure if it were not to turn out to be a hollow sham.

Whether reforms of this kind are possible within the framework of a capitalist social order raises interesting questions. It is also interesting to speculate whether international aid to facilitate such reforms would be forthcoming. Whether they are possible within the spatial framework of the present South African nation state, or whether they would need to be tackled on the basis that took in not only the present homelands but the whole southern African region, also raises interesting issues.

It only requires these questions to be raised to make the fairly obvious point that the Botha regime had neither the political will nor the capacity to pursue reforms of this order. The purpose of the reforms contemplated by that regime was to prevent, delay or modify changes of this kind. It might be objected that the distinction being made here by definition precludes the possibility that any significant changes can take place this side of a revolutionary upheaval.

It ought to be recognised that 'the revolution' began long before the crisis of the 1970s and 1980s. This revolution ought to be understood not as an event which might be anticipated and avoided (or welcomed) but as a protracted and convoluted process of conflict in which many divergent and often conflicting political elements were at work. Indeed, many of the actors in this revolution had for generations pursued quite short-term and pragmatic ends and could by no stretch of the imagination be labelled revolutionaries.

The argument that state-sponsored or state-supported changes in the political and social structures were intended to transcend the parameters of the existing order confuses cause and effect. The efforts at reform from above were candidly conservative responses to a revolutionary challenge, of which armed struggle was only one and perhaps not the most important single element. The rhythm of reform from above was dictated by the relative strengths of the political forces in the field. Reform from above was a reactive process, aimed at controlling, containing, diverting and redirecting the pressures for change emanating from below.

For this reason, the conventional wisdom which cast the issue as an alternative between 'revolution' and 'reform', in which whites held the choice, was fundamentally mistaken. In terms of this argument, wise and temperate decisions, timeously taken, which give blacks a place in the existing social order, could prevent the revolution from happening. (One expert indeed opined that the white electorate held the choice!) It was mistaken on several grounds.

The first was that it failed to understand that the agenda and pace of state reforms introduced from above were dictated by the pressures for change from below. It was mistaken, secondly, in the implication (for the issue was never clearly spelled out) that revolution and reform pursued the same kinds of ends, the former by a sudden violent assault and the latter by incremental changes and the institutionalisation of conflict. In reality, while some of the elements in the government's reform package have met the demands made by, or imputed to, opposing groups, thus confirming the belief in a convergence of intentions, the most that might be claimed is that such concessions were made in order to head off more fundamental demands.

An important part of the government reform package was developed in response to demands from the business community for less government interference in the economy, for a smaller bureaucracy, for privatisation in the economy and rationalisation of social services; in short, it was made in response to demands influenced by monetarist sentiment in economic policy. Perhaps even more significant was that the economic recession of the early 1980s was in part induced by a tight monetarist policy. To the extent that high unemployment was a contributory factor to the political unrest, it may be claimed that this unrest was a direct response to one element of the state reforms.

Furthermore, another element in those reforms, privatisation, may have contributed even more directly to political unrest. Privatisation has contributed to the escalation of costs and the politicisation of two important issues in the daily lives of the industrial African working classes: housing and transport. Both issues acutely display the contradictions in the political economy of apartheid. After the Soweto uprising of 1976, privatisation of municipal and government housing in the townships became an important strategy for creating a property-owning 'African middle class', with a 'stake in the country'. While this strategy had the effect of privatising perhaps one per cent of housing stock, it had the effect of intensifying the fiscal crisis of the black local authorities which had been brought into existence to administer the urban areas, and hence contributed to pushing up costs in these areas.

Whatever the economic effects of state reforms, the limited interest shown by Africans in acquiring a 'stake in the country' by becoming house-owners (or their limited ability to do so) pointed up the absence of any effective consultation with Africans in the 'reform process'. Such arguments also perpetuated a fallacious view of the function of the repression the state mounted against its opponents, including opponents of state reforms. It was claimed that the repression was necessary to safeguard the reform. Even the Progressive Federal Party subscribed to the opinion that the military provided an 'umbrella of peace' necessary to bring about reforms.

The reality was that the repression was directed against those elements in the society, including churchmen, trade unionists, community leaders, and a whole gamut of socialists and nationalists who rejected state reforms because they understood that these reforms retarded the development of greater participation or equality in the social and political order, and delayed the moment when the basic problems of the sub-continent, to the solution of which South Africa had so much potential to contribute, might begin.

2   National, regional and international bases of the apartheid state

The history of southern Africa during the past three centuries reflects the changing ways in which the sub-continent has been incorporated into the world economy, and the political upheavals generated in the process. Currently, not for the first time, the people of the region face fundamental changes. Despite the truism that the region is unique in its political configurations, it presents a variation on the history of that part of the world which lies outside of the metropolitan areas, shaped by rather than shaping, responding to rather than initiating, the major developments in contemporary world history. Whether or not a decisive shift is possible in that pattern of relationships will turn in some measure on the outcome of the struggles currently being waged in the sub-continent. This, in turn, will hinge on the outcome of the political conflicts in South Africa.

South Africa became a major force in southern Africa after the Second World War. Rich and powerful in the region, it exercised an influence, notwithstanding its international isolation and precarious internal political structure, far beyond its borders. The key to its social structures, its political economy, and the form of the state, lay in its racial constitution.

Racial domination in South Africa was one of the bequests of the era of colonial conquest and exploitation. Yet the political structures which evolved in South Africa were complex and atypical of other colonial settlements in the region. Unlike territories in other parts of Africa, where direct colonial rule persisted until after the Second World War, South Africa enjoyed effective political independence from metropolitan powers from the beginning of the twentieth century. South Africa's economy is largely controlled by domestic forces. Like other African countries, South Africa was drawn into the world economy by imperial powers which established political control over the region in the course of exploiting its human and natural resources. Like other African countries, too, the marks of foreign exploitation of the economy during the early phase of industrial development remain in many of the features of its contemporary economy. Unlike them, however, its wealth became increasingly controlled by domestic forces organising themselves within the framework of a powerful state.

Yet, on the other hand, South Africa in the 1960s and 1970s resembled almost in caricature form the defunct colonial regimes of sub-Saharan

Africa. Its non-white people were formally and effectively excluded from access to the central institutions of political power, and denied common political rights. Writers have tried to express the contradictory features of an independent state that has successfully perpetuated the major features of colonialism, in such phrases as 'internal' or 'settler' colonialism, 'herrenvolk democracy' and, lately, peripheral capitalism. Each label captures an aspect of the society and its politics.

South African political structures were directed over the course of more than a quarter of a century by the policy of apartheid, or separate development (as the term is often translated), which formally dictated political rights and, to a significant extent, economic opportunities according to the criteria of race. (The past tense is used optimistically.) Apartheid practice evolved out of the structures of segregation established during the course of colonial settlement and conquest. It also introduced major new features. Apartheid policy has changed over time, in response to shifts in political relationships and socio-economic interests, including the resistance of the underclasses. By the 1970s, the cumulative effect of apartheid practice marked every aspect of the society, and constituted the central element of South Africa's recurrent political crisis.

Under apartheid, Africans, Indians and 'coloureds' (the statutory designation of persons of mixed blood) were denied common political rights, and were excluded from access to the major decision-making institutions in the society. Residential, educational and many other services and facilities were segregated by law. The universities were segregated by statute in 1959, and universities catering specifically for particular ethnic groups statutorily defined were instituted. The unequal resources apportioned to welfare and service facilities enjoyed by different racial groups reflected the intention to use the state's power to prescribe different stations in life for the different racial groups.

Inter-racial marriage and sexual intercourse were prohibited by law (until 1985), a prohibition that reveals much of the sexual obsessions and fantasies of racism, but also served to politicise the population in their most intimate relations into a racially constructed social universe. Population registration codified and perpetuated the boundaries between the racial groups, a measure which fell particularly hard on people of mixed blood who attempted to 'pass for white'.

Non-whites were excluded by statute from certain occupations, though these exclusions diminished considerably during the 1970s, and by the 1980s had been almost entirely eliminated. Until 1973, blacks were denied the right to strike legally, and thereafter enjoyed it in a severely limited and restricted form. Multiracial trade unions were prohibited in 1956, though the effects of the prohibition were partly mitigated by the device of 'parallel unions' whereby white unions would represent black unions in negotiations with employers, thus giving white trade unions a degree of control over black workers' demands.

Africans had never been denied the right to organise unions, but they were harassed when they did so, and African unions were not recognised in the statutory provisions for industrial negotiation until 1979. The price set for recognition then was registration by the state and with it the possibility of cooption, an issue that raised bitter disputes in the African unions which emerged during the late 1970s.

African political activity, including union activity, was inhibited and circumscribed by the proscription of organisations and by banning orders placed on individuals, by wide police powers of detention and interrogation, an efficient system of police surveillance, and by limitations on public assembly. The Communist Party was dissolved in 1950 under threat of banning, and the African National Congress (ANC) and the Pan-Africanist Congress (PAC), the two most significant African nationalist movements, were banned in 1960. Inter-racial political bodies were prohibited in 1968 after decades of harassment. The small multiracial Liberal Party disbanded rather than accept this limitation on its membership; the Progressive Party shed its black members and entered the mainstream of white politics.

The backbone of the apartheid edifice was the tribal, ethnic or national 'homeland'. From the beginning of the twentieth century, successive governments had established reserves in rural areas scattered throughout the country and totalling about 14 per cent of its surface, as the areas in which only Africans could permanently hold land and enjoy limited political rights under the control of tribal authorities, though there were many exceptions and anomalies in the policy.

Building on these precedents, the Nationalist government elected to power in 1948 evolved a policy in which these areas, which became officially known as 'homelands' (and popularly known as 'Bantustans'), would provide blacks with full and exclusive political rights, including the right to establish independent states. The homelands would be consolidated into major tribal or, as the government preferred to see them, 'national' groupings. By 1983, four homelands, Transkei, Bophuthatswana, Venda and Ciskei, had gained independence. They were not recognised by any state except the Republic of South Africa.

Concomitant with this project to develop the reserves into fully fledged states went the systematic destruction of African claims to political (including property) rights in areas outside of the homelands. This process of destruction began long before the policy of apartheid was conceived in the form in which Verwoerd developed it, but it was only after the 1950s that it became systematically articulated and executed.

The destruction of these rights outside the homelands was defended by the argument that political rights could be acquired in the independent states established in the homelands. Arguably there was never a serious intention to make these states economically self-sufficient, and there has never been much doubt that they are the creatures and clients of the South

African state. The homelands lacked the capacity to deliver the reality rather than the simulacrum of political or economic independence from South Africa.

The trappings of independence ceremonies, separate police forces, civil services, political executives, and legislatures have not concealed the de facto hegemony of the South African regime. Indeed, most of these states survive largely because of grants from the South African Treasury, secondments from the South African public service and judiciary, and military advice and cooperation from the Republic. The policies they pursue are continuous with and complementary to the objectives of the South African state. Their economies are dominated by South African interests.

The important innovation produced by these developments was the extent to which they entrenched the position of cooperative local political elites in the power structure of the territories, and delivered to them the means for constituting a new political class. The special position they enjoyed committed these groups to maintaining the overall political structure of apartheid: with their farms, official residences and fleets of official cars, the members of homelands governments were visibly the main beneficiaries of the system.

But the list of beneficiaries is not confined to the political leadership. Trading rights and the right to own fixed property are passing exclusively into the hands of the citizens of these territories. The public services, schools and universities provide the base for the subaltern class which is indispensable to the stability of the political class. Even beyond this incipient petty bourgeoisie, Africans enjoy access to facilities which were the preserve of whites in the days before independence. But these changes represent a change in position within the structures of dependency which apartheid now means for the people of the 'independent states'. The major price paid for independence by all their citizens was to be cut off from the right to work in the major metropolitan areas of South Africa, except in the precarious role of migrant contract worker. They were particularly vulnerable to unemployment.

Moreover, the political and financial costs of independence must be measured in terms of massively increased taxation and the use of police and vigilante terror on a scale which excites comment even by South African standards. The position of particular groups, especially the peasantry, has deteriorated markedly, partly because the tightening of influx controls and the policy of resettlement or repatriation in the homelands have pushed population densities to alarming levels.

The reasons for the failure of the homelands to provide the basis for economic and political independence can be found in the history of the underdevelopment of their economies over the course of more than a century of industrial development. Since the late nineteenth century, these areas have provided a source of cheap labour for the mining, agricultural and manufacturing industries, beyond the borders of most of the home-lands, and commercial opportunities for white traders within them.

Increasingly impoverished, unproductive and overcrowded, especially since the 1920s, they had by the 1970s become sumps of underdevelopment. Millions of their inhabitants migrated during the course of the twentieth century to the industrial cities, sometimes with the connivance of the state, and sometimes in defiance of its policies, but always under arduous condi-tions, and established themselves as the major elements in the industrial workforce. Hundreds of thousands became migrant workers, domiciled in the rural areas, but working for fixed periods in the industrial areas. They included many thousands from Basutoland/Lesotho, politically indepen-dent, but otherwise closely resembling the homelands states in its poverty and dependency.

Some of the homelands are as beautiful as the Scottish highlands. Like the highlands, their economies decayed as they were dislocated by capitalist development dictated by external forces. The recruitment of their able-bodied men to work in the mines had much to do with their impoverish-ment. So too did the incorporation of their chieftaincies into the colonial administration from the late nineteenth century, sometimes after conquest, often after the penetration of their societies had been effected by merchants and missionaries. Unlike the Scottish highlands, the population of which was induced to emigrate after the failure of the rebellion of 1745, the movement of people outside of the homelands has always been strictly controlled. All Africans over the age of 16, including women, were until recently compelled by law to carry passes, which regulated their movement and access to work and living space in the industrial zones of the country and in the white-owned agricultural areas. The abolition of passes was recently announced, but new legislation is still awaited, and the practical consequences of abolition are not known. It is probable that movement and settlement will in future be controlled by other means, such as health and slum regulations, the availability of housing, and so on.

The pass system may be traced back to 1760, when it was introduced to regulate the movement of slaves; in 1809 it was revised to incorporate proof of employment in order to control the movement of 'free' labour. But it was vastly elaborated and extended after the discovery of precious minerals as a way of controlling and directing the movement of workers to the mines and other industries.

By the late 1960s, these controls were being used to force Africans who could not show that they had rights to work and live in the urban areas to return to the homelands. It has been estimated by private groups that something like three million people have been resettled in the homelands, though the South African government claims that the figure is about 400 000.

The changes wrought by these and other pressures to force people to return to the homelands are apparent in the development of great rural slums in Transkei, Ciskei, QwaQwa and elsewhere. There are huge squatter settlements at Winterveld, in Bophuthatswana, conveniently near to the industrial areas west of Pretoria. They provide evidence of the anomalies of a system in which people are forced to work in the industrial complex of the Pretoria–Witwatersrand–Vereeniging (PWV) area, but forced also by the logic of the apartheid system which created the state of Bophuthatswana and made them its citizens, to live within its borders.

Because of the poverty, lack of work and overcrowding in the rural areas, the relocation of Africans in the homelands has effectively extended the migratory labour system, initially confined mainly to mining and some sectors of agriculture, to other industries which previously had drawn the bulk of their labour from urban communities. As the example of Winterveld suggests, the shift in the pattern that developed was accomplished because homelands were established near the major industrial areas, notably in a great curve around the western periphery of the PWV region in the Transvaal, in the vicinity of East London in the eastern Cape, and near Durban in Natal.

This summary suggests the extent to which apartheid and the exploitation of black labour were interlocked. Advocates of apartheid, and indeed businessmen opposed to apartheid too, have usually denied that it was the intention of the apartheid system to exploit the African labour force. The control of movement outside of the homelands was the necessary precondition for the territorial partition of the country on racial grounds, and therefore fundamentally important in the development of autonomous and economically self-sufficient states. For its apologists, apartheid was necessary for the survival of 'white civilisation'. Apartheid was essential in ensuring the survival of indigenous culture. It had nothing to do with labour exploitation. In the dialectic of apartheid, racism would be eliminated when the races were segregated on territorial grounds.

Heribert Adam made the point well when he argued that the inescapability of apartheid gave it its totalitarian features.[1] In the years since he wrote, there were many departures from the model established during the 1950s and 1960s, but his judgement about the political regulation of social and economic life remains accurate. Urban Africans made some significant political advances during the 1970s, although few major advances were achieved in gaining common civil rights. By the late 1970s the government had recognised that urban Africans were a permanent element of the urban population, which it had denied since the early 1950s. But as we have seen, one consequence of the fluid and ill-defined concessions to urban-dwellers is that it had become increasingly difficult for people to move out of the homelands.

The iron certainty and arrogance with which apartheid's advocates held and professed their opinion during the Verwoerd period became reduced to an anxious pragmatism. But there is little reason to modify Adam's judgement. In many ways the situation deteriorated. The state acquired formidable coercive and repressive capacities, especially after the passage of the Terrorism Act in 1967, which broadened the definition of treason and increased the powers of the police.

The development of the state's coercive and repressive powers needs to be understood in the context of the resistance and opposition among blacks to the political domination of white South Africa. In a broad sense, resistance and opposition to white rule are nearly as old as European settlement in the territory. But the scope, scale and tempo of resistance changed radically after the Second World War, and became especially marked from the 1970s, partly in response to developments elsewhere in the subcontinent, and partly in response to domestic economic conditions.

Racial domination was seriously challenged after the Second World War. The challenge coincided with three developments. The first was the movements of colonial nationalism in the British and French empires, which led to the establishment of independent states across the continent. The second was the intensified effort to institutionalise racial domination in every sphere of social and economic life which the Nationalist government undertook after coming to power in 1948. The third was the rapid wartime industrialisation, which produced massive social and political changes.

The architects of apartheid often ingenuously represented it as South Africa's route to decolonisation. In fact its systematic development provoked a rising wave of protest which came to be led precisely by those elements in African society who most closely resembled the leadership of colonial nationalism elsewhere. The protests against apartheid were orchestrated mainly by the ANC, the oldest nationalist organisation on the sub-continent, a number of bodies associated with it which joined forces in the Congress movement during the 1950s, and by a rival offshoot, the PAC.

The ANC was established in 1912, two years before the Afrikaner-based National Party. Until the Second World War, the ANC was by and large a conservative body, dominated by African professional men, journalists, ministers of religion, and teachers. Until the mid-1920s, chiefs played a considerable role in it; in fact its original constitution provided for a House of Chiefs and a House of Commoners. The ANC became increasingly militant during the Second World War, under the pressure of mounting conflicts on the land and in the industrial areas.

The Communist Party of South Africa (CPSA), which was founded by whites after the First World War, became ever more deeply involved in the struggles of African industrial workers, though some of its most important members (like Govan Mbeki) were primarily concerned with the dimensions of the problem on the land. The CPSA did not strike a formal alliance with the ANC until the 1950s, but they had an overlapping membership. Contrary to a widespread myth of a communist conspiracy which controlled African nationalist politics, the party did not exercise a preponderant influence on African nationalist movements, even after their alliance was cemented. As one might expect of a nationalist movement which contained aspirant 'bourgeois' elements, the ANC was ambiguously placed in relation to the party.

The CPSA, as with other left-wing political movements in South Africa, had correspondingly complicated attitudes towards African nationalism and to the aspirant African bourgeoisie which provided it with part of its leadership. Indeed, it could be argued that the Communist Party was not, except in name, a revolutionary party before it was dissolved in 1950. Its members working in local community struggles frequently faced the problem of deciding whether to work for and accept short-term political victories which delivered tangible benefits to African workers and other classes, or whether to postpone tactical victories in favour of revolutionary struggle. In practice they went for the first alternative.

From the end of the Second World War, even before the National Party took power, a great concert of forces began to precipitate out of the diversity of groups in African society and other groups too, in opposition to racial domination. Many whites who had volunteered to fight against the Axis powers returned to South Africa in a mood of militant anti-racism, often combined with a vision of the possibilities of radical changes in the social and economic structure.

Wartime pressures against Indian traders, especially in Natal, had the effect of mobilising opposition among them; and the Durban riots of 1949, in which Africans attacked Indians and destroyed their property, impelled Indian and African leaders to seek an alliance. The Defiance Campaign of 1952 drew many of the threads of opposition together. Thousands of people of all races decided to defy racial laws, choosing as their particular target segregated public facilities, and offered themselves for arrest in imitation of Gandhi's passive resistance campaign. (Gandhi had developed the doctrine and practice of satyagraha in South Africa.) Many thousands of people, mainly Africans and Indians, were arrested and prosecuted. The opposition mounted, reaching a high point in 1955 with the adoption of the Freedom Charter at Kliptown near Johannesburg. In the next five years a movement against the pass laws, the consistent target of African protest and resistance for half a century, culminated in a campaign in which thousands of Africans burnt their passes in public demonstrations.

This mounting protest evoked a fierce response from the state. The leaders of the Congress Alliance, forged between the organisational elements which met at Kliptown, were put on trial for high treason. They were all acquitted in a trial that lasted for nearly five years. A major anti-pass campaign was launched in 1960. The police fired on a demonstration organised by the PAC at Sharpeville in the southern Transvaal, killing 69 and wounding 180. In the aftermath of Sharpeville, the deputy prime minister promised to repeal the pass laws, a promise which was never fulfilled. Instead the state organised itself to destroy its most militant opposition. The government declared a state of emergency, and banned the

ANC and PAC and a number of associated organisations.

The banning of these groups, and the repression which followed, decisively shifted the country away from the possibility of a short or peaceful decolonisation, perhaps inevitably, and dashed the hopes of liberals in the country and abroad for a multiracial pax. The ANC and PAC were similar to the nationalist movements that mobilised opposition to the colonial powers elsewhere in southern Africa and took power when they left. These two movements combined disparate followings of peasants, urban workers and petty bourgeoisie behind an educated (largely mission-educated) and Christian leadership.

The Freedom Charter illustrates the diversity of ideological and economic interests which coagulated in the Congress movement. The Charter combined demands for universal political rights, including rights to private property, with plans for socialist measures for the redistribution of property. To make the point in terms of a scholarly debate developed much later, it condensed conflicting dimensions of class and national struggles. In this it reflected the diversity among the groups who might have stood to benefit from the changes which would probably have come about had an African nationalist movement been able to come to power. It is interesting to speculate on how the alliances of which these movements were composed might have fared had they, or one of them, come to power during the 1960s; perhaps there would have been a split in the dominant political groups between radical and conservative movements on the pattern exhibited in Kenya during that decade.

The banning of the ANC and the PAC after Sharpeville foreclosed the possibility of a negotiated settlement between the state and its black nationalist and radical opponents and critics for at least two decades. State repression transformed the character of organised black opposition. African nationalist movements changed from being open mass organisations using devices such as petitions, demonstrations and campaigns to focus on grievances and to mobilise support, into clandestine organisations led by exiles with less and less direct contact within the country. During the early 1960s, African nationalists, sometimes in collaboration with liberal and left-wing groups, initiated a largely abortive campaign of sabotage aimed mainly at state installations. Many were jailed, including Nelson Mandela, who had led the movement underground.

By the late 1970s, the exiled leadership of both the Communist Party (now renamed the SACP) and the ANC became installed in several European and East African countries. After the accession to power of Frelimo in Mozambique the two movements conducted a coherent campaign of action against the Republic, designed as much to foster their clandestine domestic following as to overthrow the regime by force of arms. As they and their allies recognised, the substantive force before major reforms or revolutionary transformation occurred would need to come from within the country.

By the early 1980s, the scale and precision of attacks on state installations and personnel in South Africa suggested that a considerable organisational infrastructure had been assembled internally, or could be deployed from neighbouring states. The South African government's reprisals against the ANC in Mozambique culminated in the signing, in 1984, of an accord with the Frelimo government; it will clearly have a serious effect on the ability of the ANC to maintain an externally based military capacity. But this setback to its military capacity only emphasised the importance of the internal political struggle.

The rhythm of political conflicts was matched by developments in the region and internationally. The catalyst which escalated the South African crisis internationally was South Africa's administration of its colonial dependency in South West Africa, conquered from the Germans in 1915. South African control over the territory was confirmed by the League of Nations, which proclaimed it a 'C' class mandate in 1919.

There had been sporadic uprisings in the territory since the beginning of the century, first against German colonial rule, which had been particularly brutal even by the standards of the time. The South African administration evoked resistance too, and responded to it with brutal repression: in 1922, the South African military crushed a protest by the Bondelswarts people against the imposition of a dog tax which escalated into a rebellion, by dropping bombs from aeroplanes on their village.

The South West African issue was one of the earliest issues concerning South Africa to be raised at the United Nations. (The political rights of Indians in South Africa was the first.) During the 1950s local resistance in the territory to South African rule consolidated against the expansion of the South African Native Affairs Department into the territory. When the apartheid policy was extended to the territory under the Odendaal Plan after 1967, these protests developed into insurrection. The South African presence in the territory was declared to be an illegal occupation by the United Nations in 1966, and the International Court tardily confirmed the declaration in 1971.

From the early 1970s, South African power in the territory has been contested by a guerilla force controlled by the South West African People's Organisation (SWAPO), based partly in southern Angola. SWAPO's most significant achievement by the end of the decade was political rather than military; it established its credentials internationally as the legitimate successor to the South African regime. Internally, too, despite the attempts by the South African state to promote alternative bases for legitimacy and the difficulty of judging the extent of SWAPO's support, the movement probably enjoys more popular support than any other single party in the territory. The military struggle in South West Africa (or Namibia) strikingly illustrates the Clausewitzian dictum that war is the conduct of politics by other means. Despite the technical superiority of its military force in the territory, the South African government was unable to eliminate SWAPO guerrilla forces by military means, or to break its political significance in the territory.

The South African government sought to do this by three related strategies: firstly, by devolving considerable powers to local political groups organised on the basis of local 'ethnic' communities; secondly, by maintaining military pressure against SWAPO guerrillas, including systematic raids into Angola where SWAPO established some of its bases; and thirdly, by delaying moves made in the international arena designed to facilitate a transfer of authority on terms which might deliver a political victory to SWAPO.

Arid and thinly populated, Namibia has very considerable mineral resources, and occupied an important position in the South African defence system, particularly after Angola, Mozambique and Zimbabwe had gained independence. But the main significance of developments in the territory was that notwithstanding the Republic's massive military and economic resources it was unable to eliminate rebellion and insurrection on its peripheries, either by force of arms or by destroying the determination of its military opponents, their political support locally, or their prestige in international bodies and Western capitals.

The issues posed in Namibia during the 1970s underscored the more rapid developments which took place to the north and to the east in Rhodesia and the Portuguese colonies of Mozambique and Angola. These developments suggested that a common revolutionary trajectory could be identified in the region as a whole, and that while important differences remained in the likely trajectory of change in the Republic, there were sufficient similarities to suggest that it would follow, with its own complex variations, a path comparable to their decolonisation.

The main significance of the decolonisation of Mozambique, Angola and Zimbabwe was political rather than simply military and strategic, in the sense that these countries offered examples to the black people living in the Republic of successful resistance to white domination, notwithstanding the determination and technical sophistication of states controlled by European minorities. This was particularly important in the demise of white rule in Rhodesia.

The demonstration effect of these conflicts increasingly preoccupied South African political leaders during the 1970s. They also explain in part the resurgence of political activity among blacks in South Africa after the long political depression which had settled over black politics during the decade following Sharpeville. The success of guerrilla action in Zimbabwe and Mozambique in ending white rule in those territories contradicted the comfortable though historically ill-founded doctrine that changes in the region would not come about through armed struggle. And their importance lay not only in the methods they suggested for achieving independence, but in the alternative models of government and patterns of economic development which they offered, albeit in a somewhat illusory form.

Despite their significance as examples, however, there were marked differences between South Africa and the regions on its periphery. Perhaps the fact that they were located on its periphery is the single most important difference, which indicates that their experiences, while educative, were unlikely to provide exact models, either to groups seeking changes or to the state's decision-makers anxious to preserve the political and social status quo.

South Africa was not, like Mozambique and Angola before 1974, the colonial dependency of Europe's last, poorest and least reconstructed empire, the anachronistic survival of an eviscerated mercantile power which succumbed before a war that it could not win or afford on its peripheries and before a coup at its centre. Nor was it like Rhodesia, landlocked, predominantly agrarian, sparsely and recently settled by whites, without international standing during the last 15 years of its existence, and in rebellion against the one metropolitan power (Britain) which could, and to some extent did, act as its patron in the international arena. Notwithstanding the importance of the protracted process of change in Rhodesia and the Portuguese territories, developments in those countries went parallel to the rest of sub-Saharan Africa during the period of the 1960s. They were, to put it another way, the late starters and finishers in the common process of decolonisation.

In contrast with these territories, the size and distribution of the South African population, its highly evolved class structure, its wealth and industrial infrastructure, the importance of its resources, the scale of its military and economic influence in the region, and the size of its internal and international markets and investments, combined with its weak political legitimacy, all underline the point that more complex processes of change are at work, and that the probable consequence will not be the succession of the present state by a form of 'neo-colonialism' which characterises states established in southern Africa from the period of the 1960s onwards.

The complexity and autonomy of white rule in South Africa suggests rather that the long-term political changes are likely to be wider and more far-reaching than in the states on its peripheries. The differences cannot simply be explained by the size of the white population, proportionally much larger than most other colonial settlements, or the length of its settlement in the country, nor even by the will and determination of its whites to retain their privileges: insofar as these factors are important, they are symptomatic of a difference in the structure of the political economy of the South African state and society from other southern African colonialisms.

It is tempting to argue that the explanation for the complexity of its relationships, and the likely trajectory of their transformation in the future, are linked to the size and scale of its industrial capacity and the richness of its infrastructure. This is plausible enough, but it tends to beg the question of precisely how the social and political resources of the society became mobilised in a way significantly different from the European settlements in other parts of the sub-continent.

The sheer scale of industrial wealth in the society does not entirely help answer this problem. The really significant feature of the South African political economy, which explains its differences from that of other states in the region, is the extent to which it was controlled by a domestic political class, by the presence of a local bourgeoisie, and by the increasingly intimate links that developed between this bourgeoisie and the state.

Scholarly attempts to express and explain the relationship between a powerful state and a powerful and cohesively organised capitalism have ranged over the major contemporary theoretical positions. At one end, one might detect the view that state intervention was an unwelcome and counterproductive intrusion on behalf of the most backward sectors of the economy, or the white working class, or both. At the other end, one might encounter every variety of historical materialism, from the unreconstructed instrumentalist claim that the state was the tool of capital, to sophisticated applications of Poulantzian theory. This study cannot review all these arguments.[2] It will simply outline the position argued by David Yudelman, who shares with the writer the sense of continuity between past and present.

Yudelman's account of the relationship is both subtle and persuasive. He argues that a symbiotic relationship between the state and big business developed earlier and more decisively in South Africa than in most other industrial countries under the pressure of demands from the gold-mining industry, and because of three specific features of capital and the state: the concentration and homogeneity of capital; the concentration of political power in the hands of Afrikaners; and the divisions in the working class along the lines of race, skills and rural–urban cleavages. Moreover, most workers, white as well as black, were migrants. The *symbiosis* between state and capital prevailed even during the periods of greatest conflict between them, when capital sought to subjugate organised white labour during the early 1920s. In referring to this period he prefers to use the phrase 'symbiosis at its weakest link'. Though the documentation of Yudelman's study is limited to the 1920s and 1930s, it suggests important parallels and continuities between the struggles waged between capital and labour during that period, when white workers posed the most serious challenge to capital, and the period of the 1970s, when black workers emerged as a powerful force for the first time.[3]

By 1980, domestic investments accounted for over 90 per cent of capital formation, though foreign investments provided 20 per cent of new investment. Moreover, South African capital enjoyed a modest presence internationally, with investments in Europe, the United States, Canada, Britain and the Middle East. (In 1981, the Anglo American Corporation's investments in the United States amounted to about fourteen billion dollars.)

South African capital exerted a massive presence in the independent states of southern Africa, notably Zambia, Botswana, Lesotho, Swaziland, Namibia, Malawi, Mauritius, Angola and Mozambique.

This influence existed sometimes in the form of direct investments, sometimes in partnership with foreign capital and local parastatals, sometimes in the form of control over infrastructure and employment opportunities. It continued to operate despite the virtual cessation of diplomatic relations between the Republic and these states. The economic power of the South African Republic in the region provided the framework for the international debates, controversies, and interventions in the region.

The second significant aspect of the political economy was the close relationship between the state and the dominant economic classes, and the close involvement of the state directly and indirectly in agricultural and industrial production through parastatals which dominated the production of steel, electrical power, petrol-from-coal, armaments and other sectors. The state was intimately involved in the agricultural sector, providing capital, technical assistance, and subsidies to producers, and controlling the production and distribution of agricultural commodities. It was an important customer for a wide range of locally produced goods and services. Above all, the state was intimately involved in coercing and regulating the supply of labour, in allocating labour between different sectors of the economy, and in determining the access of labour to housing and services.

These tendencies towards state corporatism originated in the patterns of labour control which developed after the discovery and subsequent exploitation of mineral resources during the last quarter of the nineteenth century. They were amplified during the post-South African War reconstruction, and then transformed by the efforts of Afrikaner nationalists to win economic independence from British-based capital during the 1920s, and to resolve the political crisis produced by the migration of impoverished Afrikaner rural classes to the cities during the first three decades of the present century – a movement that was accelerated during the period after the Second World War, and a process that was complicated by the simultaneous mass migration of Africans to the industrial areas.

Parallel with these developments went the intervention of the state in order to reconstruct capitalist agriculture during the depression of the 1930s and after. The tendencies towards corporatism initiated during the 1920s and 1930s were reinforced during the 1960s and 1970s by the state's efforts to achieve economic autarky in the face of actual and prospective embargoes and boycotts, and by the problems it faced in trying to manage the labour conflicts which began during the early 1970s.

Alongside these processes, there has been a consistent movement towards the establishment of an Afrikaner business class enjoying close though not frictionless relations with the ruling party and state bureaucracy. The story of the growth of the domestic capitalist class is the other side of the emergence of Afrikaner nationalism to political predominance in the state. The evolution of this class has much to do with the political conflicts which have dominated South African society during this century.

There are parallels between the struggles of the Afrikaner nationalist movement to achieve political independence and economic autarky and those of African nationalist movements elsewhere on the continent, and indeed similarities between the South African state and African post-colonial states. The exceptional character of South Africa lies partly in the relative success of the struggles to establish an independent political and economic order. Yet the similarities are striking despite the differences – the continuing reliance on the production of raw materials for export, the coerced labour system maintained by state controls, as well as the colonial values embedded in white attitudes.

It was suggested earlier that one of the special features of the South African economy was the extent to which capital was domestically controlled. This does not mean that foreign capital was a negligible factor. South Africa has imported capital continuously during modern times. Probably as important as the importation of capital was the importation of foreign technology and management techniques.

It is perhaps unprofitable to distinguish too finely between the specific political proclivities of domestic and foreign capital. Both have a clearly developed sense of the importance to their interests of maintaining the political 'stability' of the regime, and in holding down the costs of labour and of other costs which might affect profit levels, irrespective of the complexion of the political leadership and the particular contours of state policy. Some foreign investors believed there was no reason why in principle political stability could not be achieved through an Africanised state, as in the former French and British colonies.

Indeed some elements of domestic capital too are relatively indifferent to the specific ethnic complexion of the political leadership, provided it can maintain political stability. Some local companies have long enjoyed a fruitful relationship with the state in independent African countries, notably in Botswana, Zambia, and more recently in 'socialist' Angola and Mozambique. Like some British multinationals, these had little difficulty in adjusting to the new regime established in Zimbabwe in 1980.

There is a wide body of business opinion inside and outside the country which believed that the government's apartheid policies 'destabilised' political relationships, though in some cases it is difficult to decide whether it was the repressive and coercive elements of that policy, or the protection it offered to white workers, which constituted the greater offence.

Nevertheless there are a number of factors that influence foreign and domestic capital to view the problems of political stability differently, and to adopt different stances towards issues connected with political change and reform. Most foreign companies with large investments in South Africa could probably survive withdrawing in the case of major upheavals, even though this might involve heavy losses which would be unpalatable to their shareholders. Few if any South African companies could do so. Even those with large investments abroad would be prostrated.

Some foreign companies are more sensitive to political disturbances than South African companies, simply because they have a wider range of alternative investment possibilities. On the other hand, some foreign companies can take a remarkably tough view of the political situation because their investments are short-term, high-risk ventures.

South African companies have a more complex view of the situation. While they clearly must base their investment strategies on their diagnoses of the prospects of political and particularly labour unrest, and have at least a crude conception of the need for some form of legitimacy, they have in the nature of the case been forced to assume a basic continuity in the political order. This complex of issues has produced among them a two-fold stance towards the state: firstly, that it should be powerful enough to contain any radical challenge to the social order; and secondly, that it should respond flexibly towards political pressures from among the underclasses to reduce the possibility of general unrest. Both stances were consistent with the demands voiced by South African businessmen, particularly the representatives of major corporations, that the apparatus of protection for white workers should be dismantled, and that statutory controls over the mobility of black labour should be removed.

It was in these latter respects that capital encountered most resistance from the state during the 1950s and 1960s. It was also in these areas that the state attempted to respond during the 1970s while trying, with decreasing success, to avoid alienating the National Party's constituency among white workers and the lower echelons of white agriculture.

The positive response of the business community to the new constitution enacted in 1983 may be explained precisely by its combination of strong government, the weakening of white electoral political forces, the promise of strengthening the political influence of the business community, and the flexibility bestowed on government in a wide variety of areas by the shift in its constituency. As well as these signs of rapprochement, the business community has also begun to explore future possibilities, for instance by holding talks with the ANC.

Foreign investors no doubt shared many of the assumptions held on such issues as these by domestic capital, though they were more cautious in giving open expression to them. In outlining the issues, it is perhaps necessary to emphasise that foreign capital has had as little interest as domestic capital in promoting changes as a step towards democratising the political system. As a class, capital is at best indifferent to democratic participation or the development of workers' rights, though it appreciates the value (under particular circumstances) of incorporating representatives of the working classes in legislatures as a way of promoting political stability and of securing the cooperation of trade unions in stabilising relations between capital and labour. Nor did foreign business interests initiate the pressures to disinvest in South Africa. Such pressures came from a particular and not especially important constituency of institutional shareholders in metropolitan countries, like churches, universities and trade unions.

The pressure on Barclays Bank to disinvest in South Africa was led by a group of British shareholders which late in 1980 set themselves up as an 'alternative' board. The boycott of South African coal imports into the United States in 1974 was initiated by unions representing dockworkers and coalminers, not by business interests. In brief, pressures brought to bear on foreign investors expressed conflicts within metropolitan societies rather than the autonomous inclinations or decisions of Western capital.

One major pressure exerted on foreign countries emanated from states in the Third World which, because of their control over natural resources, especially oil, were in the position to threaten sanctions against Western countries trading in South Africa, either directly by withholding supplies of a valuable commodity, or by diverting their custom to other countries. Nigeria was the strongest African state in a position to do so during the 1970s. Oil suppliers, both in Africa and in the Middle East, were in the unique position of having control over a commodity which South Africa cannot supply itself – oil – and this has had the effect of forcing up the price of fuel in the country. However, this in turn stimulated a vast oil-from-coal industry and intensified the search for gas and oil deposits.

Finally, the position of Western countries needs to be considered. Clearly the official attitude of Western countries towards South Africa has been influenced by the criticisms of South African racial policies, in the United Nations and other international forums, by the ending of South Africa's membership of the British Commonwealth, and by variations in the temperature of the Cold War. Overall, Western governments have adopted a disapproving attitude towards the racial policies of the Republic.

Successive American administrations have made rhetorical declarations of their repugnance for racism. But these solemn rituals of dissociation have never seriously threatened to disrupt diplomatic or business relations. On a number of occasions the United States, along with Britain, has acted either to modify or to veto proposals for international action against the Republic. The United States' stance towards South Africa is comparable to the position it adopts towards regimes like South Korea: official pressures and hints for changes were intended to forestall deeper upheavals that might threaten stability in the region and foreign investments.

The distinguished American political scientist Tom Karis put the point in essentially the same terms: 'What makes the South African situation serious and urgent for the United States is the dangerous consequences if it deteriorates further and violence spreads to both sides. If the situation becomes more polarised and black leadership becomes more radical and pro-Soviet or pro-Chinese, can the United States effectively identify with black aspirations?' Finally, 'most dangerous of all . . . are the possibilities of

East–West competition in Southern Africa, with the United States on the wrong and losing side.'[4] In general, by the late 1970s a situation had emerged in which the United States and western European countries managed to maintain relations both with South Africa and with other African states, as well as avoid acute confrontations with internal pressure groups representing racial minorities, for instance.

The most important presures emanating from Western countries have come from liberal and radical pressure groups rather than from governments, let alone the business community. Because of the weakness of these groups they have had relatively little impact on governments. It might have been expected that social democratic parties, when in power, would be more energetic than conservative governments in pressing for measures to stimulate substantive changes in South Africa. In fact while radicals in social democratic parties have attempted to steer their parties towards a more critical stance, their efforts have percolated very slowly if at all into government policy.

As with the United States, European governments, whether conservative or social democratic, have acted most effectively on the South African situation by impeding, preventing or slowing down the sale of arms and other strategic equipment to South Africa, and by establishing and maintaining cultural and sports boycotts against the country. Such actions were less damaging than controls over investment and trade might have been, and the armaments embargo has worked to stimulate the development of a local armaments industry, which by the early 1980s was actually exporting arms.

The Cold War helped smooth down some of the rougher edges of criticism of apartheid, as well as of authoritarian regimes in Latin America and elsewhere, so long as they have been 'anti-communist'. The most robust and trenchant criticism of South Africa, and support for anti-colonialist struggles in the region, have in fact come from the socialist bloc. The Cold War supplied a crude taxonomy that locates South Africa among the 'anti-communist' elements of the international community. This designation has been systematically exploited by the South African government, and by groups in Europe and the United States sympathetic to the regime.

The strengthening of anti-democratic forces in the United States during the 1970s, as evidenced in the support there for the conservative think-tank, the Trilateral Commission, and more broadly a stance on the Third World which exhibited an increasing preoccupation with 'order' rather than democracy, has emphasised the ideological links between South Africa and Western countries, especially the United States. The benefit to the South African government was an increasing indifference in Western governments with regard to assisting South African blacks to achieve common universal political rights like the franchise.

This indifference became explicit in the statement by the newly elected president, Ronald Reagan, in 1981 that he would not press for universal political rights in South Africa. Reagan's statement, and the subsequent actions of his administration, merely clarified what had become evident since the early 1970s. The dominant groups in Western countries, and especially the United States, were more interested in political stability and economic growth than in effective political participation by the underclasses or in widespread political changes.

Notwithstanding these convergencies, relations between South Africa and the United States have markedly deteriorated since 1954 when President Eisenhower bestowed the accolade that South Africa's industrial growth strengthened the Free World, and such unrestrained praise has been confined to unofficial quarters. Particularly since the Kennedy administration, the United States has adopted an increasingly critical attitude towards the Republic, and supported the total arms embargo imposed in 1978. From the mid-1980s, this movement escalated to the point where legislation was introduced to prevent investment by US companies in South Africa. But this critical stance was modified in practice in a number of ways. Indeed, it might be said that the United States acts towards certain authoritarian regimes in Latin America and south-east Asia with the same mixture of public and rhetorical disapproval, private admonition and latent support.

As with those countries, official policy in the United States was probably conditioned by its perception that the Republic is the largest and most stable domino in a precariously constructed regional game. It may be that internal instability, should it become unmanageable by the South African regime, could force a shift in US foreign policy.

To be sure, the fact that South Africa enforced statutory racial discrimination was a major problem, and made for a sensitive issue in dealing with some constituencies in domestic politics, but the fact that South African stability rested on the determination of a minority regime to arm itself to the teeth against the possibility of overthrow or substantial change was perhaps less exceptional, during the Nixon–Kissinger era, than might be supposed from considering rhetorical demonstrations against the Republic. For to a considerable extent, American foreign policy was involved in propping up such regimes around the globe. Indeed, despite its policies of statutory racial discrimination, South Africa during the 1970s was probably no more unsatisfactory than many other outposts of the crumbling Pax Americana during that decade.

One factor that consolidated a working relationship between the United States and the Republic during the 1970s was that the latter proved to be an important, though occasionally embarrassing, junior partner in American activities to exert an influence in the southern African region during and after the collapse of Portuguese colonial rule following the coup of 1974. Indeed, the Republic's collaboration in American initiatives in the region was pursued to the point of overextending South Africa's military perimeter during the second half of 1976, when South African forces undertook the ill-fated invasion of Angola, largely, it has been claimed, at Secretary of State Kissinger's prompting. It has been claimed too that the calculations which induced the South African government to embark on this adventure were based on an inaccurate reading of the American style of government; but it certainly betrayed a willingness to act as the confidante and ally of the United States. South African pressure on Rhodesia to accept a settlement was probably an important factor in getting Mr Smith to Lancaster House, and a tribute to the combined persuasive and coercive powers of Kissinger, Vorster and P. W. Botha.

Carter's election to the presidency induced a mood of pseudo-populist sincerity in the upper echelons of American foreign policy-making. The Carter administration raised hopes and fears of a distancing between the United States and South Africa. Yet, as with many other aspects of that curious interregnum between Republican presidents, the promise the Carter administration held out of giving effect to a more active opposition to the South African government was deeply flawed by irresolution.

The spirit of the administration on this issue was best summed up in Secretary of State Muskie's valedictory address in December 1980, which stressed the bipartisan nature of American foreign policy and its 'pragmatic application of democratic ideals', which meant, he explained, 'searching for concrete ways to support the efforts of those working for peaceful change . . . churches, community organisations, newspapers and courts.'

The absence from this list of trade unions, let alone clandestine political organisations or guerrilla movements, is significant, but perhaps not surprising. Indeed, it would be surprising if such organisations and movements had been included in his list, not simply because militant action by domestic groups fell outside the notion of peaceful change entertained by such spokesmen of US foreign policy, but because even vigorous action by organised or disorganised labour has uncomfortable implications for American interests, not only in southern Africa but elsewhere in the world. Such action contradicts the conception held of correct labour relations, at least by conservative Americans, who have a preference for the cooptative structures of labour relations which have characterised US industry since the 1930s. The most interesting item included in the list were the courts – the judicial arm of the apartheid state!

Perhaps the burden of their criticism of the South African system of labour coercion and control rested on their sense that it impeded the development of such cooptative structures. Even further from view in official American perceptions was the possibility that significant changes in the reduction of inequality, including racial inequality, might not be possible by 'peaceful means'. Such possibilities rested uneasily within the parameters of American foreign policy, for they brought to the surface the contradictions which lay at the heart of that policy – that the purpose of supporting reforms is to foreclose deeper upheavals.

The persisting theme in official US policy has, in fact, been this commitment to 'peaceful change'. It may be traced as far back as John F. Kennedy's encomium to the Noble prize-winner Chief Albert Luthuli in 1961, and as recently as the White House's immediate rejection of a statement imputed to Nelson Mandela in August 1985, that he saw no alternative to the use of violence in bringing about change.

In the context of the Cold War, the purpose behind American efforts to reform authoritarian regimes is to retain them in the Free World, that is to say, the anti-socialist camp, not to encourage dangerous experiments that might result in their departing from it.

During 1985, the successes of the disinvestment campaign in the United States and the decision by banks not to renew loans to South Africa suggested the possibility that a new balance of forces had begun to emerge in the United States which might affect the foreign policy. If so, this study cannot be concerned with them. It does, however, suggest that the United States may be embarked on a variation on, rather than a radical departure from, the policy which has evolved over the past three-quarters of a century. This variation may have been induced by a calculation that the South African government, controlled by the National Party and relying primarily on a mixture of repression and cooption, was no longer capable of controlling the situation, and that in the interests of stability in the region the United States ought to begin backing a horse of a different colour, or perhaps several horses of different colours.

These considerations indicate that the effects produced by the decolonisation of territories on the South African periphery, and pressures from Western states and investors during the 1970s, while important in modifying some elements of South African policy as well as the parameters of the South African political economy, were unlikely to produce on their own changes in the structure of the regime.

Whatever effects they produced would need to be calculated in relation to the internal balance of political forces. Yet in trying to understand *these* forces, it is important to stress the effects on the country of trends taking place in the international economy. The domestic crisis which emerged in South Africa during the 1970s was played out in the context of a larger international crisis. As remarked earlier, the history of the region is the history of its incorporation into the world economy. During the 1970s, the rhythm of international developments shifted. The energy crisis changed the rules of domestic politics in South Africa as in other countries. The spectre of inflation and unemployment in the advanced countries was reproduced in exaggerated form in the southern African region, exacerbated by the lack of competitiveness of South African manufacturing on the world market. Major strikes in Namibia and Natal during the early 1970s were responses to the deterioration of the most precariously situated element in the domestic workforce.

By the end of the decade there was scarcely a sector of the economy that had not experienced serious and sustained strikes from among its African workers. The rebellion of schoolchildren which began in Soweto during 1976 was directed initially at the inferior quality and repressive conditions that obtained in African education. It could be seen to be an oblique reaction to the declining employment prospects for unskilled labour.

As in earlier periods of protest and turbulence the state responded vigorously with direct repression: during 1976, more than 300 blacks died as a result of police action. At the same time the repression was increasingly accompanied by efforts to introduce measures which would reduce the levels of opposition and resistance by coopting groups in the underclasses. Some of these measures, like the recognition of African unions and the acknowledgement of the right of black workers legally to strike, were formulated by the state; others were initiated by private groups with some measure of state approval.

Among these was the establishment of the Urban Foundation, which had as one of its main aims the upgrading of housing and service facilities in Soweto and other urban black areas, including squatter camps near Cape Town. Most significant of the growing power of African labour, whether organised or not, was the continuous pressure on wages, and substantial improvements in wages in some sectors. The wages of black mineworkers, which had not improved in the six decades since 1910, trebled within five years of 1973, though continuing strikes on the mines suggested that wages were not keeping up with the demands made on them by miners' families in the rural areas, and also that wages were not the sole source of workers' grievances.

The increase in the gold price during the late 1970s masked some of the effects of the world economic crisis, but even during the short boom that followed, very heavy demands were made on revenues produced by the mines, notably for defence, and the high price of gold did not in any case have a major effect on unemployment. From the beginning of 1980, the declining price of gold and the American recession threatened to expose the South African economy to the cold winds sweeping through the international economy, this time sharpened by an increasingly powerful union movement.

These developments had deep implications for a society teetering on the brink of widespread civil disorder, particularly because they suggested that the state would need to find some alternative to its perennial recourse to repression to contain opposition and resistance. Yet the economic crisis threatened to make difficult, if not impossible, any measures which permitted blacks to achieve gains at the expense of established white interests.

The conventional economic wisdom had postulated that political reforms would follow a period of economic growth, particularly in manufacturing industries, so that whatever benefits were transferred, either in terms of wage increases or of state benefits, would come out of a growing social cake. There were in any case serious problems with the analysis on which this prediction had been based. Recent comparative studies of industrialisation suggest that capitalist development in the advanced countries pursued different 'routes'.

In a luminous paper, Stanley Trapido argued that South African industrial development followed the 'Prussian path', which required a coerced labour force, and had culminated in fascism in Germany and Japan.[5] Even if it could be said that the differences between the various routes were exaggerated, the crises encountered in the advanced countries of the West, with their complex legitimating structures, offered a somewhat ambiguous model for making predictions about South Africa.

The Rostovian model on which local forecasts were based failed to anticipate the consequences to the economies and social policies in advanced countries of the effects of stagflation, massive and growing unemployment and the 'rationalisation' and privatisation of social services, which by the end of the 1970s had begun to shred the advances achieved by workers in several major industrial countries in the West, particularly in Britain.[6] The crisis in major industrial countries in the West made the trajectory they followed during the 1970s and 1980s a dubious model for South Africa to follow if it wished to avoid major political upheavals.

It has been argued that aside from the protection offered by gold to its economy, South Africa will in the long run enjoy advantages from the oil crisis. As the costs of oil increase internationally, the country's massive coal reserves and capacity for nuclear power development, based on huge uranium deposits, and, not least important, the absence of any effective anti-nuclear pressure groups, put the country into the position of a net energy exporter.

But the character of these resources simply emphasises the importance of extractive industries and the overriding significance of the export of raw and semi-processed materials. Even before the oil crisis set in, the balance between different sectors was tilting in a telling way towards the export of raw and semi-processed materials and away from manufactured goods.

Investments in manufacturing, while growing in absolute terms, declined as a proportion of total investments during the decade which ended in 1976, and private investment in this sector declined even more sharply. While the value of exports rose over the same period, the increase was attributed to the rise in volume and value of raw and semi-processed materials. A major survey published in 1980 underscored the continuing importance of mineral exports to the economy.[7]

In some ways, for all the complexity and scale of its manufacturing sector, South Africa had by the 1970s begun to exhibit the atavistic tendency to return to the typical form of a colonial economy. It could indeed be argued that manufacturing has always been a weak sector, maintained by the state on the basis of revenues derived from the mineral sector, and that the economic downturn of the mid-1970s was simply reinforcing one of its persistent structural features. It is also significant that the manufacturing sector itself became increasingly interlocked via the structure of corporate conglomerates into an intimate and dependent relationship with mining. These tendencies have important political implications.

The critical issue posed by the South African economy for its political structure has not, since the 1960s at least, been simply a question of poverty, in the sense of poor resources or weak infrastructure, but arose from the fact that the reliance of the country on the export of raw and semi-processed materials, at prices largely dictated by foreign markets, and subject to fluctuations controlled by the rhythm of the international economy, imposed very severe overall constraints and contradictions on wages and welfare.

In such a situation, it is possible to conceive of alternative political methods of redistributing incomes from wages and welfare, but it is extremely difficult to imagine a radical increase in resources taking place that would ensure a decent standard of living for all workers. That is possibly the case in all capitalist societies. The persistent importance of raw material exports may prescribe limits to the possibilities of any significant changes in the structure of politics, and hence the possibility of change. Writers who saw South Africa moving away from a reliance on mining may well turn out to have been over-optimistic in their belief that an economy which grew on the basis of an essentially colonial relationship could, in its maturity, and because of the great wealth generated in the process, transcend the structural constraints of the institutions that set it in motion.

It might be considered, then, that there was never any serious basis for the argument that reforms comparable to those which took place in England during the late nineteenth century in the wake of the expansion of manufacturing industry are likely to take place under the circumstances found in South Africa. This does not mean that 'reform' is impossible in South Africa, but that significant reforms will probably require changes on a scale which South Africans, black and white, who call themselves moderate reformists would label 'revolutionary'.

3 The political economy of industrial South Africa

South Africa has the oldest and most highly developed industrial economy in southern Africa, and by far the richest and most powerful. Internationally, it ranks high among countries in the degree to which wealth and income are concentrated in the population. Whites enjoy the largest share of wealth, income, economic opportunity and access to education. Stanley Trapido has argued that South Africa's 'particularity' among industrial, capitalist societies lies in the fact that the majority of its workforce, who are black, are excluded from common political rights and prevented from participating in the dominant political institutions.[8] This feature of its political economy emerged out of the special circumstances of its industrialisation. During the last quarter of the nineteenth century and the first few decades of the twentieth, a pattern of coerced labour was established which precluded the extension of political rights on the pattern followed in England, France and the United States.

For Trapido, indeed, the most significant effect of the labour system on politics was that political rights acquired by Africans and other racial groups during colonial times were dismantled during the period of industrial growth and development in the twentieth century. The trajectory followed in its industrialisation, and the effects of political structures established to coerce an industrial labour force into existence, in turn shaped the way in which the state has acted to coerce and direct the labour force, and to allocate it between different sectors of the industrial economy, including capitalist agriculture.

These structures also determined the way in which the state defined and discharged functions relating to the welfare needs of the different sectors of the labour force. Welfare and subsistence functions were directly linked to and integrated with the controls over the labour force, as an adjunct to the coercive measures used to create and maintain it. Consequently the state has been confronted by a series of problems in managing the workforce and the communities in which the workforce became established. The measures it undertook to mobilise and control labour virtually precluded the possibility of extending political rights to Africans as a way of establishing some degree of legitimacy for the state.

For these reasons, attempts to legitimise the social order by extending the franchise or by giving access to common political institutions were virtually foreclosed. The pattern of industrialisation since the last quarter of the nineteenth century has thus limited the prospects of political and social reform via the extension of political rights during the twentieth century.

The evolution of the coercive industrial labour system was influenced by the practices established during European settlement at the Cape and European expansion into the interior during the seventeenth and eighteenth centuries, and in the trekker republics in the Transvaal, Orange Free State and Natal (prior to British annexation). But the labour system which was established in the South African mining industry cannot be represented unproblematically as a continuation of the system of slavery, abolished in 1833, and other forms of coerced labour developed in the hinterland and in the trekker republics. To be sure, political and economic relations on the land, particularly in the Transvaal and the Cape, gave rise to forms of coerced and repressed labour which might have served as precedents for the mining industry and, with variations, other sectors of the industrial economy. But pre-industrial relations in South Africa do not convincingly explain the development of coercive controls during the period of industrial development, or the consequences for its political institutions.

The pre-modern history of every industrial country provides evidence that traditional political and social relationships, including serfdom and slavery, indenture and tenancy, affect the evolution of social and political relationships in the course of industrialisation. Such social relations provide historical precedents and legitimations for the command structures of industrial society, its habits of deference, obedience and discipline. But we cannot explain the exclusion of the workforce from political rights as a consequence of such pre-existing social and political structures.

Some of the literature on South Africa exaggerates the effects of conquest and slavery in shaping social and political formations. It should be noted that the whites did not conquer the country in the way that the French conquered Algiers; the process in South Africa was more slow-moving and complex.

To be sure slavery did have important effects. But again it ought to be recognised that slavery in South Africa contrasts sharply with the slave states of the United States and most of the West Indies. In those societies the social and economic order was in substance constituted through the institution of slavery, whereas in South Africa slave-holding was confined to the western Cape, affected the ancestors of a small minority of the black population, and was terminated in 1833, more than a generation earlier than in the United States. Slavery totally encapsulated the lives of the ancestors of the Negroes (and the white Southerners) as it did of Caribbean society, and shaped the social structures that emerged subsequently. In contrast, a vast area of 'race relations' in South Africa grew up outside of the framework of the slave society. Consequently, quite unlike what happened in Negro society, very large areas of indigenous African culture survived the establishment of white power in southern Africa. Yet a considerable body of the theory of race relations in South Africa is constructed on the assumption that it can be viewed as a variant form of these societies, perhaps because the claims of American Negroes to speak for black South Africans can thereby be legitimised.

Insofar as politics is affected by cultural features, these areas of indigenous culture need to be taken into account in understanding patterns of resistance and conflict. They also explain why most whites have resisted an assimilationist strategy, which only makes sense if the proponent of assimilation is a member of the dominant culture. It might be noted that the strength of indigenous African culture has had contradictory effects. It has on one hand provided potential sources of political power. But on the other it has also tempted many Africans into a form of isolationism. And while the existence of these cultural traditions has been a source of strength, it has also been a source of strain. The theoretical justification of apartheid was based on claims of cultural distance.

In contrast to slavery, the quasi-feudal relationships established on the land in the Transvaal during the nineteenth century preserved, and indeed reinforced, the direct access of the black peasant labourer to the means of production. This meant that, in contrast with the slave, who was himself a chattel, the African peasantry needed to be prized away from this access before they could become available for mobilisation as a fully proletarianised labour force. It will become evident in subsequent chapters that this problem vastly complicated the evolution of labour relations in South Africa.

The traditions of slavery and conquest are also frequently summoned to explain the exclusion of blacks from the franchise. But the question of admitting the majority of adult men and, later, women to the franchise, and to participation in the central political institutions of societies (at least before the era of decolonisation), has only ever arisen anywhere, including most of the now advanced industrial countries, in the context of industrialisation. What needs to be understood is not simply how traditional structures of social and political control were maintained during the period of industrialisation in South Africa, but how and why they were adapted and transformed (when they were) to suit the particular requirements of the new industrial economy.

Until the discovery of diamonds at Kimberley during the 1870s and of gold along the Witwatersrand during the 1880s, European settlement in South Africa was comparable in size, social structure and economic activities to colonial settlements elsewhere in southern Africa. The bulk of the white population was concentrated in seaport towns established from the seventeenth century onwards. During the eighteenth and the first half of the nineteenth century, groups of Dutch-speaking trekkers settled in the interior, engaged mainly in pastoral activities, hunting and trading. The people they initially encountered were groups of San and Khoi, hunters and herders. The San were almost exterminated during the eighteenth century in a deliberate campaign of genocide. The Khoi became incorporated into the agrarian labour force. As white settlers penetrated the interior, they encountered well-organised chiefdoms and kingdoms of Bantu-speaking people engaged, like themselves, in pastoral activities, hunting and trading, and, in particular localities, in the mining and smelting of iron and gold.

The advances made by the trekkers, who identified themselves as boers (farmers), into the interior during the eighteenth century, and in the process of establishing the trekker republics (briefly) in Natal and (more permanently) across the Orange and the Vaal during the mid-nineteenth century, were achieved by a combination of war and diplomacy with these groups.

But though the boers demonstrated again and again their military skills, organisation and the superiority of their guns over spears, forcing the Basotho south of the Caledon, defeating (though not breaking) the Zulu, and pushing back the Swazi from the Transvaal highveld, boer political domination did not fundamentally transform the social and political structures of the Bantu-speaking people with whom they came into contact. Comparably, the British colonial order established its control over the border areas of the Cape, in Natal, and through war and diplomacy in Basutoland. Missionaries and traders had a marked effect in opening these societies to the influence of Christianity and commerce. But, before the end of the nineteenth century, these influences developed within the interstices of the traditional communities, working by a slow attrition rather than a decisive assault to undermine them. It is a mark of the transformation initiated by trading and missionary activity during the pre-mining period that a vigorous African peasantry emerged to take advantage of the market opportunities which opened up, and that this stratum was in turn destroyed by the demands of the mining industry for labour.

Mining

It was the mining industry, and particularly gold-mining, which rapidly and profoundly transformed the social and political structures of colonial South Africa. The social and economic order established with its centre on the goldfields of the Witwatersrand produced an effective absolutism over the pastoral and agrarian communities of southern Africa which by the turn of the century had coerced hundreds of thousands of labourers into employment on the mines. To be sure, there were precedents for coerced labour. The Dutch had imported slaves to the Cape soon after its occupation in the seventeenth century. Although the indigenous people of the interior were not enslaved, masters and servants laws and an early version of the pass laws were imposed on them during the nineteenth century to discipline and control the movement of rural labour, as well as to solidify relations in the border areas. In the Transvaal, the *inboek* system, in which captives taken in campaigns against local tribes were indentured to farmers, provided another precedent for labour controls. Indentured Indian labour was imported to Natal to work on sugar plantations. So there were ample precedents in the pre-mining era for the labour system which came to be the main feature of the mining economy. But the peculiarities of mining, particularly gold-mining, required a radical extension and elaboration of earlier forms of labour recruitment and control, which quite transformed the social and political landscape.

For at least the first thirty or forty years of its existence, the fundamental condition for the profitability of the gold-mining industry was a large, cheap and totally controllable labour force. The goldfields of the Witwatersrand were the most extensive known deposits in the world, but the quality of the ore grades was among the poorest. Moreover, the extraction of gold from the ore became extremely difficult once the surface outcrops had been exhausted, and as mining was carried out at deeper levels. These problems induced a series of crises in the industry during the 1890s. Small-scale producers were forced out by groups which could raise the massive amounts of capital required to develop deep-level mining and to import, install, and operate the elaborate crushing and extractive plant needed to produce the metal in marketable form. The price of gold was externally fixed in the financial capitals of the world, without any reference to the costs of its production. Any mining company which remained profitable despite these bleak constraints was forced to pay ruthless attention to the costs of production. The element in these costs which it was possible to control was the wages of the labour force. Both control over the process of recruitment and control over the conditions of living as well as working became vital to the profitability of the whole elaborate enterprise.

A two-fold solution was adopted. The problem of control was broached at the Kimberley fields and transferred to the Witwatersrand. Ostensibly in order to prevent the theft of diamonds from the diggings and, it was claimed, to check the alarming incidence of alcoholic inebriation among black workers, the Kimberley managements established barrack-like compounds in which black workers were housed, and where access and egress were strictly controlled. But while Kimberley offered a method of controlling labour once it was *in situ*, it provided no long-term solution to the problem of inducing large numbers of workers to offer their labour at wages that might help the mines to remain profitable.

Some of the labour on the diamond mines was drawn from the agricultural labour force displaced from the land by the increasing density of European settlement and the spread of commodity relationships. The main source was the Basotho, who had been forced out of their rich wheatlands north of the Caledon and into the Maluti mountains by the Free State boers during the 1850s and 1860s. This force, it could be argued, was produced by the logic of colonial, and particularly boer, conquest, expansion and settlement. The goldfields required more elaborate and radical innovations to mobilise a labour force. In 1894, while Rhodes was prime minister, the Cape parliament passed the Glen Grey Act, which provided for a system of individual land tenure in the Transkeian Territories, thus ensuring that some elements in the community would become landless, and imposed hut and poll taxes which forced such individuals to enter the labour market. Similar systems, including restrictions on African rights to acquire land, were developed in other parts of the country, and variations already established in British and Portuguese colonies created the conditions for recruiting labour over wide areas of the sub-continent.

Recruiting agents scoured the territories thus affected, ensuring that the workseeker would be assisted in finding his way to the Transvaal goldfields. The system was initially conducted by a variety of small-scale recruiting agents and by traders who, by encouraging purchase on credit, could increase the turnover both of their stocks and of human labour. The system soon exhibited disutilities to the mines. Agents sometimes 'sold' labourers whom they had recruited to other agents in the course of their movement to the fields, thus pushing up the costs incurred by the mines. Moreover, mines frequently competed with one another for labour, often recruiting deserters from other mines. Some agents maintained their own labour compounds (occasionally rented from the mines) and collected the workers' wages. In order to solve these problems, the Chamber of Mines set up the Witwatersrand Native Labour Association (WNLA), which recruited labour on behalf of all its members and distributed it among the mines according to their requirements.

The mineworkers signed contracts, enforceable in criminal law, in terms of which they worked on the mines for a period of the year, usually nine months, and then returned to the land. During these periods of 'rest' between contracts the worker was expected to engage in agricultural production, which would provide him and his family with their subsistence. On the mines, managements supplied food and accommodation to the workers, which made it possible to effect considerable savings in the costs of workers' subsistence, and created in the compounds conditions conducive to enforcing total controls over the workforce. Conditions in the compounds were initially so appalling that the British governor of the Transvaal after the South African War, Alfred Lord Milner, considered the reduction of the mortality rate among black miners to be one of the most important issues which faced him, and he expressed considerable satisfaction in the results of his efforts to draw up regulations specifying minimum standards of nutrition, accommodation, and medical attention. After Union, these regulations were consolidated in the Native Labour Regulation Act of 1911, one of the foundations of the spartan fabric of welfare measures evolved by the South African state to maintain the African workforce in sufficiently good condition to withstand the rigours of the labour it performed.

The migrant labour system which evolved on the Witwatersrand mines made it possible to hold the wages of mineworkers constant over a remarkably long period of time. Black miners' wages actually fell over the period between 1910 and 1942. They did not increase in real terms between 1910 and 1973, when they more than trebled in the wake of widespread strikes and a sharp increase in the price of gold. This instance of wage constancy becomes doubly remarkable when it is realised that the wages of Africans in manufacturing industry, though lower than the wages paid to white workers, tended over time to increase in response to rises in the cost of living and the pressures of industrial action, notwithstanding the repressive powers which the state has used against African workers in all sectors of the economy. The system of migrant contract labour, housed in compounds, must count as one of the most perfect instruments devised in modern times for controlling the wages of industrial labour. By the 1920s, the main features of the mine labour system had been established. At its base was a force of African migrant contract workers drawn from most of the South African reserves, from British protectorates and colonies in Basutoland, Bechuanaland, Swaziland, and Nyasaland, and the Portuguese colonies in Mozambique and Angola. This element in the labour force performed the heaviest work. Black workers were precluded (by statute from 1911) from performing the crucially important task of blasting. And though the chain of command in the workforce incorporated a system of African 'indunas' and 'boss boys', the key supervisory roles were performed by white workers.

Housed and fed in compounds, their contracts forcing them to oscillate between reserves and the mines, black mineworkers were sealed off from the rest of society as effectively as though they were prisoners. Of course, as with prisoners, many escaped into the workforce in other industries where wages were higher and conditions of life less closely regimented. Also comparable in another respect with prison society, mineworkers developed informal associations, sometimes linking the workforce into networks extending back into the reserves – as with the Witzieshoek Vigilance Society which was founded before the First World War, and which played an important part in the resistance to government 'betterment schemes' in Witzieshoek reserve during the 1940s and 1950s. In the compounds and underground, informally organised hierarchies developed, sometimes encouraged by mine managements to reinforce their precarious controls. Miners were in these circumstances very difficult to organise, and strikes were violently repressed, often by forces of armed policemen. Despite these difficulties, African mineworkers struck, rioted, assaulted white miners, and in other ways took collective action to express their interests. On two historic occasions, in 1920 and in 1946, they brought production to a standstill on mines stretching across the entire length of the Reef. The resurgence of working-class action, which took place from the early 1970s after a long period of relative quiescence, was mainly initiated by mineworkers. Industrial action by mineworkers, and generally by contract workers, reflected their responses to the circumstances on the land no less than to conditions in the mines and in the compounds. The stopes at which they worked lay at the end of a path that stretched back hundreds and sometimes thousands of miles, to a family, a few head of livestock, and a patch of land, though many were effectively without land.

The migrant labour system produced an indelible deterioration of the political economy of the reserves, partly because of the measures taken to coerce the labour force into existence, partly because of the defensive measures undertaken by the peasantry (e.g. by raising sheep to help pay taxes), but mainly because of the deleterious effects produced on subsistence economies by the absence of a major proportion of the able-bodied male population for most of the year. Historians disagree about the rate at which the reserves decayed as a consequence of the changes induced by the mining industry. Certainly, by the early 1930s, both the government and the mining industry were deeply disturbed about the high rejection rate, due to ill health and malnutrition, among new recruits seeking work on the mines.

A number of government commissions considered the problem, and the Chamber of Mines itself conducted a private inquiry which remains one of the most interesting and detailed studies of the deterioration of the Transkeian economy. All the inquiries attested to the overcrowding, overstocking and declining productivity of the reserves. Areas which previously exported grain began importing it from the 1920s. Sheep were widely introduced during the first decade of the twentieth century by people who hoped that the proceeds from the sale of wool might help pay taxes. In subsequent generations, sheep have damaged rich grazing and ground cover, and what the sheep left unharmed, goats have destroyed. The ownership of livestock became concentrated in the hands of local elites – chiefs, headmen and schoolteachers. White traders early took advantage of their superior knowledge of market conditions and of health regulations to acquire cattle cheaply, and in many areas grazed their cattle on commonage in the reserves. Increasingly people bought from trading stores the food, including maize, which previously they had cultivated and stored or marketed, as well as expensive and less nutritious tinned food. Tribesmen became indebted to traders, often buying back at inflated prices maize they had earlier sold to the stores. Women entered wage employment, leaving children in the care of siblings or grandparents. Numerous investigations by government departments, the mining companies, mission hospitals and academics during the 1930s and 1940s revealed a radical decline in standards of health. Studies conducted in widespread areas, including Bechuanaland and Swaziland, suggested a high correlation between malnutrition and the extent of migrancy.

The measures introduced under the Glen Grey Act, the limitations placed on the amount of land available to African peasant cultivators, the restrictions placed on squatting under the 1913 Land Act, and the effects of the Land Act of 1936, have all contributed to undermining the subsistence economies of the reserves. But, as Colin Bundy has shown in an important study, they also destroyed the African peasantry which had begun to emerge during the 1870s in response to increasing market opportunities, especially in the eastern Cape. By the 1920s, this group had largely disappeared as a significant social stratum. Many African political leaders, writers, scholars and professional people emerged from the remnants of this class. But the majority were forced into the ranks of a landless proletariat.

The Native Land and Trust Act of 1936 was purportedly intended to provide for the economic development of the reserves. But the 'betterment schemes' introduced under that legislation at best improved the position of tribal elites, by then incorporated into the central apparatus of the Native Affairs Department as petty administrators of government policy. Betterment schemes appeared sensible enough on the surface. They were aimed at preventing overstocking and overgrazing, the exhaustion of land through continuous cultivation, by measures such as stock culling, limitations on ploughing, fencing, and the development of pilot projects. In practice, the measures inflicted such serious penalties on peasant producers that from the time of their institution there has in some areas been almost continuous rebellion on the land. At the bottom of the problem lay the shortage of land made available for African occupancy in terms of legislation introduced from before Union, and particularly the Natives Land Act of 1913 and three Acts, of which the Native Land Act was one, in 1936.

The measures adopted to secure a cheap and controllable labour force involved a close relationship between the mining interests and the state. The companies which came to dominate the Kimberley diggings, and which later transferred to the goldfields of the Witwatersrand, exercised considerable influence over the Cape government during the 1890s. The Glen Grey Act and the programme of railway construction undertaken during the last decade of the nineteenth century were two of the most important consequences of the symbiotic relationship between the Cape government and the industry. But though the mining industry stood at the zenith of its political influence in the Cape during the 1890s, it was not without its critics in Cape politics, even before the Jameson Raid of 1895. John X. Merriman, later prime minister of the Cape, summed up the loathing felt for the parvenu society built on gold at Johannesburg in such well-chosen invective descriptions as 'a plague spot with its shoddy prosperity and its hideous criminal vulgarity'. In the Transvaal, the loathing was even more intense. The Transvaal Republic was a well-established though impoverished political society, controlled by a self-righteous and puritanical class of rural land-owners. The Republic's independence was already under threat in the legal form of the British suzerainty formula imposed after the War of Independence of 1880-1. The main attraction of the mining industry to the boer political leadership lay in the revenues which it could deliver to the state, and the profits its growing markets could provide to agricultural producers. It is probable that President Paul Kruger intended to cream off the surpluses produced by the mines in order to develop indigenous manufacturing; certainly, he and the group of businessmen and bureaucrats associated with him took every opportunity to reap harvests in the goldfields, directly through taxation, and indirectly through the concessions system which made the state the direct beneficiary of industrial production of a wide range of commodities. The fact that few of the leading members of the mining interests or indeed the bulk of the new workforce were Transvaal citizens, and that even fewer demonstrated the sober piety which might have ingratiated themselves with Pretoria or the platteland (country districts), made it all the easier for Kruger to regard the industry as a resource to be exploited rather than an interest to be cosseted.

The crisis which emerged during the 1890s in fact developed around the issue of the franchise for the 'Uitlanders'. Possibly the situation might have persisted at a temperature below boiling point had it not been for the crisis to profits precipitated by the need to shift to deep-level mining and the technical problems which this posed to the industry. Whatever the reason, an influential number of mining magnates of Johannesburg decided that they needed a government more sympathetic to their problems than the one led by Kruger. They decided to overthrow the government by launching a column led by Rhodes's friend Dr L. S. Jameson from Bechuanaland. The Jameson Raid was abortive. The Raid ruptured relations between the British and Transvaal governments, and the mining interests put pressure on the British government to try to secure the franchise for the white foreigners on the goldfields. Whether the British government intended to provoke a crisis on the dimensions to which it eventually grew is not clear, but by late 1899 the Republic declared war on Britain. The Orange Free State joined forces.

The war intensified the transformation initiated by the opening of the goldfields. It broke the power of the boer agrarian class which had controlled the republics, and paved the way for the creation of a powerful British colonial administration intent on modernising the state and fostering the mining industry.

During the period of reconstruction which followed the war, Milner established the elements of a powerful bureaucracy, including a native affairs department, an efficient police force and an impartial judiciary. The concessions system was dismantled. Crown Colony rule in the Transvaal lasted barely five years before the introduction of responsible government, but it had an indelible effect on the subsequent political and social history of South Africa. Although political parties with strong links to the old agrarian interests which had controlled the republics regained power in the Transvaal and the Orange River Colony, their power was reconstructed within the framework of the colonial states.

The political consequence of the defeat of the boer republics was to advance the position of the mining industry, which entered a period lasting nearly a quarter of a century of almost unchallenged political power in the country. Milner saw himself as a servant of Empire, first and last, and his administrative reforms were designed primarily to secure British hegemony by encouraging immigration. But, as Shula Marks and Stanley Trapido have argued, the innovations he introduced in the administration served precisely the political requirements of the mining industry.

Milner's policies worked equally to serve British political interests and the interests of the mining industry.[10] He sought to open the country up to British immigration, especially in the Transvaal, so that when the franchise was eventually introduced it would work to uphold and not to threaten British interests in South Africa.

He hoped to delay the establishment of responsible government, and with it the prospect of an Afrikaner majority, until British immigration, combined with the acculturation of Afrikaners to British ways via the educational departments he set up, could counteract the elements loyal to traditional Afrikaner leaders and hopeful of the restoration of the former republics. There was no fundamental contradiction between a state capable of generating the economic conditions for rapid immigration and one that upheld the mining industry as the dominant political and economic interest.

In the event, Milner's plan to delay responsible government until he was certain of a British majority was frustrated, by a poetic justice, because of the efforts to which he went to solve the labour shortage that developed on the mines after the war. Milner imported Chinese indentured labour to the goldfields. The outcry against Chinese labour, both in South Africa and in Britain, was an important issue in the British general elections of 1906 and helped to garner votes for the victorious Liberal Party. The new Liberal government pushed the Crown colonies in the former republics towards responsible government. By 1909, there were Afrikaner ministries in these two states, and a pro-boer government dependent on the Afrikaner vote in the Cape.

This outcome thwarted Milner's hopes for a British South Africa, but it did not undercut the political power of the mining interest. That interest exercised considerable influence over the British electorate of the Cape and the Transvaal, through the positions of leadership assumed in them by men like Jameson, Percy FitzPatrick, George Farrar and other reformers who in 1895 had plotted the downfall of Kruger's Republic.

More important, perhaps, the leaders of the Het Volk party, which controlled the Transvaal after 1907, proved to be more sympathetic to the mining interest than might have been expected. Generals Smuts and Botha, the main figures after 1907 in Transvaal and Union governments, had been strong supporters of Kruger, and among the toughest of the *bittereinders*. They had continued the war for eighteen months after Pretoria had fallen, but they were keenly aware of the benefits of the large revenues the mines could deliver to the state, and continued the work of modernising the state which Milner had begun. Smuts understood clearly the importance of protecting the industry against political attack from the workforce, and used troops to suppress the disturbances that accompanied the strike of white mineworkers in 1907. Botha was a bon viveur who got on well with the leaders of the mining industry, and despite the fact that in the new Union of South Africa the political interests of mining were represented through the Unionist Party until 1921, the government maintained the close relationships which Milner had established with the industry.

So despite the political volte face of the years between 1907 and 1910, which scotched Milner's hopes of perpetuating British rule in South Africa, the mining industry maintained its position as the dominant force in the industrial economy and continued to secure the government's cooperation in protecting its interests. Imperial preferences were retained until the mid-1920s. They did not disadvantage the mining industry, but exposed local manufacturers to British competition. The system of labour recruitment and organisation initiated before the South African War was reformed, consolidated and refined in post-Union legislation. Mining retained its privileged position in relation to government until the Nationalist–Labour Pact took office in 1924. Even thereafter, when successive governments stimulated local manufacturing and granted increasing subsidies to agriculture, the mining industry long remained the jewel in the South African industrial crown. The practices evolved in mining, especially in the organisation of the labour force, have had a lasting effect on the entire sub-continent. The long period of mining's predominance imposed on the agrarian societies of the region and on the emergent manufacturing sector a structure primarily intended to serve mining. Some of the consequences can be seen in the transformation of boer society after the South African War.

The defeat of the boers had calamitous consequences for many thousands of burghers in the former republics and for Afrikaner colonists in the interior of the Cape whose position on the land had become precarious even before the outbreak of hostilities. The fact that mining dominated the economy during the period after the war, and remained the ascendant force during the period in which the industrial infrastructure was developed, intensified their problems, and cast them into social and economic roles that deeply marked the forms of social stratification which subsequently developed in South Africa.

The pace of industrial development sharpened a crisis in white agrarian communities which had been slowly emerging since the early days of the Dutch settlement at the Cape. The name which preachers and politicians gave to the crisis was *achteruitgang* – retrogression – or, more simply, poor whitism. It had many dimensions, of which the major economic feature was landlessness. The principal cause of landlessness lay in the relative ease with which land had been occupied and indigenous labour appropriated during colonial and republican times. Boers very often did not take out titles to the land they occupied as they settled the interior. The problem was masked while the frontiers remained open and new land could be settled, but from the 1860s in the Cape and the 1870s in the Transvaal, a distinctive stratum of landless boers became evident as a feature of the countryside. The very extensive farms, and the practice of many Transvaal boers of holding two farms, one on the highveld and one on the lowveld for winter grazing, meant that a land shortage would emerge once territorial expansion was no longer possible. Children often settled on the family farm particularly if they were unable to acquire their own. Their descendants came to constitute the *bywoner* class, the landless occupiers of rural property with whose owners they could claim kinship ties and for whom in earlier days they performed important services. The Dutch system of inheritance encouraged the fragmentation of farms and the emergence of dwarf holdings. It was difficult to exploit these holdings effectively in many parts of the country, where climate and soil dictated extensive rather than intensive land usage.

The slow commercialisation of agriculture during the second half of the nineteenth century extruded many whites to the margins of the rural economy. The opening of the diamondfields induced many landless whites to enter the diggings, where they found employment as washers and sorters. They also went to the alluvial diggings in the eastern Transvaal and to the Witwatersrand. Well into the twentieth century men moved from one alluvial field to another in search of their elusive fortunes. Many entered the lucrative transport-riding industry. The completion of the railway line to Johannesburg in the mid-1890s, and the rinderpest epidemic of 1896, which killed hundreds of thousands of draught animals, threw them onto a depressed labour market which had little space for white men (burghers or citizens, after all) who would not be coerced like the African mineworkers.

Charles van Onselen has shown that they demonstrated considerable ingenuity in opening up small-scale industrial and service enterprises on the goldfields. They pioneered brick-making and the cab-driving trade in Johannesburg, only to be squeezed out by companies linked to the mining industry or with political influence in government circles. The problem was greatly aggravated during the South African War and after. Lord Roberts, the commander-in-chief of the British forces, devastated vast areas of the two republics in an effort to starve out the boer guerrillas. When boers who had been put into concentration camps returned to their farms they found them in ruins, their homesteads dynamited, their stock slaughtered, and their land often occupied by African squatters. Many poor whites who had earned a poor reputation for their fighting skills surrendered early to the British – the so-called *hensoppers* – and served in the National Scouts, raised by the occupying power. In the early post-war years, no group attracted more calumny from the general body of Afrikaner society.

The Milner administration and Transvaal industrial and commercial interests were little interested in restoring the decaying remnants of what they saw as an archaic social order to its position on the land. Milner wanted an energetic and compliant British, or anglicised, class of commercial farmers on the land, not an independent rural squirarchy surrounded by a retinue of *takhare* (backwoodsmen). Equally, the post-war administration was hostile to the possibility of restoring poor white farmers to the soil where they might batten on the state for relief.

Yet, as we shall see presently, the conditions of initial industrialisation provided little scope for the development of commercial agriculture holding more than a fraction of the white population on the land. The mass of Afrikaners were fated to migrate to the urban areas. The problems they encountered there illuminate the political conflicts that developed in and around the workplace which made it possible for their support to be mobilised for segregation and for apartheid. The structure of the industrial labour force which emerged under the dominance of mining provided little space for an unskilled white labour force. The successive waves of Afrikaners who left the land from the turn of the century onwards found it difficult to enter the supervisory jobs on the mines, which were initially monopolised by immigrant workers, usually with experience of the Californian and Australian goldfields, the Cornish tin mines and, above all, the exclusivist practices of English craft unionism. Squeezed out of the small industries which they had pioneered before the war, Afrikaners in the cities were highly vulnerable, particularly during depressions, and were often constrained to subsist on wages obtained from public relief works. In 1907, when white, mainly immigrant miners struck, Afrikaners were recruited as scab labour, and thereafter entered the mining industry in increasing numbers.

The special position of white workers on the mines requires some comment. White workers performed supervisory roles and jobs like blasting, which became reserved to them by statute. Contrary to a widespread belief, this racial stratification in industry was not simply a sop to white prejudice, or a form of relief work imposed on the mine managements by a politically powerful white working class. A privileged stratum of workers who could exercise control over the African workforce was as necessary to the maintenance of control and discipline in the workplace (especially underground) as the presence of a subaltern class of *colons* in other parts of colonial Africa. All the same, the wages which whites could earn on the mines, between ten and twenty times those paid to black mineworkers, were a constant source of friction between the mining companies and white workers. Whites, who constituted around a seventh of the labour force, accounted for up to 40 per cent of the mines' wage bills. Especially during periods of rising costs and a static or falling gold price, mine managements tried to reduce the proportion of white to black workers on the mines, commonly by increasing the number of Africans working drills under the supervision of a single white overseer. Such efforts to change the ratio had a two-fold consequence: they increased the workloads and responsibilities of white supervisors, and they threatened the collective interests of white workers. In 1922, a move to change the ratio took the Witwatersrand over the brink of civil war.

In 1921, the mining companies unilaterally changed the ratio in order to save costs in a situation in which the gold price was falling and costs were rising. The ensuing strike precipitated the extraordinary episode of the 1922 Rand Rebellion, which had far-reaching consequences for the mining industry's position in the political economy, for white workers' relations with the state, and for the shape of government over the following decade. Early in 1922, about 22 000 white workers went on strike. By March, the strike had developed into an insurrection. Armed strikers occupied working-class districts along the Reef. The prime minister, Smuts, ordered a force of 7 000 troops, bomber aircraft and armoured cars, to put it down. The strikers suffered 153 dead, and more than 500 wounded in four days of fighting, during the course of which artillery shelled, and aircraft bombed, working-class districts in Johannesburg, where the revolt had its centre. Five leaders were sentenced to death and hundreds to fines and prison terms. The brutal suppression of the strike intensified the political crisis with which Smuts's government had been wrestling since the end of the First World War. The suppression of the strike alienated a good deal of the government's support in working-class districts, and opened the way for an alliance between the National and Labour parties, catching Smuts in the pincers of an opposition made up of white farmers and workers.

The Nationalist–Labour Pact of 1923 laid the basis for an electoral victory for the alliance in 1924. The 'civilised labour' policy, which provided employment in the public service for whites at 'civilised' rates of pay, was one of the major consequences of the Pact victory. Another consequence was a significant shift in the state's policy towards industry and towards organised labour, though it should be noted that Smuts had contemplated both possibilities. The first involved the decision to develop an infrastructure that would stimulate the local manufacturing industry, a policy of protectionism for industry, and increased subsidies for agriculture. The second involved the creation of machinery for 'industrial conciliation', which had the effect of institutionalising the white labour movement, thus enhancing its negotiating power, but at the cost of blunting its militancy. The Industrial Conciliation Act passed in 1924 made it difficult for white workers to strike legally. Conciliation boards were established on which unions, employers and government officials were represented, and to which disputes had to be taken for arbitration before a strike could legally be called. This measure induced bureaucratic tendencies in the unions which decreased their effectiveness. By the late 1930s, the Mineworkers' Union had become corrupt and inert, largely the instrument of the Chamber of Mines. Afrikaner workers who entered manufacturing industries during the Second World War turned to unions organised under the auspices of Afrikaner nationalist cultural associations, such as the Federasie van Afrikaanse Kultuurvereniginge (FAK). The Labour Party gained access to political office in 1924, but it was a pyrrhic victory. The party declined as a workers' party as the union movement ossified. By the late 1930s it was represented in parliament exclusively by middle-class members. By 1948, the party had virtually conceded the political leadership of the white working class to the National Party.

The commanding position which the mining industry held for so long in the South African political economy has had several major consequences for subsequent social and political relationships, even after manufacturing overtook mining as the leading sector of the industrial economy. Some of these will briefly be considered here. The location of the goldfields on the Witwatersrand generated a large and diverse population in the towns and cities established on the Reef, and especially in Johannesburg, where the mining houses had their headquarters. The main lines of communication, particularly railways, which in the absence of navigable rivers provided the most important means of transportation, were dictated primarily by the transportation needs of the mining industry, and later by the markets provided in the heavy concentrations of population in the area. The particular form of the transport network had a fundamental effect on the access of long-established communities to transportation, and hence their access to the new markets. The line between the Cape and the Witwatersrand followed a path which diverged from the direction of European settlement in the Cape during the nineteenth century, bypassing many small towns and farming communities, as well as the densely settled African communities in the eastern Cape and Border areas.

The seaport towns of Durban, Cape Town and Lourenço Marques (now Maputo) were all founded long before the mining areas were opened up. They had developed local industries, markets and economic hinterlands prior to and independently of the industrial growth of the interior. But from the 1890s, these areas, all linked by rail to the goldfields, became increasingly locked into the mining economy, serving as entrepots for the transportation of men, equipment and goods to and from the mining areas, and subject to the rhythms of the gold-based economy. When the gold price fell, or the industry faced a crisis, the effects percolated throughout the economy. East London and Port Elizabeth, serving the old-established wool- and grain-producing areas of the eastern Cape and Border areas, were relatively retarded by their distance and indirect links to the goldfields. Even though manufacturing industries developed there from the end of the First World War and there was massive growth during the Second World War and after, their major markets lay in the dense settlements of the Pretoria–Witwatersrand–Vereeniging area.

Most financial institutions, banks, insurance companies and industrial corporations continue to maintain their headquarters in Johannesburg. The untidy conurbations which spread out from the original Reef continue to form the core of a changing economy, notwithstanding signs of decline in its original centre. During the 1960s and 1970s, parts of this area, including Johannesburg, have exhibited the signs of decay and economic stagnancy which are the features of all old-established metropoles. Since the 1960s, the most important new industrial undertakings have been occurring on the borders of the 'homelands'. The towns which spread across the 60-mile length of the Reef have decayed as the goldmines which brought them into existence declined. The Witwatersrand has been superseded as the main gold-producing areas by the richer fields that opened up in the Orange Free State after the Second World War. And Pretoria makes the major decisions concerning the political economy, but the Witwatersrand continues to be the centre of gravity of industrial South Africa.

A study of corporate power demonstrated that Johannesburg remained during the 1980s the major centre of economic power in the country; that one of the three secondary centres was Pretoria (the other two were Cape Town and Durban); and that three of six minor centres were located in the southern Transvaal.[12] It is there that the largest settlements of the most affluent classes of whites live; it is also in these areas that the densest and most securely established settlements of Africans have grown up. The African population of the Witwatersrand has become the largest and most politically assertive element in the new industrial workforce in the country and potentially one of the most important consumer markets.

Although the Kimberley diggings and the Witwatersrand goldfields attracted a large number of small entrepreneurs, controls very rapidly passed into the hands of a few large companies. The registration of the De Beers Consolidated Mines, Ltd in 1888 represented the alliance between the last survivors of the ruthless concentration which drove out the small producers – C. J. Rhodes, and Wernher and Beit, on the one hand, and Barnato on the other. In 1917, the Anglo American Corporation was formed under the control of the remarkable Ernest Oppenheimer. In 1929, he became chairman of De Beers, thus uniting in one corporation the leadership of a massive proportion of South Africa's gold and diamond industries. In turn control was extended into many other branches of mining, into manufacturing, land, estate and investment. The Anglo American Corporation is exceptional in the scale and reach of its operations, the continuity in its leadership, and the coherency of its corporate strategy. But it was characteristic of the extraordinary concentration of economic power which took place in the mining industry, and subsequently in other sectors of the economy.

Nearly 600 gold-mining companies were formed during the period 1887–1932; only 57 of them remained in existence after 1932. Most became controlled by six groups of companies. The concentration of power was a marked feature of the industry from the earliest days. As we have seen, two major factors influencing its development were the need for massive capital investments to develop the industry after the crisis of the mid-1890s, and the strategies adopted to recruit and control African labour on terms optimal for profitability.

Agriculture

The rapid growth of the industrial labour force and the urban population, which followed the establishment of the mining industry, promised to lift the sluggish agricultural economies of southern Africa out of the doldrums in which they had previously existed. The markets that opened up offered commercial farmers opportunities which many were able to exploit to full advantage. The highveld areas of the Transvaal and the Orange Free State rapidly developed as centres of commercial farming, supplying food to the mining areas. A much wider area of the sub-continent was developed as a source of agricultural supplies to the industrial areas, including Southern Rhodesia and Bechuanaland.

However, a number of constraints rapidly emerged to limit these opportunities, tending to stimulate a system of controls over labour which were comparable in purpose, though different in form, to those which emerged in the mining sector. Some of these constraints were produced by problems inherent in the soil and climatic conditions of the sub-continent – low and unreliable rainfalls, light soils, and frequent droughts. Others had their origins in the methods of organising agricultural production, the system of inheritance, and patterns of rural settlement. But most importantly, the trajectory of industrialisation and the political consequences of industrial development on the basis of mining created restraints which limited the opportunities that the industrial revolution offered South African commercial agriculture.

The collapse of the vigorous class of African peasants and the wholesale transformation of the Afrikaner *bywoner* class into an industrial proletariat have been noted. The white farmers who managed to survive and prosper through the depressions of the 1920s and 1930s did so, like the mining companies themselves, by paying ruthless attention to costs, and particularly the costs of labour. As with the mining industry, this required invoking the aid of the state to control and regulate the movement of labour. Increasingly, too, the state's support was invoked as a source of subsidies, low-interest loans, credits, relief, technical assistance and marketing. The cumulative effect of these developments was sharply to stratify the white farming community and to maintain a force of poorly paid black labour. By the last quarter of the twentieth century, control over agriculture had come to lie in a small group of powerful land-owners, commonly incoporated into companies, behind which trailed, like a comet's dust, a cloud of impoverished farmers who might have done better in industrial employment.

In trying to take advantage of market opportunities, farmers experienced a number of problems. Farmers were induced to invest in equipment, initially imported, on a scale that frequently led to overcapitalisation. The cost of agricultural machinery increased during the twentieth century at a rate higher than the price of agricultural produce. Above all, despite its growth, the internal market for agricultural production remained disappointingly small. As early as 1908, the Transvaal and Free State were forced to seek export markets for agricultural produce. The reasons for this lie partly in the small populations, especially the urban populations, in industrial employment, but also in the condition of the labour force. The largest element in the industrial workforce until the end of the Second World War was the African mine labour force, the numbers of which had by then risen to something like half a million. Housed in compounds and supplied rations by the mine managements, this element of the workforce provided a limited and restricted market for agricultural produce, despite its size. The African labour force in secondary industry, which by the end of the Second World War had outstripped the mine labour force in numbers, was another important market for agricultural producers. But like miners, Africans working in manufacturing lived perilously close to the breadline. The element in the labour force which constituted a more promising market for agricultural produce was the white working class, but they were not numerous or affluent enough to provide a mass market. The stratum of middle-class whites which emerged in the shadow of the mining houses, commerce and industry did eat well, but were also too few in number to create a mass domestic market. Moreover, until the 1960s, a good deal of produce was supplied from market gardens within cities' boundaries or close nearby, and by small-holders supplementing wages and pensions. Indian squatters and Italian or Portuguese market gardeners were active from before the First World War in supplying the need for fresh produce in the larger cities. In the 1960s, the old market gardens became happy hunting grounds for speculators in suburban property development.

Farmers were compelled to look to distant export markets, particularly in Europe, where they were exposed to the full brunt of the international economic crisis after the First World War. During the 1920s, especially after the Pact government took power, the state increased its subsidies to white farmers, but this action was insufficient to prevent the collapse of many enterprises. The crisis of the depression of the early 1930s shook thousands of white farmers off the land in the wake of collapsing prices on the international market. The government introduced measures comparable in intention, though not in detail, to the New Deal measures undertaken in the United States. In essence the South African system involved fixing production quotas each season, determined by a centralised, state-controlled decision-making process and marketing machinery. Farmers were guaranteed their 'costs of production' within the limits prescribed by the quota. The boards paid the difference between these costs and the price of produce on the international market. They also undertook the complex tasks of arranging contracts and marketing produce.

The full consequences of the system, which became increasingly elaborate over the course of the following half-century, are difficult precisely to determine. Subsidies and other supports probably worked to extend the scale and intensify the mechanisation of production. Because only a minority of farmers had the resources which qualified them to take advantage of the system, state supports probably worked to reinforce the stratification of white agriculture between an extremely small number of very affluent farmers and a large group which found it more and more difficult to live off the land. Although all governments have proclaimed the importance of the agricultural community in maintaining 'white civilisation', government policies may have worked, if anything, to accelerate the process of stratification, and hence the exodus of whites from the countryside. Indeed, during the Second World War, the Social and Economic Planning Council recommended that the number of farming units should be reduced and their efficiency improved.

After the National Party came to power in 1948, with massive support from the rural white community, there were expectations that the state would make efforts to reverse the depopulation of the rural areas. Indeed, the new government intensified controls over the movement of African labour, and increased and rationalised financial and infrastructural supports for the agricultural interest. But notwithstanding these efforts and rhetorical flourishes about the need to halt the depopulation of the white rural areas, Nationalist policy did not significantly reverse the stratification of the white farming sector and it may have worked, through the rationalisation of production and marketing which it encouraged, to reinforce it. By the early 1960s, the top 1 per cent of farms accounted for 14 per cent of gross sales, and 16 per cent of farmers accounted for 65 per cent. The bottom third of farms accounted for less than 5 per cent of sales, and brought incomes which were little better than a skilled artisan could earn.

The difficulties facing commercial agriculture go some way to explaining the extraordinarily low wages paid to African farmworkers, about a third of the wages paid to black workers in manufacturing industry. They might also explain the repressive influx controls imposed to regulate their movement away from the rural areas, the exclusion of farmworkers from regulations governing industrial labour, and specifically their exclusion from statutory wage determinations. The general backwardness of the agricultural sector also explains the arduous nature of the work performed, the use of child, prison and female labour.

Above all, the backwardness of this sector helps explain the development of the system of labour tenancy which was only gradually phased out during the mid-1960s. The central element of the system, though it varied in its application from place to place and over time, was the contract which obliged the tenant to work for a certain number of days per annum for the farmer. The labourer commonly enjoyed access to the land on which he could cultivate crops and run stock. Sometimes, though infrequently, a tenant might receive no cash wages at all; but everywhere the system was in operation it ensured that wages could be held very low. Labour tenancy resembles in many ways an earlier system, which some scholars have described as 'squatter peasantry', which was prevalent in colonial times. The essence of that system was that the African occupiers of farms over which the colonist gained title paid him rent, whether in cash, kind or labour service. Land-holders were frequently absentees. Their control over the labourers lay ultimately in the military power of the settlers, and its immediate sanction lay in the violence the owner could inflict on the peasant occupier.

The system broke down under the impact of industrialisation. Given the stimulus to agricultural production which followed the opening of the diamondfields and goldfields, land-owners were induced to develop a labour system more appropriate for producing goods for sale on the market than was provided in a system in which the land-owner secured his income from what was in essence a form of ground-rent. During the last decade or so of the nineteenth century, the colonial and republican governments placed increasing restrictions on the rights of Africans to purchase land, and limited the number of squatters permitted to live on white farms. The latter measures were somewhat ineffective in achieving their purposes, but after the South African War, when Free State farmers in particular faced massive squatting on their lands, they pressed the colonial governments to stiffen the measures. Various statutes introduced before Union were consolidated into the Natives Land Act of 1913, singly the most important piece of legislation affecting African rights passed during the early years after Union. The Land Act prevented the sale of land between Africans and whites, limited the amount of land available for the African reserves, and most importantly, restricted the number of squatters on European farms.

The Act was put into immediate effect in the Orange Free State, where it had a devastating result on Africans. In his *Native Life in South Africa* (1916) Sol Plaatje recorded incidents of families, driven from the land, burying their dead on the roadside. The Beaumont Commission, which investigated the effects of the Act, reported in 1916 considerable evidence of the massive dislocations created on the farms and in the reserves within a year or so of the passage of the Act. An African witness told the Commission, 'We have never seen so much trouble since we were born. We are everlastingly moving from one place to another. We are very tired and annoyed.'

Squatting persisted well into the twentieth century, and indeed into the 1960s and 1970s in parts of Natal, and sharecropping in parts of the Transvaal till the mid-century, but the era of the semi-independent sharecropper and squatter had passed by the end of the First World War as decisively as that of the independent African peasant producer. The labour tenancy system which replaced these older forms outwardly resembled the system of squatter peasantry in so many ways that it is understandable that it should sometimes be seen as an evolution of the earlier forms. But it has been forcibly argued by a number of scholars, notably Michael Morris, that a sharp break was involved in the transition from the one form to the other, and that the change was dictated by the effects which an industrial economy dominated by mining produced on a relatively backward agricultural sector.[13] For where the system of squatter peasantry had rested on the payment of ground-rent (either in cash or as labour service) by labourers using their own implements and forms of labour organisation, labour tenancy was a form of coerced wage labour in which part of the wage was paid in kind.

One index of the change was that the labour tenant worked the owner's land, and his own , with the owner's equipment. Another token of the shift was that it became quite common from the end of the 1920s for farmers to calculate the value of in-kind payments in terms of their cash value, and indeed agricultural societies sometimes advised and made recommendations to their members of the value and levels of these in-kind payments prevailing in particular districts.

Labour tenancy resembled the mine labour system in a number of respects. At bottom both were methods of securing a cheap form of labour through two parallel sets of structures. The first set constituted the legal and juridical controls which forced labourers to enter into and remain within the labour force. The second set constituted the elements of welfare and subsistence to which the labourer had access (land and stock in the reserves for the migrant mineworker, and on the farm for the agricultural labourer). Restrictions on movement, which took a variety of forms in the course of the twentieth century, and the contract enforceable in criminal law, were essential features of both systems. Both were characterised by a system of migrancy, and though there were differences in the form it assumed in the two sectors, both were driven by a common economic logic. In the case of commercial agriculture, the farm labourer would often find work in nearby towns during 'off' seasons.

The farm, like the mine compound, approximated to the model of the 'total institution', and indeed the whole life of the labourer could be kept under surveillance and control by the farmer. Unlike the miner, who was separated from his family, the presence of the family on the farm provided an additional hold over the labour force. The most immediate form of control which the farmer could exercise over the labourer was physical violence, no less important despite the fact that it was illegal. The fact that violence was illegal no doubt placed constraints over the behaviour of farmers, and from time to time the worst cases would come to the courts. No doubt too, a farmer with a reputation for violence would find it more difficult to recruit and maintain a labour force. But such limitations did little to modify a situation in which farmers regarded the right to punish labourers as an inherent element in maintaining control. As well as the incidence of individually exercised violence there are cases in which, during periods of intense conflicts, farmers have taken, or threatened, collective action to ensure their labour supplies. Helen Bradford has analysed the virtual lynch law that developed in Natal during the 1920s, when the Industrial and Commercial Workers' Union (ICU) recruited members from among the agricultural labour force.

Writing of the intense struggles on the land during the 1920s, she refers to the 'bloody violence which made up the very fabric of rural society, and suffused with its spirit all relations between landlords and labourers.' Farmers regarded the police as inadequate instruments of control over their labour force, and small farmers in particular preferred to 'rely on their own brute force to discipline Africans who had not accepted the right of white farmers ruthlessly to abuse them. Thus in an economy in which black labour power came cheap, black bodies were the site on which white farmers exercised their blood-stained power.'[14] In 1949, faced with disturbances in the nearby Witzieshoek reserve and a coincident shortage of labour, farmers in the Harrismith district of the Orange Free State disingenuously demanded that they should be permitted to arm themselves and enter the reserve to *rus hulle uit* (root them out). In fact a contingent of the South African Police entered the reserve, and in clashes with the African community, 16 lives were lost and the majority of the able-bodied inhabitants decamped across the border into Basutoland.

Aside from the regulations controlling the movement of labour, successive South African governments have acted in various ways to ensure access to labour. After the Second World War, when white farmers already beset by a profound transformation in the agricultural economy were faced with severe labour shortages, the state made prisoners available as farm labour, and to facilitate the procedure, prisons were built on farms. Such arrangements emphasise the intimate relationships between the agricultural interest and the state; in particular localities, this intimacy was visible in the personal relationships between farmers, magistrates and policemen.

It is difficult to generalise about the agricultural industry and the conditions of labour. For the most part, it is probably the most depressed sector of the labour force in the country. Yet there are variations. At a conference on farm labour held in Cape Town in 1977, a number of farmers gave impressive evidence of the efforts they made to ensure that their workers were decently housed and clad, and their children educated in schools which are constructed on farms, and which the farmers, with state subsidies, help maintain. The state itself subsidises housing on farms, though not lavishly. But farmers with a humane interest in their labour force are in a small minority, and even they made it clear, sometimes inadvertently, that they claimed the right to regulate the moral conduct of the workforce.

The mechanisation of agricultural production and the concentration of controls over the industry which were developed during the 1930s have had a marked effect on African labour on the land. The shift away from the use of labour-intensive methods and towards the use of mechanised equipment has reduced the demand for African labour, and further weakened the position of Africans on the land. True, the process may have been retarded in some sectors of the industry, and probably overall in the less profitable or well-organised white farms, where reliance on poorly paid labour is probably a more attractive alternative to investments in the very expensive and sophisticated equipment sometimes required. But generally, farmers have come to require a core of workers skilled in the use of machinery, and seasonal demands for labour have been met by recruiting casual labour, often from the homelands. The ratio between permanent and casual labour has shifted in favour of the latter. During the 1970s, there was a marked tendency for black agricultural workers and their families to be resettled in the homelands.

Manufacturing

Despite the low tariffs and preferential treatment for imported British goods which prevailed until the 1920s, manufacturing industries developed rapidly during the period following the establishment of the goldmines, and by the end of the Second World War had outstripped goldmining as the leading sector of the economy. But the manufacturing industry faced problems comparable to those confronting agriculture in that the peculiarities of the mining industry imposed a specific stamp on manufacturing and commerce. Like agriculture, manufacturing industries had small internal markets, and their activities were governed by the uncertain rhythms of the mining economy.

Moreover, as noted earlier, the small-scale manufacturing enterprises which developed in the Witwatersrand found it difficult to survive in a climate dominated by the mining industry. Conditions for local manufacturing nevertheless improved during the period following the end of the First World War, and especially after the Pact government took power. The government imposed high tariffs on imported goods and, most important in the long run, established the Iron and Steel Corporation (Iscor) in 1926, even though it had before it a report that the steel industry was not likely to be profitable. Iscor was in fact to become a major force in generating the basis for a local manufacturing industry before the Second World War. It was also the first important instance of a state-controlled industrial production enterprise, and it provided a model for many similar ventures developed after 1945.

In the short term these developments stimulated investment in manufacturing industry. Under the stimulus of state support during the mid-1930s, manufacturing was set for major growth during and after the Second World War. The major social effect was the development of a local entrepreneurial class on the one hand and the growth of an industrial workforce permanently, if precariously, living in the metropolitan urban areas of the country.

The shift in the state's relationship to manufacturing industry was prefigured during the First World War by the emergence of a number of financial institutions, insurance companies and burial societies with a nationalist Afrikaner flavour, motivated explicitly by the intention to expand the economic opportunities available to Afrikaners. The funds to establish these institutions were derived partly from the Helpmekaar ('Help each other') movement which had been established after the 1914 Rebellion in order to pay for the defence of rebels. The Afrikaner Broederbond was set up at the end of the First World War. By the 1960s, it had assumed the global function of coordinating the political, economic and bureaucratic structures of Afrikaner nationalism. In the long run, Afrikaner entrepreneurs became the main beneficiaries of the development of the powerful state support for secondary industry, but they were not the leading elements in manufacturing, even after the Second World War. Indeed Dan O'Meara has argued that 'Afrikaner capital', formed mainly in commercial agriculture, has always predominated in financial, rather than in manufacturing activities.[15] The interweaving of controls over the different sectors by the 1960s makes it a rather pointless exercise to try to disentangle the political structures within each sector. Mining began quite early to invest in manufacturing through the establishment of finance companies, and in some sectors companies with a major interest in mining took a leading role in developments outside of the sector. To take a leading but by no means unique example, the Anglo American Corporation acquired interests outside of mining from the late 1940s, and by the 1960s was investing internationally as well.

The state's policy of stimulating manufacturing from the 1920s and 1930s was, it has been argued, paid for out of revenues derived from the taxes paid by the mines. It was in effect a policy by which mining subsidised manufacturing. According to some interpretations, the constraints placed on the mining industry by high taxation forced the industry to retain the low wages and consequently also the coercive and repressive practices which had developed earlier, long after they were necessary to maintain the profitability of the industry. Trapido argues that had it not been for this burden, the industry would have been able to increase miners' wages from the 1920s or 1930s.[16] This argument was based largely on a case presented on behalf of the mining interest, and has been challenged on the grounds that the taxes carried by the mines did not increase appreciably during the 1930s. Undoubtedly, other factors may have intervened to explain the continued reliance of the mining industry on a cheap labour force subjected to contracts and housed in compounds. One such factor might have been the pressure by white farmers on the government to impose on all sectors a labour policy which would not threaten labour supplies to the white farms. After the Second World War, some major mining companies, including the Anglo American Corporation, pressed for the development of a workforce settled in villages in the vicinity of the mines. This development was largely thwarted by the post-1948 Nationalist government, which limited the proportion of the black workforce permitted to live with their families.

Local manufacturing industry grew rapidly from the mid-1930s. It was particularly favoured by the United Party government, which was formed in 1934 with considerable support from local industrialists. According to economists using the Rostovian paradigm, the industrial economy entered the 'take-off' stage during the middle-to-late 1930s. But it was really during the Second World War that the major development and expansion of the manufacturing industry took place, especially after 1943. Local industries were stimulated by the virtual cessation of imports from Europe, and by the opportunities to produce war materiel which opened up with the country's entry into the war, and by the development of technical research and the increasingly scientific management of manpower. In 1920, capital investments in manufacturing stood at R48 million, compared with R138 million invested in mining.[17] By 1930, manufacturing investments had grown to R80 million, and by 1940 to R152 million. In the following decade, they multiplied more than five-fold to R823 million, while investments in mining rose at a comparatively sedate pace to R293 million.

The number of Africans employed in manufacturing grew in step with the growth in investments, from 35 065 in 1916 to 55 638 in 1925, and to 69 895 in 1930. The most rapid and sustained increase in employment took place between 1936 and 1945, nearly doubling from 107 674 to 207 797. By 1980, the number of Africans employed in the sector had reached 780 200. The urban African population followed the pattern of growth in employment:

Urban African population

Year	Population
1911	508 000
1921	587 000
1936	1 142 000
1946	1 689 000
1951	2 329 000
1970	5 000 000

The wages of workers in manufacturing were considerably higher than those paid to mineworkers and agricultural workers, though it must be borne in mind that most workers in manufacturing had to pay the costs of subsistence – rent, food and transport – out of their wages. Nevertheless, wages in manufacturing were impressively higher than in the other sectors, and the differential has increased steadily over the course of the century. In 1916, workers in manufacturing earned about 15 per cent more than mineworkers. By 1925, they were earning about 25 per cent more, by 1956 2,25 times as much, and by 1966 over two and a half times as much. Only after the increase in miners' wages during the early 1970s did the tendency begin to reverse, and even so, mineworkers earned about 70 per cent of the real wages of workers in manufacturing. Comparisons with agricultural workers are difficult to make because of the 'in-kind' element in farmworkers' wages, but workers in manufacturing earned something between five and six times the cash wages of agricultural workers.

This difference does not mean that black workers in manufacturing were affluent. On the contrary, a considerable proportion of the workforce received wages which fell short of providing the costs of family subsistence. The desperate poverty of the workforce underlay many of the political battles carried out in urban African communities. Their poverty also constituted a grave problem for the state, including local authorities, which had to confront the dual issues of managing political conflicts and the social and economic problems that flowed out of the condition of the working class.

The fact that wages were significantly higher in manufacturing than in the other sectors impelled the state to develop an elaborate machinery through which it could effectively allocate labour between the different sectors. The instruments of labour allocation via the use of influx controls and labour regulations which were established during Milner's reconstruction were further consolidated after Union, and elaborated during the 1920s in response to the increasing importance of manufacturing. These controls can partly be understood as a consequence of the threats of labour shortages which manufacturing industry posed to the agricultural and mining sectors. But it is important also to situate labour regulations within the broader context of the need for political controls over a growing industrial proletariat living in urban areas. The urban labour force was unenfranchised, uprooted from the land, housed in wretched conditions, poorly fed, and denied access to most of the amenities of civilised life. Missionaries and social workers made efforts from the early 1920s to ameliorate conditions. A petty bourgeoisie began to emerge during the 1920s, but they enjoyed no privileges compared with the rest of urban African society. Opportunities for accumulating property or moving out of a condition of desperate poverty were very small, and were often blocked by white entrepreneurs. In general, the mechanisms which developed in liberal capitalist industrial societies to legitimise social inequalities did not evolve in South Africa. The regulation of the lives of urban Africans thus assumed considerable importance in the maintenance of political controls.

Despite the poverty, hardships and a repressive state, politics in urban African society was a richly tumultuous process. Although an element of the labour force in the manufacturing sector was housed in compounds comparable to the mine compound, a significant and growing proportion settled in and around the major cities in communities which created wider opportunities for political expression and organisation, class stratification, and cultural transformations and interaction than existed in the total institutions of farm and mine compound. In part, these opportunities emerged out of the contradictions which the presence of urban Africans exposed within and between different sectors, classes and strata: between the great interests dominating the three main sectors in the economy, but also between large interests and small-scale white entrepreneurs, between capital and labour, and even between different levels in the state itself, particularly between central government and local authorities. The presence of a large African labour force in the cities challenged the white-controlled local authorities in a number of ways, for neither they nor the central government could ignore the need for housing, services and welfare, or the threat to public health of the conditions in which they lived.

African workers in manufacturing precipitated a powerful reaction from white workers, especially from newly urbanised Afrikaner workers. Fearing competition and displacement from their jobs, and competition for living space in the industrial towns and cities, white workers supplied a mass base for the Afrikaner nationalist movement, and hence crucial political support for the policy of apartheid. Cumulatively these issues have underlain the major political problems of twentieth-century South Africa. The development of a 'native policy' and the changing forms which it has assumed have largely been dictated by the problems of labour allocation, social control, and the preservation of the support of white workers in the face of African competition.

Initially, local authorities adopted the simple solution of clearing blacks out of the overcrowded cheap quarters near the city centres, and used slum clearance and health regulations to demolish housing and to push their inhabitants to sites at some distance from the city centres. These measures have reverberated on government policy over a broad front: the Stallard Commission, which in 1922 recommended the policy of urban segregation to which all governments have subsequently adhered in one version or another, was based on an analysis of overcrowding in the poorer quarters of Johannesburg. As in other countries, the arguments used to justify slum clearance schemes rested on the threat to public health which they constituted. In reality, these justifications often masked the fear of public disorder or the withdrawal of political support from enfranchised groups – in this case, white workers. Pushing the African proletariat to well-demarcated segregated areas in the urban areas, sometimes under close state surveillance, provided a superficial solution to these threats, real and imagined, which emanated not only from black workers, but also from the reactions of whites who faced competition in the workplace and for living space.

But segregation proved to be more difficult to accomplish in the larger cities than it first appeared, even after the massive programmes of removal and relocation which were instituted during the 1950s and 1960s, and which imparted to some areas (District Six in Cape Town, Sophiatown and, later, Pageview in Johannesburg, as well as parts of Durban) a resemblance to European cities subjected to saturation bombing. These removals were begun in an ad hoc way in Johannesburg within twenty years of its foundation, and have continued ever since. Yet they have never entirely succeeded in their purpose. Even when it worked in some degree, the policy of segregation in the major cities produced and intensified a series of contradictions in the industrial economy. For instance, the residential location of workers at long distances from the workplace increased transport costs, and hence put pressure on wages, thus provoking transport boycotts and industrial conflicts, which in turn widened the opportunities for African political organisations to become involved in community issues. On the other hand, it has also been argued that the wretched conditions of life in many of the urban settlements were major factors in disorganising and dislocating the potential for political power which lay in urban African people.

Perhaps as important as the contradictions which followed the efforts to preserve the major industrial cities as white areas through such mechanisms as segregated housing, was the elaborate social structure which evolved in and around the urban areas, and which was strongly influenced by the structures of segregation and the forms and levels of economic exploitation. This had a particularly important political consequence in the freehold areas in the larger cities, where Africans, Indians and coloureds acquired the right to own fixed property. Many of these areas were expropriated during the 1950s, and their populations settled elsewhere. But, surprisingly, some communities successfully resisted such efforts and remain to this day. The common features of such communities were the complexity of the class and occupational structures which emerged within them, and the development of new styles of politics and culture. Rentiers, traders, transporters, craftsmen, shebeen-owners, entertainers, intellectuals, prostitutes, schoolchildren and criminal gangsters, generated a variety of forms of political conflict, confrontation and collaboration, for which there was no comparable social base in the mine compound or on the farm.

Most important, perhaps, the urban areas became the sites of family-based communities. During the earlier period of industrialisation, men were numerically predominant in the urban populations, but especially from the 1930s the crisis in the rural economy impelled increasing numbers of families to migrate to the cities. The freehold areas provided some refuge for them, but it is interesting to note that from the 1930s municipalities created locations which made increasing provision for families. The housing, both private and public, was never developed in sufficient quantity or at low enough rentals to satisfy the need for it, but it provided the precarious base on which family communities could establish themselves.

During periods of especially rapid transition and urbanisation (for instance during and after the Second World War, but more or less continuously up to the present time), communities of squatters have settled on the outskirts of the major cities. They constituted a particularly acute challenge to the authorities, politically and in other ways. From the 1940s onwards, the authorities, initially local bodies, but later the central government, adopted two complementary strategies. The first – outright removal from the area – has been the preferred method of dealing with squatting near Cape Town during the 1970s and 1980s involving workers bringing their families from Transkei. The other strategy comprised resettlement in a variety of emergency and permanent housing schemes, where people could be more readily subjected to administrative and police controls. Notwithstanding these efforts, the successful squatter movements created bridgeheads for permanent settlements in and around the industrial urban areas.

Despite these developments, it would be wrong to exaggerate the possibilities that opened up for political organisation and action, or for the consolidation of working-class settlements into autonomous communities in the urban areas. Working conditions were poor, hours long, wages low, and living conditions sometimes appalling. Before 1980, Africans were excluded from the machinery of industrial conciliation. Although their right to strike legally was never prohibited outright, sustained police action against trade unionists, as well as against left-wing and nationalist groups, directly repressed the capacity for political organisation. In the townships, wretched and overcrowded living quarters, poor and often non-existent services, limited forms of representation on advisory boards, the absence of a viable fiscal base for local authorities, the temptations of alcoholism, and the predations of footpads and gangsters, all combined to reinforce more overt and direct forms of repression.

Police raids to control illegal possession of alcohol (only legalised during the 1960s) and to arrest pass offenders, as well as to contain 'disorder', further undermined the coherency of community-based political action. The exploitation of tenants by landlords in the freehold areas was matched by the exploitation by tenants of sub-tenants in state-owned housing. Municipal and central government housing schemes were for the most part characterised by a bleak and utilitarian efficiency, rather than by any effort to create hospitable or aesthetically interesting environments. Above all, urban housing of any kind was grossly inadequate. Regulations over housing were pervasive. In the new townships established by Verwoerd during the 1950s and 1960s, an effort was made to establish tribal zoning. Enclaves of migrant contract workers living in compounds in locations have on several famous occasions (most notably in 1976) acted to antagonise political tensions in the townships.

But when all that is said, the controls were difficult to establish, and at best precariously maintained in urban areas. The very factors which worked to undermine the possibility of effective political action, including racial zoning itself, at another level worked to reinforce the resolve to resist. The opportunities for successful political organisation, riot, boycott and strike, were probably more propitious in these areas than in any other sector of the economy. Perhaps only the peasantry in reserves situated in more remote areas of the country – Pondoland, Zeerust, Pietersburg, the Transkei – rivalled urban-dwellers in their capacity for effective collective political action. But theirs was a different kind of action, more akin to resistance against changes undermining their position than the activities of an increasingly politically sophisticated proletariat, often working in complex symbiosis with a petty bourgeoisie.

4 White power in the twentieth century: from party government to Bonapartist rule

The National Party has dominated South African party politics for some forty years. It has had an effect on the political structure of the country which would be difficult to exaggerate. Its leaders claimed to define the political interests of the Afrikaner people long before the party took power in 1948. The party mobilised succeeding generations of Afrikaners into the only political commitments they have known, as political actors, voters and state servants. It revived doctrines from the times of the trekker republics which asserted that an organic relationship existed between the Afrikaner people and the state, and on coming to power the party has viewed the state as its own property. Its leaders make claims for the party which are seldom heard outside of fascist states and the countries of the Eastern bloc. It has virtually become synonymous with the South African state and white domination. Yet the party is not a self-generating and frictionless automaton. It grew powerful in a symbiotic relationship with a variety of other parties and interests, and within a specific set of social and economic relationships. It evolved within a particular framework of institutional power and control. Likewise, the policy of apartheid, which was originally formulated as the expression of the party's doctrine of race, evolved out of an established framework of segregation, labour coercion and repression.

Notwithstanding its great power the party has operated within specific limitations. Its organisational strength lay in its linguistic and cultural exclusivism, and the sense of identity it evoked among Afrikaners. But this exclusivism made it difficult for the party to gather support among English-speakers. Indeed, paradoxically, its strength within the Afrikaner community has never rested on a consensus among Afrikaners. It developed out of intense conflicts between rival Afrikaner groups, each claiming to express the fundamental interests of the Afrikaner volk. The party alienated many Afrikaners who achieved political influence and wealth within the framework of policies of reconciliation between themselves and English-speakers. The party's linguistic and cultural exclusivism made it vulnerable to internal schisms between rival groups seeking its 'purification'. Above all, it has continuously encountered difficulties in representing and organising itself as the inclusive embodiment of the political interests of all whites.

The success of the policies of economic nationalism initiated by the party and related cultural and economic associations during the 1920s in the long run established an Afrikaner bourgeoisie. By the 1970s this class had gained a predominant position in the commanding heights of the economy. But while this class owes much to the relationship it enjoys with the party and the state, it also frequently found that party policies restricted its entrepreneurial opportunities. The recent attempts to initiate political reforms originate in some measure as responses to the criticisms made by this bourgeoisie. In turn, these efforts have deeply affected the party's relations with its working-class support. In common with other whites, many young Afrikaner intellectuals have found the moral and political boundaries of the apartheid state stifling and repressive. Indeed, while the success of the party in mobilising support from all classes in the Afrikaner community has led many writers to conclude that class is irrelevant to the explanation of political allegiances in South Africa, one of its major pre-occupations has been the management of class interests within white South Africa.

The rapid but uneven economic growth of the 1960s and 1970s helped widen the rifts between classes in Afrikaner society which in earlier years it had been the party's greatest triumph to manage, conceal and regulate. Perhaps the deepest irony of all is that the logic of its policies has under-mined the relevance of the parliamentary and electoral conflicts through which the party generated its mass support during its rise to power. The siege mentality and the development of the garrison state over which the party's leaders presided in order to resist the advancing tide of African nationalism inexorably thrust the chiefs of security to key positions of power and authority. Party rule, even in one-party states, rests above all on civilian control over government policy. The close involvement of the military in shaping policy and in reconstructing the state's institutions threatens to usurp that control.

In this chapter, the history of South African party politics will be reviewed. It will become apparent that one-partyism lies deep in the structure of the political system, and began to emerge long before the National Party took power in 1948. The reasons for this are a matter of controversy. It could be argued that the system of racial domination and exclusion foreclosed any possibility of a genuinely competitive politics, and that agreement among whites to exclude blacks from participation in the political system provided a basis for a precarious consensus between white political groups otherwise deeply divided. It could also be argued that although different sectoral and class interests might have been affected in different ways by the system of labour control and allocation which became the significant feature of the South African state, these interests could be made to accommodate the divergent interests of different sectors of capital and could be made congruent with the interests of the white working class in securing and maintaining a privileged position in the labour market.

It may be the case that the common political interest of whites in a system of racial domination has worked to limit political conflicts between white political organisations and interest groups. However, it would be simplistic to elevate a single factor into the basic determinant of political formations. Party politics cannot be explained by a single set of causes. The system of racial domination has been a central, almost obsessive issue in the political discourse of white parties and interest groups. But it has also formed the issue defining real and enduring cleavages between political groups, as well as the basis for agreements and alliances among them. Other issues and interests have operated to reinforce, modify and redefine the basis for political action. The history of party politics offers an interesting view of the process in which social and economic interests, political organisation and ideological forces have interacted to define and redefine white interests. Insofar as party politics provided the framework for the hegemonic project of white power during this century, that project has assumed its particular meaning via the conflicts and agreements reached in the arena constituted through party political debate and conflict. In other words, 'white domination' was not given a priori; it was defined in the process of political discourse between and within parties, as well as in other institutions.

Parties were the political media through which social groups with access to the franchise were able to achieve national political power. Class, region, religion and language provided the bases for political organisations to launch themselves into the political arena. Sometimes, as in the Orange Free State during the period after Union, these reinforced one another to produce a coherent and tightly knit political identity. In others regions, like the Witwatersrand, the site of a cultural and linguistic melting pot and of intense class and racial conflicts, a variety of political organisations competed for support. And, at the national level, men engaged in the tricky operation which Bertrand de Jouvenel called 'la grande politique', the art of assembling and maintaining coalitions of diverse interests.

Political parties became significant forces in white politics during the twentieth century, evolving most rapidly during the crucial years between the end of the South African War and the beginning of the First World War. Although there were parties before 1899, it is difficult to speak of party rule anywhere in South Africa during the nineteenth century. Groups of notables appeared in the Cape parliament after responsible government was granted to the colony in 1872. The Afrikaner Bond, founded in 1879 on the basis of farmers' associations, developed a powerful political machine in the rural constituencies of the Cape, and commanded the allegiances of most Afrikaners in the region. Cape governments increasingly relied on the support of the Bond, but its leader, 'Onze Jan' Hofmeyr, never formed a government. Until the election of 1898, governments were based on delicate coalitions between groups of notables, normally with Bond support. Sir Gordon Sprigg, who was prime minister four times, never had a party. The election of 1898 was won by Rhodes's Progressive Party, which mobilised a large proportion of English voters in the colony and received the support of many African voters in the eastern Cape. The Jameson Raid, in which Rhodes was deeply implicated, ruptured the delicate consensus between political groups, and polarised opinion both in parliament and in the constituencies. The war of 1899–1902 breached relations between pro-Boers and Progressives almost beyond repair.

The South African War seriously weakened the Bond, for it stretched to breaking point the complex and ambiguous attitudes of the 'loyal Cape Dutch' towards Britain and British institutions on the one hand and to the republics on the other. The Bond was also weakened in a material political sense, for many of its supporters were disfranchised for rebellion during the war ; and the moderate pro-Afrikaner groups organised as the South African Party, which depended on the Bond for their support in the country, lost the first post-war election to the Progressive Party, now led by Jameson, the Raider himself. By the time the last pre-Union election in the colony was held in 1908, the South African Party under the leadership of John X. Merriman won the election on the basis of an alliance with the Bond in the constituencies. The duality of Merriman's ministry, its leadership based in parliamentary groups and its electoral strength drawn from the Bond, was reminiscent of the style of nineteenth century Cape politics. It was the last such election, and Merriman lost the contest for the premiership of the Union, partly at least because he did not command a mass party in the constituencies.

If party rule in the one British colony in South Africa was a precariously balanced set of parliamentary factions during the nineteenth century, it did not emerge at all in the other. Natal was granted responsible government only in 1893, and became dominated by groups of notables, all English-speaking, and representing the merchants of Durban, Zululand cane-growers, and Midlands farmers. These groups were fiercely pro-British during the war, but the strength of regionalism prevented them from organising links with the British parties emerging elsewhere. Indeed, unlike the Cape and Transvaal Progressives, Natal politicians accepted unification with great reluctance and deep misgivings, for fear of being swamped by an Afrikaner majority. Most seats in Natal were won by independents in the 1910 elections, and though they joined Botha's South African Party when it was formed in 1911, they continued to maintain a strong regional identity. The subsequent history of Natal parties has continued to exhibit the strength of regionalism there.

The political life of the two boer republics across the Orange and the Vaal were dominated by factions of notables, representing the dominant agrarian classes of the Free State and the Transvaal countryside, though from the 1890s industrial and financial interests became prominent in the Transvaal Volksraad. In the Transvaal, two factions emerged. The 'progressives' put up candidates for the presidency in opposition to Kruger, and sometimes criticised his policy, but they did not gell into a party. In both republics, there were powerful institutional inhibitions on the emergence of parties. Both had strong executive presidencies, the incumbents of which (especially Kruger) were tough and cunning politicians, using a combination of cajolery and bullying to control opponents. Kruger stood at the apex of a system of patronage; the concessions system, which controlled the licensing of a variety of products, from dynamite to alcohol, could be used to reward supporters within the Transvaal's nascent bourgeoisie. These patron–client relationships extended into the political relationships on the land, which were dominated by a rural class (of which Kruger himself was a powerful representative) whose power lay in military prowess and extensive land-holding.

After the discovery of gold and the rapid inflow of finance and the influx of entrepreneurs and workers, a social base for a new opposition to Kruger's presidency emerged in the 'British' population of the Transvaal. But the Uitlanders, as they became known, lacked the franchise, and Kruger found ways of delaying giving them the vote. Without it, the Uitlanders lacked the means of public political organisation. The representatives of mining, financial and commercial interests negotiated directly with the administration, or through the intermedium of sympathetic Volksraad members. The Jameson Raid severely strained the relations between Kruger and local British interests.

The war of 1899–1902 generated a rapid development of political parties in the Transvaal and the Orange Free State. The *bittereinder* leadership of the boer forces, particularly Botha, Smuts, Hertzog, De la Rey, and Beyers, consolidated political organisations in the devastated countryside, among the dispirited communities of the defeated boers. These leaders' power lay in their brilliant military skills, the allegiance which they had built up among the commandos, and their ability to negotiate advantages with the British on the basis of very limited resources. In 1903, they refused seats on the nominee Legislative Council set up by the British administration, potentially a cooptative trap, and worked instead to develop a political base for winning responsible government. In the Transvaal, this base was Het Volk ('The People'). In the Free State, it was Orangia Unie. Het Volk won the 1907 elections with the help of a mainly English-speaking party, the Responsible Government Association (confusingly known as the 'Nationals'), with which it entered a coalition. Against it stood the Progressive Party, virtually the mining interest in political form.

Despite the similarities between Het Volk and Orangia Unie, Free State politics began moving at a tangent to the more complex and dynamic society of the Transvaal. Where the Transvaal leaders resolutely pursued the pragmatic goal of responsible government, Orangia Unie leaders spoke of winning back their independence. The Transvaal leaders set the pace in the move towards Union; the Free State followed with reservations. The Transvaal won responsible government in 1906; the Free State did not gain it until 1907, and then only in order to qualify formally as a participant in the National Convention which debated the terms of Union. In the election of 1908, Orangia Unie swept the countryside, and took power in the colony without the need for a coalition. Het Volk leadership began moving towards 'conciliation', while Orangia Unie's leaders began to formulate their conception of Anglo–Afrikaner relations in terms of the notion of 'equal rights'. Writ large in the arena of pan-South African politics, these themes and the organisational structures which evolved with them had a significant effect on party politics for decades to come.

By Union, a loose alliance of Afrikaner leaders had emerged as the political directorate in the country, though regional particularities dictated different balances of political forces in each province. The Free State was an agrarian society, with perhaps the least evolved capitalist agriculture in the country, where sharecropping, 'kaffir-farming' and farming-on-the-half were widespread. In the Transvaal, with its prodigiously wealthy gold-mining industry, large industrial labour force (black and white) and a now enfranchised British population, the political balance of forces was much more complex. The complexity of class politics was beginning to reshape the structures of political allegiances: Smuts had intervened in the strike of 1907 with the help of troops. Cape politics prior to Union was even more delicately balanced, with Merriman's ministry resting on the support of the Bond.

The movement towards Union had been supported by a variety of former adversaries, and for a variety of reasons. The British parties, reflecting with some modifications Milner's aspirations, believed that unification would provide the political framework for economic growth and immigration, and hence consolidate South Africa for capital and empire. They found Smuts and Botha's objectives of creating a powerful centralised state, willing and competent to coerce black and white labour, and to regulate industry in a spirit of close collaboration with capital, were perfectly compatible with these purposes. They had indeed hoped for a 'best-man' government of men who would put the 'national interest' above party, but were disappointed. The 1910 election was fought on colonial party lines. The first government was a somewhat creaky coalition of Het Volk, Orangia Unie, the Cape's South African Party–Bond alliance, and the Natal independents. The former Progressive parties combined to form the Unionist Party, which became the official opposition. Its leaders included many luminaries of the mining industry, high finance, and commercial interests. In local political situations, in particular on the Witwatersrand and in the larger coastal cities, the political struggle in the constituencies was frequently a naked class war, with Unionist bosses fighting Labourite mineworkers. (At Georgetown in 1910, a predominantly mining district on the Witwatersrand, Sir George Farrar, after whom the town was named, fought and beat the Labour candidate, T. Mathews, at the polls, and dismissed him from the mine.)

It soon became apparent that political divisions between government and opposition were less important than between different elements in the coalition. In particular, Hertzog became concerned that the theme of conciliation which Botha placed at the centre of his election campaign was incompatible with his own demands for equal rights, and within a few months of the formation of the South African Party in November 1911 Hertzog was dropped from the cabinet.

Early in 1914, Hertzog formed the National Party. In effect, the party was Orangia Unie under another name. Its parliamentary support initially lay exclusively in the Free State. But it was developing connexions in the other provinces, especially in the Cape interior, in the western areas of the Transvaal, and among Afrikaner workers in Witwatersrand constituencies. The outbreak of war in August 1914 accelerated the growing divisions within Afrikaner politics. Districts in the western Transvaal rose in a rebellion led by General Beyers, the commander-in-chief of the Union Defence Force; both he and his fellow *bittereinder* General De la Rey, by then a senator in the Union parliament, were dead before the uprising was ended. The government put down the rebellion with commandos loyal to Botha within two months, but the political consequences for Smuts and Botha were less easy to deal with. An army officer, Jopie Fourie, who was executed for treason, became transformed into a martyr in the struggle for Afrikaner independence. The bullet-ridden, blood-stained jacket which General De la Rey was wearing when he was shot as he drove through a police roadblock (murdered, said some) became a feature at political rallies, as did General Beyers's widow. The extent of the political disaster for Botha and Smuts became apparent in the general election of 1915. Large areas that had formed the centre of gravity of Botha's electoral support among Afrikaners now voted for the National Party – the whole of the Free State outside of Bloemfontein, country districts in the western Transvaal, and the Cape interior. Moreover, the rebellion stimulated a strong republican movement which promised to give expression in the Free State to the old idea of independence. In 1919, the provincial council of the Orange Free State overwhelmingly supported a motion calling for independence from the British connexion. Funds collected for the defence of rebels became available for political, philanthropic and cultural activities. Soon after the war, a movement towards the establishment of Afrikaner businesses was floated.

In the aftermath of the rebellion, the outlines of contemporary Afrikaner power began to become visible. Of course, events do not dictate historical developments as though the body politic were driven along by a series of shocks. The rebellion revealed the deep suspicions among Afrikaners of the new state which was growing within the integuments of a society undergoing a radical transformation. By the outbreak of the First World War, the men on the peripheries of the industrial economy were experiencing the full weight of its effects on the life of the countryside. Then, as later, the golden age of the republics seemed to beckon the possibility of a restoration, not only of the forms of political independence which they had formerly enjoyed, but also the social and economic autonomy of an agrarian arcadia. The newly centralised state did little to foster such sentiments, illusory as they were. The rhetoric of conciliation overlay the reality of an intimate collaboration between the state and the mine-owners, the hardships of life in the mining areas, and the anxieties of farmers pushed into the unfamiliar world of commercial agriculture. The state was closely involved in promoting the interests of 'progressive' farmers, and thus in pushing the backward elements off the land. The elements most resistant to this process (landless farmers, woodcutters, and other unreconstructed remnants of colonial South Africa) were passed by in the rapid modernisation of the society, and left to stagnate.

It is worth noting that while the National Party undoubtedly benefited from the ferment generated in the rebellion, it did not actively sponsor the entry of rebels into politics, or indeed seriously entertain the restoration of nineteenth-century political forms. At the party's Transvaal congress in 1917, a motion was proposed to exclude rebels from lists of party candidates. And though the proposal was roundly condemned and defeated by indignant delegates, it is interesting that no rebels were nominated for parliamentary seats in the 1920 elections. Like other populist nationalist parties, the National Party sought to inherit a centralised state, not to break it up.

The war, the rebellion and the 1915 election shifted the balance of forces in parliament. The Unionist Party, enthusiastically pro-British, virtually ceased to act as a parliamentary opposition. The small Labour Party split over the war issue: its right wing supported the war effort, while its left departed from parliamentary politics to form the International Socialist League. Some of its members emerged at the head of the Communist Party when it was formed in 1921.

The 1920 elections forced a major shift in the government party. The Labour Party won 20 seats at the expense of the Unionists, and the National Party gained significantly from the South African Party. After a brief and unsuccessful attempt to unite the South African and National parties, the Unionists disbanded and joined the SAP. Smuts called another election in 1921 and heavily defeated Labour. In the aftermath of the 1922 strike, the foundation was laid for its re-emergence as a junior partner in an alliance with the National Party in the Pact government which won the election of 1924. Labour's re-emergence was short-lived, however, and the party split in 1927 and thereafter declined as an effective force in parliamentary politics. In 1929 the Nationalists gained a plurality of seats, though Labour continued to hold some cabinet posts.

In 1932, in an effort to form a national government, negotiations were opened between the two major parties, and the coalition swept the country in the general elections called in 1933. D. F. Malan, the Nationalist leader in the Cape, had supported the coalition with reservations, but when Smuts and Hertzog began moving towards uniting the two parties, Malan formed the Gesuiwerde Nasionale Party (the Purified National Party) with its support located mainly in the Cape hinterland. Smuts and Hertzog formed the United South African National Party, which sought, as its name suggests, to encompass every significant element in white politics. As during the period after Union, the attempt to centralise political organisation within a single party stimulated the development of factions and regional groupings. Like Hertzog's party in the period after 1914, Malan's Nationalists soon broke through its regional base.

The Dominion Party and the Home Rule Party remained limited mainly to Natal. The Home Rule Party was formed in 1932 as a devolutionist reaction against the changes in the Commonwealth registered in the Statute of Westminster. It also reflected the worries in Natal about the rapprochement between the SAP and the National Party. It won two seats in the 1933 general election and then faded away. The Dominion Party, formed in 1934, was somewhat similar, but was better led by Colonel Stallard, the architect of South Africa's policy towards blacks in the urban areas, and it survived as a parliamentary party for more than a decade.

The United Party contained almost as diverse a set of elements as were represented on its fringes. In the cabinet was J. H. Hofmeyr, the main hope of the small and unorganised group of liberals; also included was Oswald Pirow, whose admiration for Adolf Hitler was not long to be contained within the confines of the United Party, and he was soon to form his own imitative movement, the New Order. The United Party assembled the largest parliamentary majority yet seen, and gathered into its ranks every significant strand of opinion in white South Africa. From its formation, however, the consensus on which the party was based depended on the condition that it did not define its position too clearly on certain crucial issues. The article in its constitution dealing with the republican question, perhaps the central issue in white politics at the time, was a masterpiece of ambiguity which satisfied neither republicans nor anyone else. Organisationally, the party resembled the South African Party at the time of its formation in 1911; it was an aggregation of different interests weakly contained at the centre. As with the South African Party, the uneasy consensus held until the next war broke out.

The government enjoyed the benefits of the economic recovery that followed after 1932. It reorganised commercial agriculture on lines similar to the American New Deal, and energetically threw itself into a programme of industrial development which favoured local manufacturing. Above all, it embarked on a legislative programme which would entrench and embellish the segregationist policies followed by previous governments. Africans were placed on a separate voters' roll, and special representation of African voters by white MPs was instituted. The indirectly elected and purely advisory Natives' Representative Council was established. A new Land Act was passed which made provision for the release of land in the reserves, and for 'betterment' schemes. These measures could all find support from white parties and interests, though the Nationalists found much to criticise in the legislation on African affairs. Yet by the time of the 1938 election, the worm was in the bud. Malan's party won 27 seats, mostly in the Cape country districts, and seriously threatened United Party majorities in a number of others, especially in the Orange Free State, where Hertzog's support lay.

As with the party Hertzog had founded in 1914, Malan's party advanced as an electoral party, winning support at the grassroots of Afrikaner society by exposing contradictions in the consensus upon which the United Party rested. Malan's party exploited the manifold grievances of Afrikaners, and developed a political structure that integrated the party with cultural, economic, religious and philanthropic organisations which, on these different terrains, laid the basis for an organic identity of party, people, and state, in contrast to the mechanistic, aggregative consensus on which the United Party was based. The United Party's strength lay in its capacity to form alliances between national and provincial leaders which papered over the deep political differences between them. In large measure it depended on the charisma of the generals, Smuts and Hertzog, who led it, and on their willingness to cooperate.

The declaration of war in September 1939 broke the basis of the alliance by rupturing the relations between the generals. In 1914, the constitutional doctrine had held that when Britain was at war, so was the Empire. In 1939, the Dominions enjoyed the right to decide whether to declare war, at least according to some authorities. Hertzog wanted to take the issue to the country, but in a much-debated decision the Governor-General asked Smuts to form a government, and South Africa declared war on the Axis powers on 4 September. This time there was no rebellion, though Smuts was sufficiently fearful of the possibility to call in all privately owned firearms. Hertzog sought to mobilise support against the war. The Ossewabrandwag clandestinely trained its members in the use of arms. Some committed acts of sabotage; others, including a future prime minister, B. J. Vorster, were detained. A crowd of small parties formed during the season of schism that followed – some, like N. C. Havenga's Afrikaner Party, or Pirow's New Order, founded by former United Party cabinet ministers.

The breach in Afrikanerdom seriously damaged the United Party. In an ominous prelude to the election of 1948, the party lost 18 seats to the Nationalists, and might have lost more had not the Afrikaner Party split the vote in a number of constituencies. Although the United Party gained a comfortable majority, and formed a government in coalition with the Labour and Dominion parties, it was never to solve its central problem of restoring its crumbling authority among Afrikaner political groups. The Nationalist victory of 1948 revealed the full extent of its failure. In fact, the victory was precarious; the Nationalists won the election because they reached an electoral pact with the Afrikaner Party, and formed a coalition government, but in 1952, in time for the next election, the Afrikaner Party dissolved and was absorbed into the National Party. In 1953, the National Party increased its representation in parliament, and before the following election created six seats in South West Africa, all of which returned Nationalist MPs. Henceforth, parliamentary elections in South Africa ceased to function as serious contests for political power.

Despite its narrow majority, the party embarked after 1948 on a vigorous and controversial programme which laid the legislative basis for the apartheid state. By 1953, parliament had passed Acts dealing with the prohibition of racially mixed marriages and sexual relations between different racial groups, the suppression of communism, group areas, population registration, Bantu education, Bantu authorities, separate representation for coloured people, and a series of prohibitions defining occupations Africans would not be permitted to enter. It tightened the pass laws. It introduced the Criminal Law Amendment Act to expand the powers of the police, and introduced the Public Safety Act. Much remained to be done to complete the apartheid edifice, but in those five years after 1948 its main features were established.

The Separate Representation of Voters Act of 1951, which removed coloured people from the common roll, raised a serious constitutional crisis. The Appellate Division of the Supreme Court ruled that the Act was invalid on the grounds that it had not been passed by a two-thirds majority of both Houses of Parliament in joint session, as required for legislation which amended the 'entrenched clauses' of the constitution. (The franchise rights of people of colour in the Cape constituted the one subject of these clauses; the status of English and Afrikaans as official languages was the other.) The government retaliated by passing the High Court of Parliament Act, which in effect gave parliament, sitting as a court, the power to review legislation invalidated by the courts. The Appellate Division, in turn, declared this Act to be invalid. In 1955, the government reconstituted and enlarged the Appellate Division and the Senate in order to produce the majority required to revalidate the Separate Representation Act.

The battle over this issue lasted for five years. Even after 30 years, it still stands out as a demonstration of the willingness of the party to abrogate the few political rights remaining to non-whites, in the teeth of massive opposition. It also demonstrated the willingness of the party to override the conventions and procedural rules of parliamentary government when these stood in its way, ignoring mass protests, including perhaps the largest and most sustained among whites since the rebellion of 1914. The issue itself, as we shall see presently, was less important to most of the white opposition than the procedural matters it raised, and the implications it held for equal language rights. Nevertheless, along with the systematic development of the policy of apartheid, the struggle over the rights of coloured voters was an ominous prelude to the era of one-party rule which it ushered in.

The election of 1953 was the first in which all significant groups of Afrikaner nationalists were united in the National Party, and the last in which political parties seriously contended for political office in elections. All the same, internal problems remained in the party. There were regional divisions between the Cape and the Transvaal branches, and there were resentments against Verwoerd, then Minister of Native Affairs, which led to speculation that he would resign. But they were not serious, and presented minor problems to party unity compared with the difficulties faced by the parliamentary opposition. The white opposition in 1953 comprised the United Front, an inappropriately named mélange of the United Party, the Labour Party and the Torch Commando. The last was a massive but unstable popular movement, formed to protest against the Separate Representation Act, which at its height claimed a quarter of a million members, and like many such movements, was prone to internal division. The United Front was fissiparous, riddled with ambiguities, and threatened by regional splits, particularly in Natal, where enthusiasm for the Torch Commando became fused into support for the secessionist 'Natal stand'. Although the Torch Commando and the 'Natal stand' soon fizzled out, the decade was not a happy one for the United Party. In 1959, its conservative and liberal elements parted company, and the Progressive Party was established by some of the ablest young MPs in the party. The party system was settling into the form it subsequently assumed of a massive and coherently organised National Party surrounded by a fringe of smaller parties – of which the United Party was the most important – representing particular regional, sectoral and class interests, without the capacity to challenge the hegemony of the Nationalists.

Its power over political institutions entrenched in parliament, the National Party consolidated itself during the next decade by penetrating the major state institutions. Preference was increasingly given to party men in appointments and promotions in the armed forces, the police and public service, the diplomatic service, the South African Broadcasting Corporation (SABC) and the judiciary. In some areas, the Gleichschaltung was achieved by a slow war of attrition against non-Nationalists. Competent policemen or consular officials would find comparative juniors promoted over their heads, and resign. In other areas, notably the army, the Nationalist take-over had the aspect of a bloodless purge. Many regular officers had been on active service during a war which the Nationalists opposed, and had at least sympathised with the Torch Commando.

But the dominance of the party was not achieved simply via parliamentary control and through penetration of state institutions. It slowly established hegemony also in the major institutions of the political economy, though this stage of its development, as will be seen, involved a certain diffusion of power which was later to contribute to dissension within the party. By the 1960s, Afrikaners (mainly, but not exclusively, Nationalists) had achieved controlling positions in sectors of the economy, especially mining, manufacturing and finance, which before the war had been controlled by English-speakers. Of course, agricultural interests in most regions had long been committed to the kinds of policies which the Nationalists vigorously pursued after they came to power, for these policies promised to secure for white farmers the controls they demanded over the movement of African labour out of the rural areas.

The Nationalist entry into the commanding heights of the mining, financial and manufacturing industry was the product of a broad strategy which had evolved since the end of the First World War to develop a specifically Afrikaner interest (grossly underrepresented) in business. Institutions which linked agricultural cooperatives to financial institutions on the one hand, and to the party on the other, served to give these interests cohesion. So too did those state corporations directly involved in production, like the Iron and Steel Corporation (Iscor) and the publicly owned transportation and communications networks. The legislative programme of apartheid generated an elaborate bureaucracy which provided many opportunities to exercise patronage. Among these were the Native (later Bantu) Affairs Department, which proliferated a series of administration boards, the Group Areas boards which decided on the racial zoning of cities and towns, and the Censorship Board and its regional committees. The National Party was not especially venal in respect of patronage; before 1948, similar opportunities opened up to 'Smuts men', but they existed on a lesser scale. The United Party's administration was less specifically tied to party doctrine, or to put it differently, party doctrine itself was more diffuse. The scale of government was relatively small until after the Second World War. But such factors as these help explain why the Nationalists, having won electoral power, were able to entrench themselves so effectively within the state institutions, as well as command the ideological and material resources which mobilised popular support among Afrikaners.

Perhaps even more importantly, by the early 1960s the political system was being radically transformed by the gathering strength of the black opposition, and by the continental and international ramifications of decolonisation, which simply eclipsed traditional party formations. The massacre at Sharpeville, the banning of the ANC and the PAC, and the emergence of militant resistance in the form of the African Resistance Movement, Poqo and Umkonto we Sizwe, were indications that henceforth the significant political confrontations were going to concern the survival of the political order itself. It is sometimes argued that Nationalist policy itself provoked the kind and intensity of the resistance, but it is difficult to imagine any other white government acting very differently. No existing white party, let alone any parliamentary party (and very few whites anyhow), challenged the legitimacy of the political order, though the Liberal Party outside of parliament and the Progressive Party within it were seeking alternatives to apartheid. In general, white parties, and especially the United Party, had little room to manoeuvre. Their problems were exacerbated by Verwoerd's tour de force (even if it was based on a miscalculation) in taking South Africa out of the Commonwealth, thus removing from parliamentary politics the central, if somewhat inchoate, issue of the British connexion.

The referendum which was held in 1960 on the issue of a republic was plebiscitary in form and in substance, and set the style for the elections that followed. White party politics became the sounding box for the National Party, which in turn rallied with little dissent from its members to Verwoerd's unblushing statement of purpose: 'We want to make South Africa white. . . . Keeping it white can only mean one thing, namely domination, not leadership, not guidance, but control, supremacy.' Nationalist policy placed the United Party at a disadvantage. The United Party avoided its crudity, preferring the euphemisms of leadership and guidance. It stressed that the possibilities of inter-racial harmony and goodwill were jeopardised by government policy. But in a time of crisis to white domination, it is not clear that such formulae offered any meaningful alternative to Nationalist policy, without undermining the whole project of white power and privilege. The United Party was anyway unwilling to represent black interests against whites. True, it opposed most of the legislation which established apartheid, and the draconian security legislation that went with it. But its opposition was necessarily limited.

Firstly, the United Party, while in power, had created precedents for much of the legislation which the Nationalists used to establish apartheid. Even the removal of coloureds from the common roll, which drew such opposition from the United Party, had its precedent in the removal of African voters from the common roll in 1936. The main difference, aside from the limited representation offered to Africans in the form of 'Natives' Representatives' and the Natives' Representative Council, was that in 1936 the United Party had been able to secure the necessary two-thirds majority, an important difference to be sure, but not one that suggested that the party was vitally concerned with the political rights of blacks. The United Party found itself in a contradictory position in attacking legislation like the Group Areas Act, for when it had been in power, it had passed the Asiatic Land Tenure and Indian Representation Act, which though less far-reaching and limited to Indians, was little different in principle.

The other difficulty which the United Party faced in opposing the Nationalists concerned the constraints over the electoral strategies it could pursue in order to win back Afrikaner support without alienating English-speaking support in the urban areas. In pursuing the first objective, it was forced into a position of me-tooism on issues relating to colour; in retaining support in urban areas, and especially in affluent middle-class constituencies, the party presented its liberal face. These problems were compounded by the party's difficulties in maintaining a viable political career for Afrikaner politicians as it lost seats in rural areas. From the mid-1940s, the party was increasingly forced to go carpetbagging in safe English-speaking constituencies. For instance, Deneys Reitz, who sat for many years for Barberton in the eastern Transvaal, ended up as MP for Parktown. Sometimes the consequences were very damaging for party morale, as politicians exploited opportunities to cross tricky traverses in their political careers. Thus, Mr 'Blaar' Coetzee, sometime member of the National Party, won a United Party nomination in a Witwatersrand seat against the wishes of the local constituency organisation, and thereafter defected to the National Party.

The strains in the party began emerging during the mid-1950s and reached a climax in 1959 when eleven MPs, mostly representing urban seats, challenged the leadership to take an unequivocal stand on the issue of apartheid. Fourteen MPs resigned, and eleven of them formed the Progressive Party late in the year. The new party affirmed its commitment to protecting fundamental human rights, irrespective of race, and the rule of law; it rejected religion, race and sex as criteria for debarring any citizen from 'making the contribution to our national life of which he or she may be capable', a somewhat ambiguous affirmation compatible with, but not committed to, universal political rights; and it declared its commitment to maintaining the unity of the state. The party opened its membership to all races. In 1968, when multiracial parties were prohibited by statute, the Progressives decided to continue as a white party, unlike the Liberal Party, which disbanded.

In the elections of 1961, the Progressive Party lost all but one seat, that held by the remarkable MP for Houghton, Helen Suzman, who carried on the parliamentary struggle against racism single-handed for a decade before other Progressives got to parliament. The significance of the party during the 1960s should not be underestimated. It helped shift the focus of political debate among whites away from the sterile exchange of claim and counter-claim for different versions of white supremacy, and towards issues concerning political participation. The issue was not new in white politics, and the Progressives were perhaps the most conservative group to commit itself to change in these areas. A long line of white liberals and leftists, mainly in the Communist Party, the Liberal Party (formed in 1953), radical trade unionists, and the Congress of Democrats, had raised such issues earlier and in less ambiguous terms. The significance of the Progressives was not that it was especially bold or innovative, but that it had a platform in parliament and in the press from which it could debate the issue, a platform effectively denied these other groups. It also attracted the sympathy of some elements of the business community. It was able to use these platforms effectively because it could pose authoritatively the case that the legitimacy of the social order in South Africa would increasingly hinge on the rights of blacks to participate in the political system and as effective actors in the capitalist economy. It was also fortunate in attracting a remarkably talented group of whites. Insofar as a reform movement could be said to have been generated within the boundaries of white politics since

1948, it was the work of the Progressive Party.

The Progressives had little effect on the government during the 1960s. Its political significance in the medium term lay in the effects it produced on the parliamentary opposition, though it was not until the early 1970s that even this became evident. Indirectly, however, the issues which the party raised influenced the debates within the National Party between *verligtes* and *verkramptes*, which arose after Vorster took over the premiership in 1966, and which precipitated the split in the National Party in 1969.

The formation of the Progressive Party exacerbated the internal problems of the United Party. The latter, on one front unable to advance against the Nationalists, was now threatened in the English-speaking urban constituencies. In the elections of 1970, the Nationalists began picking up English-speaking support. To sharpen the United Party's problems, a division emerged between two factions. The one, which was centred on the Witwatersrand, and therefore potentially vulnerable to Progressive inroads, attacked the party's participation in a parliamentary commission into national security that had led to bannings, deportations and harassment of liberal and radical political groups. To exacerbate the problem, this faction (labelled 'Young Turks' – the South African political lexicon is not exactly original) seized the party leadership in the Transvaal, revamped its tired constituency organisation, and mounted a campaign in which the party regained eleven seats from the Nationalists – the party's only significant advance since losing power. This modest victory turned out to be catastrophic for the party, for it forced the split between the 'Young Turks' and the party conservatives into the open. Within a few months, the Young Turks had formed a new party, the Reform Party. In 1975 they had joined the Progressives in the Progressive Reform Party, later renamed the Progressive Federal Party. The United Party dissolved, and its rump reformed as the New Republic Party. The NRP supported the new constitution in the referendum of 1983, and at the time of writing is in disarray, with little support outside of Natal.[18]

The split in the National Party emerged in a different context, but also bore on the issue of the political rights and economic role of blacks, and particularly the problem that the issue posed internationally and in the context of relations with the rest of Africa, which during Verwoerd's premiership were non-existent. B. J. Vorster, who succeeded to the premiership after Verwoerd's assassination, was the principal agent of changes in government policy. He was anything but a liberal. He had been a commandant in the Ossewabrandwag during the Second World War, and had been detained. He failed to win a nomination in 1948 because of his membership of the movement. He entered parliament in 1953, and rapidly rose to ministerial rank, making his reputation as a tough police minister, responsible for the series of police actions against African nationalist and left-wing organisations during the late 1950s and early 1960s and for steering the General Law Amendment Act of 1962 through parliament.

Moreover, Vorster did not waver on apartheid. He preserved the main features of the apartheid state established under his predecessor, and indeed brought the policy to fruition. He presided over the establishment of the first 'independent' states in the homelands. The policy of reversing the flow of Africans from the rural areas to the cities began to take measurable effect during the early 1960s and continued into the 1970s and 1980s. Vorster did not liberalise, let alone reverse, government policy in any of its major features. Yet there were differences between him and Verwoerd, both in nuances of policy and in style, which stimulated discontent within the National Party, and there were deeper changes taking place in the politics of Afrikaner nationalism that reinforced the divisions.

From the late 1960s, Vorster attempted to end the Republic's international isolation by establishing diplomatic and trade relations in Africa, the Far East, and Latin America. Secondly, the rapid economic growth of the 1960s prompted industrial and commercial interests to press for a relaxation, though not abandonment, of state controls over the movement of black labour and over their entry into skilled jobs reserved for whites. Vorster was much more accessible to businessmen than Verwoerd had been, though he did not try to institutionalise the relationship as did his successor, and the state tolerated many unofficial breaches of job reservation. Indeed, by the mid-1970s, Vorster was publicly defending the entry of blacks into skilled and semi-skilled jobs.

These two issues – Vorster's 'outward' foreign policy and government flexibility on job reservation – provoked discontent within the cabinet and the party. The issue came to a head in 1969 with the resignation of Dr Albert Hertzog (the General's son) over the issue of the introduction of a television service. Other apparently peripheral issues, such as the visit of a New Zealand rugby team which included Maori players, tended to obscure the seriousness of the divisions. The formation of a new party, the Herstigte Nasionale Party (Reconstituted National Party) was evidence that the split was serious. The name chosen for the new party significantly echoed that ('Herenigde' – Reunited) chosen by Malan in 1940 to signify the purification of his party. The new party imitated the populist rhetoric of the old Malanite party, and claimed the mantle of authentic grassroots nationalism. 'A nation', declared Albert Hertzog in heroic style, 'is born in times of struggle, not in times of prosperity.' The outlines of this new populism had already been established some years earlier by Dr 'Ras' Beyers, a romantic figure in right-wing Afrikaner trade unionism. Beyers asserted that 'at the turn of the century, our fathers fought off the yoke of British rule. They succeeded. But now we are under even worse and more distasteful rule – that of our own people – the self-styled "elite" Afrikaners, the "chosen" ones.' All the resentments of lower-class Afrikaners were concentrated in that bitter speech. The HNP presented itself as the 'soul' of Afrikaner nationalism, and the National Party as the skeleton. There were tales of whole constituency organisations defecting, and of seething discontent among the rank and file.

In the event, the HNP did not seriously challenge the National Party during the 1970s. It was not until 1981 that it made serious inroads into Nationalist majorities, and even then failed to win a seat. Its important effect was to undermine party unity and to retard efforts by Vorster and his successor P. W. Botha to legitimise some of the features of apartheid policy in the urban areas and to liberalise labour policy. The HNP did not manage even to dominate the political groups on the right of the National Party. That position was assumed by the Conservative Party, first formed in 1979 after the Nationalist leader in the Transvaal, Dr Connie Mulder, had been expelled from the party. The defection of a cabinet minister, Dr Andries Treurnicht, and a handful of Nationalist MPs in 1982 gave the Conservatives a platform which the HNP never achieved.

The factionalism in the National Party and the threat of grass fires in the Transvaal country constituencies go some way to explaining the features of Botha's constitutional proposals which began taking shape during the early 1980s, for they would have the effect, if fully implemented, of denying or at least severely limiting an institutional base for nativist and populist movements within Afrikaner politics. One of these is the provincial system, which provides an arena where party forces might be mobilised against national leaderships: almost every significant party revolt has succeeded or failed on its initial performance in a party's provincial base. Every South African party is organised on the basis of strong provincial elements. The provinces are about the right size for a party organisation; neither so small that they do not count in national politics, nor so large that the relations between party leaders and members cannot be established or maintained. Moreover, though the provincial councils do not seem to have been specially important in providing a base for the Afrikaner 'right', they have provided a niche within the bureaucracy hospitable to conservative elements in the educational system, for it is at this level that primary and secondary education for whites has been administered since Union.

To follow the twists and turns of events in a process which is developing at the time of writing would be impossible. Rather, an attempt will be made to sum up the structure of the party system as it has evolved over the past few decades, for it is in the party system that 'white domination' achieved concrete articulation, and it is in the transformations of the party system, and possibly the supersession of party politics, that the clues to political changes generated within the framework of the established political order may be found. Over the century, party politics evolved through three stages: from the weak and fissiparous coalitions which until 1948 attempted to reconcile the diverse and often antagonistic political forces contained within them, towards a system dominated by the National Party, highly organised and centralised, strongly authoritarian and, until the 1970s, well-disciplined. Under the pressures from below for inclusion in the political order, and in response to elements within the political order for some degree of legitimacy and liberalisation of the political order and the economy, the system began to develop into a militarised version of state corporatism. This third development threatens to eclipse party politics as the authoritative source of political decision-making in South Africa. Significantly, the lexicon of new constitutional structures, machinery and procedures, abandons 'parliamentary' terms in favour of corporatist ones, some, like the President's Council, with a distinctly Latin American flavour. These tendencies will be discussed in greater detail in Chapter 10.

The combative terminology of party warfare has long given way to the tougher language of insurgency and counter-insurgency. Party conflict has never enjoyed the legitimacy it has in the Anglo–American democracies or in the 'old' Commonwealth. The hegemony the Nationalists have recently achieved over the 'centre' of white politics, the advance of the military to the key positions in state policy and decision-making, and the hysteria provoked by black opposition and resistance, by decolonisation in the region and by insurgency, have reduced the legitimacy of party conflict even further. Opponents, including parliamentarians, of Nationalist policy have often attracted the innuendo of treason.

The constitutional developments of the late 1970s are likely to have profound effects on the structure of party politics. In particular, they are likely to reduce the position of the parliamentary opposition and of inter-party conflict and intra-party debate even further. Indeed, it is probable that one of the motives behind the developments was to dampen opposition within the National Party and in the conservative parties on the NP's right to changes contemplated in education and labour policies. The liberalisation of apartheid's economic strategies has as a necessary corollary the limitation of the political rights of whites most vulnerable to the changes it is likely to usher in.

And while the proposals entrench the present National Party leadership firmly within the state structure, they will in all likelihood also reduce the autonomy and identity of the party as the source of political authority in white politics. The President's Council, which was established in 1981 to formulate a new 'constitutional dispensation', though undoubtedly dominated by Nationalists, was not simply a party committee writ large, nor were its leading lights old party apparatchiki. Its membership represented commercial, industrial and professional interests and a wide range of putative expertise outside of party and parliamentary life. (It also included coloured and Indian members.) The establishment of the President's Council coincided with the disestablishment of the Senate. The demise of this body, elected by a college of provincial councillors and members of parliament, and roughly reflecting the strength of parties in the provinces, was a token of the impending decline of parties before a corporatist reconstruction. A similar shift is indicated in the rise of technicist ideology in various branches of the state. The creation of a strong executive presidency, and a tricameral legislature with the Houses representing whites, coloureds and

Indians in 1984, is likely to undercut the position of opposition parties. It is also likely to corrode the significance of parties as the base for political recruitment, for many alternatives have opened up to policy and decision-making areas. The extensive intrusion of the military into political life has reinforced these tendencies. The national leadership of the National Party, which engineered these changes in the structure of government, is likely as a consequence to be less vulnerable to challenges from within the party. But in the longer term, it is probable that party leaders will increasingly reflect the imperatives of military and corporate strategies. Indeed, it could be argued that P. W. Botha's ascent to the premiership in 1978, from his position as Minister of Defence, was the sign that this had already taken place. Secondly, one can predict that the authority of the party as the political expression of white opinion will decline. Thirdly, it seems probable that the military itself will increasingly become entangled in the management of issues hitherto preoccupying parties.

The decline of party politics as the authoritative base of white politics is intimately bound up with a whole range of structural changes that have been taking place in southern African society over the past few decades. These have had the effect of corroding the alliances established during the 1920s, between Afrikaner business, agriculture and white workers, which generated the base for the 'monolithic' party that emerged during the 1940s and 1950s. Although white workers were never the dominant partner in the alliance, the attention given to securing their immediate interests in high wages compared with black workers and in job security (a combination necessarily requiring job reservation) served as the lynchpin of the class alliance which provided the political base for Afrikaner unity. The partial breakdown of the alliance became visible in the splinter parties and groups which emerged from the late 1960s. The HNP and the Conservative Party are by no means worker parties, but their rhetoric of struggle and their criticism of elitism in Afrikaner society, combined with their attacks on monopoly capitalism, strike a response among Afrikaner workers confronted with a rapidly changing technology and set of social relations in the workplace. This response has been most clearly visible among white mineworkers who stand at the face of these changes. But it is echoed in the situation of many other workers.

Afrikaner nationalism during the twentieth century has exhibited many of the features of populism, albeit truncated by the exclusion of the majority of the population from common political rights. It proclaimed the superior values of the countryside over the alien city; of the simple rural life over the squalor and moral turpitude imputed to urban industrial society. Even its stereotypes of African society were cast in the mould of a tribal arcadia threatened with disintegration by social change. Afrikaner nationalists mobilised the resentments of small businessmen and farmers against the remote forces of metropolitan and monopoly capital. The nationalist movement exploited the fears of landless farmers facing the prospect of proletarianisation, and organised the efforts of white workers seeking a privileged position in the labour market. Like populisms elsewhere, the Afrikaner variety exhibited an ambiguous and shifting attitude towards capitalist institutions. Engaged on one hand in developing, fostering and protecting local industry and commercial agriculture, yet on the other hand hostile to great foreign interests to the point of threatening to nationalise the mines, these attitudes characteristically cannot be reduced to a clear set of principles or programmes.

By the 1960s, the strands of interests gathered together in the party were beginning to unravel. The new class of Afrikaners – the 'chosen ones' who were the targets of Ras Beyers's enmity – holding important positions in business, the professions, agriculture and the state bureaucracy, had become increasingly remote from Afrikaner workers in factories, shops, mines and offices. They could be distinguished by their wealth and a lifestyle out of reach of ordinary workers: expensive cars, aeroplanes, holiday cottages that might be mistaken for mansions, holidays abroad, chic couture, and expensive educations for their children. The political representatives of the new class became wealthy while in office. Verwoerd left a tidy though not enormous estate. Nico Diederichs, who had threatened to nationalise the mines during the 1930s, became in turn Finance Minister and State President, and died a millionaire.

Some celebrities in business and politics might keep alive the folksy camaraderie or churchy primness which was formerly the stock in trade of the social and political leadership of Afrikaner populism, and the vulgarity of the nouveaux riches might serve to link the new class with the aspirations of the embourgeoisified working class, with their ski-boats, caravans and face-brick villas. But the institutions of party, church and community served less and less effectively to provide an integrating force. The opportunities for social mobility which economic growth and effective political controls afforded to white South Africans during the 1960s induced a marked condescension among the elite towards the poorer elements in the white community. During the late 1970s, most pretences at inter-class cordiality began to be abandoned. One cabinet minister declared that had he held office during the 1930s, he would have used influx controls to keep the poor whites out of the cities. One of the implications of the restructuring of the state during the 1980s was that whites would have to pay for their own education, as blacks did, a sign that the most significant avenue of social mobility available to white workers' children was becoming restricted. And, above all, the strategy for state reconstruction includes proposals for introducing an explicit class bias into the franchise arrangements for local and regional authorities.

5 The logic of labour coercion: influx control and political domination

All contemporary states are directly or indirectly involved in labour regulation. But the South African state is distinctive among capitalist states in the extent, scope and directness of its intervention in this arena. It early assumed control over the movement and allocation of the African workforce between different sectors and regions. Unusually, labour controls also led to the institution of state controls over aspects of community life which in liberal states were left to informal social controls. State interventions in the labour sphere, as well as over administration, provision of services, law enforcement and planning, became fused into a complex unity reminiscent of the absolutisms of the eighteenth century rather than of the liberal states of the nineteenth. In the latter these controls came to be distributed between the market on the one hand and social controls on the other, with the coercive functions of the state limited to narrow 'law and order' issues.

The controls the South African state acquired became among the most important, controversial and onerous features of its regulatory functions, and the inner rationale for both domestic and regional policies of control over the allocation of land and over the movement of people between the rural and urban industrial areas. These controls were singly the most serious issue in the relations between governments and their black subjects, providing from before the First World War down to the 1980s some of the most intense confrontations (including the one at Sharpeville) in their political relations.

Some elements of labour regulation in contemporary South Africa originated during colonial times. But those early forms of regulation and control were essentially concerned with the labour problems of an agrarian society. By contrast, modern labour regulation had its origins in the problems faced by the mining industry, and in the repercussions which the labour demands of mining had on other sectors of the industrial economy. The system that developed during the twentieth century was dictated by the specific problems of labour mobilisation and control in the era of industrial capitalism, specifically the mining industry.

From the beginning of the twentieth century, the state assumed a major role in regulating the supply of labour and allocating it between different sectors of the economy. As part of that function, the state came to assume control over the internal movement of people, and to prescribe the domicile and place of residence of the different racial groups, as well as a whole range of private and public relationships.

This feature of the contemporary South African state emerged after the South African War. Milner's 'conquest state' established in the Transvaal the foundations of the modern South African state, including the structure of its judiciary, police force, local authorities, taxation, customs, a regional labour recruitment system and a native affairs department. The state assumed a direct role in controlling the movement of labour.

Its intervention was based on the cordial and intimate relationship established between the state and the mining industry, which was profoundly to influence both future relationships between the state and industry, and also the role it assumed towards labour, black as well as white. The intimacy of the state's relationship with the mining interest was enhanced by the absence of the franchise in the Transvaal before 1907. Smuts and the Randlords could forge a relationship undistracted by the need to placate a white working-class electorate. In fact, however, it was black workers, not white, who became the major target of state strategies of control, for white workers along with other whites got the vote in 1907.

After the establishment of the mining industry, state intervention in the organisation and control of African labour passed through two main phases. From the 1890s, it was mainly concerned with mobilising an industrial labour force by limiting access to land and other resources. From about the 1920s, the state extended its reach, instituting controls over African settlement in the urban areas. Influx controls have subsequently embraced two spheres: control over access to the urban areas and over movement and settlement within the urban areas. The need for these controls and their increasing complexity were dictated partly by demands for cheap labour and partly by competition for labour between different sectors of the capitalist economy. Each sector had distinctive labour needs, and required a specific intervention from the state to ensure adequate labour supplies.

Between the 1890s and the end of the First World War, the state was chiefly involved in mobilising the labour force for the mines, and with meeting the demands of white commercial farmers for wage labour. The main instruments of labour coercion during that period were the Glen Grey Act of 1894 and the Natives Land Act of 1913. These Acts generated the pressures required to push African peasant cultivators and squatters on white farms into wage labour.

The Glen Grey Act introduced individual land tenure, which broke up collective tribal ownership in certain areas, and created a class of landless people. It also introduced a variety of taxes. The Natives Land Act restricted the rights of Africans to acquire land to about 7 per cent of the surface area of the country. The Native Labour Regulation Act of 1911 established global controls over migrant labour, including the enforcement of contracts and the regulation of conditions in the compounds. In combination, these measures had the effect of prising large numbers of peasant cultivators off the land and prescribing the conditions of their existence as a migrant labour force.

By the end of the First World War, Africans were moving into the urban areas at a rapidly increasing rate, partly under pressure of impoverishment in the countryside, and partly because of the higher wages being offered in the growing manufacturing sector. The wide disparity in wages paid to African workers in different sectors impelled agriculture to summon the state to assume the function of regulating and distributing labour between different sectors of industry (mines, commercial agriculture and manufacturing).

In response to these pressures, the state from the early 1920s expanded its activities, beyond coercing the industrial labour force into existence, to embrace the functions of allocating labour between different sectors of the economy.

During the same period, the state assumed direct control over communities of urban Africans, growing numbers of whom were working in manufacturing industries. The movement of Africans into the urban areas was accompanied by political upheaval and social dislocation, by strikes and riots, and the beginnings of a working class movement. In the haphazardly settled slums and locations of the new industrial cities, there was intense poverty, overcrowding and disease. Their poverty and lack of rights to participate in the administration of the cities have marked the subsequent history of urban African communities down to the present.

These developments underlay the formulation of an urban native policy which has proved remarkably resilient during the subsequent half-century. This policy rested on two strategies of control. The first involved state control over the entry of workers into the urban areas. The second involved regulating the access of Africans to housing and other amenities. The establishment of these strategies marked an important shift in the state's control over labour. From being a simple labour pump, the South African state became during the 1920s the cardiac and nervous systems of the industrial economy. This new policy received legislative expression in the Natives (Urban Areas) Act of 1923. Together with the Native Administration Act of 1927, which consolidated previous controls over the movement of Africans in the country, this Act created the basis for all subsequent government policies relating to urban Africans.

Two reports produced during the 1920s provided the basis for the new policy. The first, which emphasised controls over entry into the urban areas, was proposed by the Stallard commission of inquiry into local government, published in 1922. It stated its position unambiguously in the famous, or infamous, dictum that the African was required in the urban industrial areas 'to minister to the needs of the white man and should depart therefrom when he had ceased so to minister'. The Stallard doctrine rested ostensibly on the claim that Africans belonged in the rural areas, but Paul Rich has persuasively argued that like the apartheid policy for which it formed a precedent, Stallardism was essentially a doctrine designed to 'circumscribe the economic functions and conditions of social existence of an urban, African workforce'.[19]

The Stallard doctrine provided an important guide to the policy of successive governments, but it should be stressed that it was never applied in an undiluted form. Indeed the existence of permanently settled urban African communities is evidence of its modification. In order to understand this, it is necessary to recognise the central contradiction in the nature of this African 'ministry'. The labour power required by the white man was unavoidably accompanied by real human beings. The increasing demands which different sectors of the industrial economy made for African labour intensified the contradictions, for they contributed inevitably to the destruction of the rural economy, and therefore also to the range of social groups in the reserves which became dependent on the earnings of black workers. At the heart of the contradiction in Stallardism lay the simple fact that it promoted and encouraged the proletarianisation of the labour force, and thus undermined the social and economic system in the reserves which might sustain or subsidise it on a temporary basis in the towns. But although Stallardism did not prevent the emergence of a permanently settled African workforce in the urban areas, it had a profound effect on the character of their communities.

Insofar as it became established as a principle of state control over urbanisation and urban life, the Stallard doctrine worked to make African labour homogeneous, and to reinforce contract migrant labour. Stallardism inhibited, though it did not prevent, the stratification of urban African communities. It did not distinguish between different classes and strata in African society, and it also encouraged competition between urban workers and migrants. Therefore it dampened any tendency for social and economic stratification to take place.

The assumption on which it rested – that Africans were impermanent elements in the 'white' towns – had two major implications for future administration both in the rural and in the urban areas. The first, not fully articulated until Verwoerd's time, was that Africans should exercise whatever political rights they enjoyed in the reserves, and not in the towns. The second was that in the urban areas they should be the mere objects of administration, subject to arbitrary and discretionary powers of the state. Stallardism was in essence a system of control over entry into the urban areas. It provided no explicit guidelines for the government of urban African communities. In theory it provided for a form of managerial control over the lives of urban Africans. In practice it created the conditions for arbitrary and authoritarian controls above and near-anarchy below.

As a consequence of the doctrine, hardly any elements of civil government emerged in the urban areas. In Johannesburg, African housing was controlled until the late 1920s by the Parks and Recreation Department (along with the zoo) and the main instruments of administration were slum-clearance regulations. The city established a Native and Non-European Affairs Department during the late 1920s, a move which routinised its administration, though there were instances of corruption from time to time, especially during the 1920s and 1930s. Its officials were sometimes dedicated and sympathetic to their charges, but as in the traditions of colonial services elsewhere, their paternalism barely masked the authoritarianism which lay at the heart of the system.

An alternative and complementary 'native policy' to Stallardism, liberal in kind, developed along lines recommended by a government interdepartmental committee, the Godley Committee, set up in 1920 to inquire into the pass laws, which reported in 1923. In contrast with the Stallard Commission, which proposed close controls over entry into the urban areas, the Godley Committee recommended that African labour should be permitted to move freely into the towns and cities, subject only to the obligation to register and to carry a registration certificate outside of the ward in which the African was a resident, and to produce the certificate on demand and on obtaining employment. In contrast with Stallard, the Godley Committee emphasised the 'economic' purposes underlying its proposed controls over urban Africans. The Godley inquiry also recommended the exemption of property-holders, voters, and certain classes of workers (artisans and clerks) from the obligation to carry passes. It thus encouraged the stratification of urban communities.

The alternative emphases set out by these two reports for the management and control of urban Africans became the basis for the 'native policies' of rival political parties and for political controversies over the 'native question' in white politics. The conflicts between parliamentary parties, and particularly between the Nationalists and the United Party, tended to coagulate around these differences. The National Party favoured the direction set by Stallard, and indeed Verwoerd's doctrine of apartheid was a systematic development of Stallardism. The United Party followed the Godley line. But the differences between the two ought not to be exaggerated; they were differences in emphasis rather than of principle.

The Natives (Urban Areas) Act of 1923, which established the legislative framework within which government policy down to the present has been developed, catered for both directions, including provision for the exemption of the groups mentioned by Godley. Moreover, while party policies emphasised one or the other direction, no party when in power relied exclusively on either position. Thus, although United Party policy was similar to that formulated by the Godley Committee, it used influx controls during the 1930s to limit urbanisation and to expel surplus labour. The Native Laws Amendment Act of 1937 was the first piece of legislation that acknowledged the existence of permanent urban-dwellers, but it also provided for tighter influx controls. It thus combined features both of

Godley and of Stallard.

The United Party relaxed influx controls during the Second World War in response to the demand by manufacturing interests for labour. This demand was strengthened by the rise of manufacturing as a powerful pressure group in the United Party after the beginning of the war, when Hertzog's departure from the government weakened the influence of the agricultural interest. The shift also reflected the social revolution which accompanied war-time industrialisation.

In 1945, the government passed the Natives (Urban Areas) Consolidation Act. This Act was designed to establish machinery that would improve conditions of residence for blacks in urban areas, clearly a move away from Stallardism. But like other such moves, before and since, it also provided for tightening controls, for instance in the registration of contracts, and the regulation of influx and of the conditions of residence. Among its provisions was the prohibition placed on African acquisition of land, except from other Africans.

The direction set by Godley was reinforced by the Fagan commission of inquiry into 'native laws', which was constituted in 1946 and reported in 1948. The Fagan Commission was charged with investigating ways of creating an institutional framework within which a permanently settled urban African population could be accommodated. The Commission argued that urbanisation was an 'economic phenomenon' which could be guided and regulated, but not prevented or reversed, and that Africans had to be accepted as permanent features of the South African urban landscape.

It recommended that the labour force should be stabilised, though it stopped short of proposing that migratory labour should be discontinued. Among the recommendations it made to secure stability was the proposal to establish 'native village councils' which would have administrative responsibilities to maintain law and order under the jurisdiction of white-controlled local authorities.

It proposed improvements in financing urban housing for Africans, including provision for government loans to local authorities, and it drafted legislation that would empower local authorities to compel employers to contribute towards housing their employers. It also suggested that the different aspirations of various strata in the urban African community should be acknowledged in the provision of housing. Indeed, its concern to distinguish between the common day labourer and the trader, schoolteacher or clerk, ran throughout its report.

This concern was most clearly expressed in the Commission's response to the objection that the pass laws discriminated on the grounds of race. It recommended that all inhabitants of the country, including whites, should be made to have an identical document which, in principle, they might be required to produce on demand. The task of distinguishing between whites and 'settled' Africans, well known in an area, from 'other natives' could be left to administrative practice. The Commission suggested that while the former two groups would seldom have to produce their documents, 'other natives' (recent arrivals from the rural areas, persons without fixed addresses, the unemployed, and vagrants) would be advised to carry their documents at all times! This recommendation holds considerable interest to the student of state reform. The idea of a common document resurfaced during 1984. So too has the sentiment that what was objectionable about controls over movement was the use of race as a criterion, not the controls themselves.

The Fagan Commission also accepted the established structure of racially segregated residential areas in the medium term, but left open the long-term possibility of mixed areas, a position that drew the criticism that it was in favour of racial integration. This laissez-faire attitude helped the National Party win support among newly urbanised Afrikaner workers who faced competition from Africans for jobs and, among the poorest classes of whites, for housing too.

In fact, the proposals of the Fagan Commission were less radical, and a less radical departure from current practice, than its critics made out. Far from favouring a relaxation of influx controls, the Commission suggested that labour bureaux should be created over wide areas of the country in order to coordinate and regulate the flow of labour to the towns and to distribute it in the most effective way. The Commission thus lay the foundation for a national system of labour allocation. It only departed significantly from historical precedent and current practice in its investigation of ways to reduce the offence caused by the pass laws to the settled, relatively well-established strata of the urban African community. But even this proposal had its precedent in the Godley report. The Commission was, like other major attempts to formulate the basis for a new policy, a pragmatic adaptation of a basic formula designed to control African movement and settlement.

The Fagan Commission reported at the least opportune time for the United Party government, a few months before the general elections of 1948, which brought the National Party to power. The implications of its recommendations for relaxing the pass laws were a factor in attracting support for the Nationalists from newly urbanised Afrikaner workers and from farmers deeply concerned for their labour supplies. The National Party took maximum advantage of the chaotic conditions in post-war cities to advertise the perils of such a policy, and the benefits to white workers and farmers of the party's policy of apartheid.

Nationalist policy on urbanisation had been sketched in a report prepared for the party by Paul Sauer, a subsequent cabinet minister. Sauer recommended the intensification of controls over influx into the urban areas. In general, the Sauer report lay in the direction set by the Stallard Commission, but it went beyond Stallard in proposing that races should be segregated on territorial grounds. The basis was thus prepared for the development of Verwoerd's plan for total segregation. In the shorter term, the Sauer report clearly expressed the ascendancy of the agricultural sector in the array of interests represented in the National Party and in the post-1948 government.

While it is not being claimed here, as many critics have done, that there were no differences between the policies of pre- and post-1948 governments, it is suggested that the two themes in 'native policy' were complementary rather than mutually exclusive. Post-1948 Nationalist policy was in this respect more systematic, and more ruthlessly pursued than previous government policy, and it was distinctive too in the changes it produced in administration of the rural areas. But it rested basically on an extension of Stallardism, on which all government policies since the 1920s had rested in greater or lesser degree. Governments tended to shift from one set of strategies to the other, depending on the rhythm of the economy, and the relative strength and influence of the interests competing for state intervention in the labour process on favourable terms. Broadly, Nationalist governments emphasised influx controls, while United Party policy was inclined towards permitting urbanisation. But, as we have seen, governments might shift the emphasis or even reinforce both emphases simultaneously.

Moreover, the liberalisation of policy did not imply a relaxation of labour control but a change in its form and focus. During the Second World War, pass offices, which regulated influx, were set up in the rural areas. Together with the labour bureaux, which operated to distribute labour, the government was in a position to control the movement of Africans out of the rural areas at the source of the supply. In substance, this development, undertaken under the aegis of the most liberal government ever to hold power in post-Union South Africa, anticipated the introduction of labour bureaux in the homelands during the 1960s as part of the establishment of apartheid.

This duality was also evident in the way in which apartheid policy evolved. In 1952, the law was amended so that no African could remain in the urban areas for longer than 72 hours without a permit, unless he was born and resided permanently there, or had worked for 10 years, or had been legally resident in the area for 15 years. The effect was to threaten all but a tiny minority of Africans in the urban areas with the possibility of exclusion. On the other hand Verwoerd, the apostle of total separate development, extensively expanded the physical infrastructure of urban African settlement during the 1950s and 1960s. Though he and his senior officials never wavered from the position that Africans could not hope to enjoy the right to stay permanently in the urban areas, he admitted that they might be there for a very long time! Ironically, although the Nationalists decisively rejected the Fagan Commission report, Verwoerd, as the Nationalist Minister of Native Affairs from 1950, put into effect its recommendation that a levy should be imposed on employers in order to pay for African housing.

By the early 1960s, the policy of apartheid had produced a large surplus population in the countryside. But the tightening of controls over movement out of the rural areas, and Verwoerd's refusal to consider the possibility of granting permanent rights to urban Africans, did not simply work to homogenise the African labour force in the country as a whole. On the contrary, the effect of Verwoerd's policy was to deepen and intensify the distinction between those Africans who had won exemptions from measures excluding them from the urban areas, and those who had not. From the early 1950s, the form of the distinction changed in such a way as to differentiate between 'permanent' and 'temporary' residents in the urban areas. While this distinction did not confer de jure rights on the first group, it laid the foundations for their claims to acquire such rights, a claim which became stronger during the late 1970s. Like the Fagan Commission's recommendation that a 'common document' should be introduced, the acquisition of de facto rights provided an important precedent for the strategy of state reforms instituted during the 1980s.

Hindson's important study of influx controls suggests that while there have been different emphases in policy, the shifts in strategies have taken place within a frame of common assumptions in relation to the changing needs of capital, the conflicting interests of various sectors, and the shifting tempo of political struggles, including the struggles of the African workforce.[20] Hindson argued, against the proponents of the 'cheap labour' thesis, that influx controls during the twentieth century worked not merely to reinforce a racial division in the workforce – though it certainly did that – but also to differentiate between two groups within the African workforce, one of which became increasingly entrenched as 'insiders', whose interests and life chances diverged increasingly from those of the 'outsiders', excluded from permanent rights in the urban and industrial areas. Both processes have been at work, with different emphases, from the 1920s down to the 1980s, irrespective of whether governments placed the main emphasis of controls on influx or on housing and employment. The urban insiders became the focus of attention for reformist administrators during the late 1970s.

During the 1960s, the government announced a policy of industrial decentralisation which established growth points in the homelands and the national states. An important consequence of this policy, which located surplus workers on the periphery of the industrial areas as part of a national labour strategy, was the increasing centralisation of control over labour. Until 1971, local authorities exercised jurisdiction over the pass laws and considerable powers over urban locations and townships. In 1971, these powers were directly assumed by the Bantu Affairs Department, which in 1973 set up a number of regional Bantu Affairs Administration Boards. This centralisation of control was intended to create a more uniform national policy. Its most important result was to centralise control over the supply of labour and to coordinate it with economic fluctuations.

As homelands governments and (during the 1970s) 'national states' became established, labour bureaux were located within their borders. Along with this development, the emphasis in administration shifted from direct physical control over movement to control over housing, and was accompanied by an expansion of housing within the homelands states close to industrial areas created on their borders. This development brought into existence a class of long-distance commuters, living in the homelands but working in the Republic and travelling daily or weekly to work. The transport struggles of this class have produced sometimes bizarre consequences in the politics of homeland repression. In Ciskei, for instance, vigilantes fired on commuters using the South African Railways trains instead of buses with links to the Ciskeian establishment.

The juridical and political powers conferred on the homelands states in the process of their becoming national states, formally independent of South Africa, sharpened the boundaries between the various sectors of the African labour force, and institutionalised the differences among the elements of a segmentalised labour force in the form of differing citizenship rights.

The issue of citizenship has become a crucial one for Africans enjoying the right to live permanently in the urban areas, and perhaps even more important for those living in the homelands. For the first group, to have accepted citizenship in a national state carried the real possibility of alienating the right, precarious and ill-defined though it might be, to be present in the urban areas of South Africa. The development of national states, and with it their power to prevent and control the movement of their citizens beyond their territorial borders, as well as the corresponding power of the South African government to subject migrant workseekers to immigration regulations, might be seen as an attempt to normalise influx controls by casting them in the form of controls over inter-state movement. The implementation of this aspect of the policy might also be seen as an effort to devolve onto the national states the increasingly difficult task of managing the unemployed within their borders.

The Bantu Homelands Citizenship Act of 1970 provided that every black who was not a 'citizen' of a self-governing territory would become a 'citizen of the territorial authority area to which he was attached by birth, domicile or cultural affiliation'.[21] J. Dugard[22] has argued that since 1976, the South African government has

resorted to the fictional use of statehood and nationality in order to resolve its constitutional problems. New 'states' have been carved out of the body of South Africa and been granted independence, and all black persons affiliated with these entities, however remotely, have been deprived of their South African nationality. In this way the government aims to create a residual South African state with no black nationals. The millions of blacks who continue to reside and work in South Africa will be aliens, with no claims to political rights in South Africa. In this way, so the government believes, Blacks will be given full political and civil rights in their own states and a hostile international community will be placated. . . .

Hindson argued that the labour bureaux in the rural areas provided 'more efficient channelling facilities for a shrinking proportion of the surplus rural population'. Their effect would be to 'enforce idleness upon a growing surplus population trapped permanently in the countryside'.[23] The Bonapartist features of the national states become readily understandable in the light of the repressive functions imposed on them to control the surplus population as a consequence of this policy.

Yet, if the duality in the system of influx controls is properly understood, it becomes possible to see that the increasing readiness of the South African government during the 1970s to accept the presence of an African workforce permanently resident in the urban areas was the obverse of increasing controls over movement from the homelands and the national states, and of the powers which the state has assumed to relocate surplus people in the rural areas.

During the late 1970s, a series of tentative steps was taken towards a formal, de jure recognition of the permanency of urban Africans, though it ought to be stressed that the issues raised by such proposals were fraught with conflict within the higher reaches of the government. The development of the policy affected interests in government and in the state apparatus, as well as shook the National Party.

The Department of Community Development, which controlled the Administration Boards, came increasingly into conflict with such departments as Manpower, which expressed an institutional interest in relaxing controls over the movement of labour in order to improve its productivity. Despite the inhibitions imposed on it by such conflicts in the state, let alone between the government and its right-wing critics, the government's search for a strategy of 'stabilisation' became an increasingly public preoccupation during the late 1970s and early 1980s.

This shift in strategy was prodded into existence by progressive critics, by business leaders, and by judgements in a number of court cases. Perhaps above all, it was stimulated by the memory of the loss of life and property, international credibility and the growing tempo of armed struggle and internal insurrection which followed the events of Soweto in 1976. These issues were immeasurably intensified during the more or less continuous civil commotion of the early 1980s.

The strategy of stabilisation which developed after 1976 was based on the recognition of permanent African urban communities and the consequent attempt to establish appropriate political, fiscal and administrative structures. The policy was largely the work of two groups, the Riekert Commission (1977–9) which formulated its principles, and the Grosskopf Committee (1980–1) which considered the legislative implications of the Riekert Commission. The reports of both groups stressed the permanence of the urban African population, and addressed themselves to questions of defining this population and of regulating the future entry of people into the urban areas.

In a phrase remarkably reminiscent of the Fagan Commission of 1948, the Riekert Commission asserted that 'continued urbanisation should be regulated but cannot be halted'. The two reports asserted that the existing rights of urban-dwellers (formally, exemptions from exclusions) should be respected. They recommended that persons with a stable income sufficient to maintain a family and secure adequate accommodation, as well as persons who had resided in urban areas for five years or longer, together with their spouses, children and dependants, should be allowed to remain. Both recommended that the 72-hour prohibition, the cornerstone of government policy towards urban Africans since the 1950s, should be abolished. The use of the term 'rights' to refer to the bundle of statutory exemptions from exclusion, which had been introduced from the 1923 Urban Areas Act onwards, was a significant indication of the new note in government thinking.

Yet it should also be evident that, like the Fagan Commission, these reports did not point to a radical rupture with past policy or administrative practice. Nor, despite their affirmation of the rights of African workers freely to move between urban areas, did they in any sense propose to eliminate controls over influx into those areas. Even changes in terminology, like the use of the term 'orderly urbanisation' in place of influx control, suggest that the new policy was intended to maintain continuities with older ones. These proposals, like other elements of the 'reform' package which was being made up during the late 1970s and early 1980s, rested on and were designed to modify, not eliminate, the structures of the apartheid state which were created during the 1950s and 1960s.

The modifications which Riekert and Grosskopf introduced were intended to improve the productivity of labour or comparable economic functions on the one hand, and to reduce the levels of opposition to the state on the other. In broad terms, the condition for the recognition of a permanently settled African workforce was the maintenance and reinforcement of the political structures of the homelands states, many, though not all, the citizens of which had been excluded from the list of claimants to the right to live permanently in urban areas.

Many changes had already taken place in social and economic structure, and in political and administrative relations, particularly during the 1970s, which enabled the government to introduce more 'flexible' elements in its labour policy. Some of these were made possible by a realignment in the relationship between the state and the private sector, which has come about as a result of changes in the structure of the capitalist economy.

Contrary to some opinion, much of this flexibility has been made possible precisely because of the enduring effects of earlier policies of control over the structure of class and race relations. For instance, the policy of segregation which evolved during the course of the twentieth century indelibly shaped the spatial structure of the urban environment. It was difficult to imagine that this structure would dissolve, merely by the act of removing the statutory instruments which created its juridical framework, without radical changes in the political forces that brought those instruments into existence. Of course, there *have* been changes in the character of those political forces, particularly in the structure of capital (towards more concentrated control over the economy), in the increasing strength of organised black labour, and in the relations between the two. But it is unlikely that modifications brought about through a strategy of liberalisation (for instance, through the suspension of formal statutory controls, privatisation, deregulation and decentralisation) would produce fundamental changes in social structure, economic opportunities and political power. Many of the effects of past policy, achieved through state coercion, are likely to be maintained in modified form through the operation of market forces.

Before exploring these problems, it is worth situating these changes in the perspective of the history of segregation. It will be recalled that Stallard was worried that if Africans acquired the right to reside permanently in the urban areas, they would also inevitably win civic rights in those areas, including the right to the municipal franchise. Writing his report during a period of intense conflict between white workers and the gold-mining companies (his report was published in the year of the Rand Revolt), he was concerned about the possibility that white and black workers might join forces on issues of common interest. He realised that if urban Africans were to gain political rights in the urban areas, such as the right to participate in municipal elections, the institutional basis for joint action would be laid.

After three-quarters of a century of segregation, the chances of this happening at the grassroots have been reduced. In the cities of the Transvaal the foundations have been laid of metropolitan and regional structures in which Africans might, and indeed do, enjoy limited political rights in racially segregated areas. But the effects of segregation and apartheid policy on the spatial and social configurations of these metropolitan areas have reduced the likelihood that white and black urban communities will easily reach political alliances based on common interests. The 1983 constitution made provision for multiracial representation on regional and metropolitan councils and it is possible that non-racial representation might be instituted in some areas. However it is almost certain that because of the structure of these councils, party organisation will be excluded from them.

These considerations make it possible to understand why the Riekert Commission not only did not question the need for influx controls, but actually made recommendations for revising the administration of influx controls which would complement the measures operating through the labour bureaux in the homelands. The revised forms of influx controls which Riekert proposed would require monitoring both workplace and place of residence of the African worker. The owners or occupiers of premises would similarly be obliged to show that residents had the right to permanent or temporary residence.

Undoubtedly modifications might yet be considered which would either weaken or strengthen the controls over the movement of labour between the homelands and the urban areas, or shift the balance of controls one way or the other between the urban areas and the homelands. As a result of the Riekert Commission's recommendations, movement between urban areas, but not from countryside to city, was made easier. From the late 1970s, the state authorities took more and more seriously the problem of constructing viable black local authorities in urban areas. But none of these elements in the problem were new, nor were any of the solutions that were considered during the late 1970s and early 1980s without precedent. The plans for the development of local authorities had their precedent in policies that had evolved from the 1920s onwards. Indeed, the current prospectus for reform is a modernised version of the kinds of solutions proposed by Godley, and recommendations rest on the assumption that labour controls are a necessary element of the political economy.

For decades, migrant workers from the reserves, the white farms, the homelands and the national states, have tried to establish their families in the urban areas by squatting. Far from being symptomatic of a breakdown in an otherwise orderly process of urbanisation, squatting has been a major route to urban settlement, and perhaps the most important route to family settlement in urban areas in Third World countries. In South Africa and in other countries with restrictions over the movement of rural people comparable to its influx controls, squatting was perhaps the most effective strategy for achieving a foothold in urban society.[24]

No South African government, whether 'reformist' or 'reactionary', has willingly countenanced squatting, though in periods of intense crisis in the countryside and demands for labour in the cities, the state has tried to control squatting by re-housing groups with some claim to being in the cities, usually by screening out unemployed squatters and expelling them from the urban area. The harsh treatment of these families by state authorities, for instance by bulldozing shelters and deporting workers, their wives and children, back to the national states, has been represented by liberal critics of the South African government as a retrogressive anomaly in the process of state-directed 'reform'. This view is based on a misunderstanding of the character of state reform. Such actions should rather be seen as the corollaries of a policy deeply rooted in the complex history of influx controls. That policy, like its precursors, was wide and flexible enough to embrace a certain range of political and administrative reforms. Indeed, the remarkable resilience of the South African state, despite its weak legitimacy, may be explained in part by its capacity to shift between the two forms of labour control.

In September 1984, the State President announced measures to abandon the policy of protecting coloured people in the western Cape against

African competition for jobs. He also announced the government's intention to introduce 99-year leasehold titles for Africans in the Cape Town metropolitan area. Presumably this change was intended to consolidate the position of Africans in the urban areas of the western Cape. Yet in his statement, the President made it clear that the change in policy did not imply any concessions to squatters. The policy of 'controlled urbanisation' which began to emerge during the early 1980s was aimed at preventing squatting.

In 1984, disturbances of the same kind as but probably on even greater dimensions than the Soweto uprising of 1976 broke out in the Vaal triangle, and then widened to many other parts of the country, including the homeland of QwaQwa, where migrant workers rioted. In October, troops were used to back massive police action in Sharpeville and Sebokeng in the southern Transvaal and throughout the eastern Cape. Such events suggest that the policy of stabilisation had failed to meet the needs of urban Africans.

It might be claimed that the measures undertaken by the state to consolidate the position of urban Africans have been remarkably tardy in their execution, and that this explains the renewed conflict. It is true that the Grosskopf Committee, which reported in 1981 on draft legislation to give effect to the Riekert Commission's proposals, remained confidential in 1984. But it would be a mistake to interpret the problems faced by the state during the mid-1980s as the result of the slow progress of political reforms. The problem lay in the repression of any political initiative which was seriously intended to eliminate the structures which have been generated since the 1920s, including the liberal versions enunciated in turn by Godley, Fagan and most recently by Riekert.

Those structures, it has been suggested, allowed for considerable flexibility in the control over the movement and allocation of labour. But in general, though there may have been considerable variations within each strategy of control, measures which allowed for stratification of the urban labour force have also required the use of controls over entry into urban areas, including controls exercised from the homelands. The measures which by the mid-1980s the government had introduced to stabilise urban African communities, not only remained within the framework of apartheid, but were meaningless outside of that framework.

The consolidation of the position of urban Africans within that structural framework necessarily requires the reinforcement and elaboration of the controls over movement from the homelands. It could also be argued that the efforts of state and private bodies like the Urban Foundation to improve the quality of life in African urban areas rest upon the basis of the apartheid state, and can only have any real effect in those areas on the basis of limiting access to the urban areas.

In July 1986, the government scrapped influx controls. It also passed the Restoration of South African Citizenship Act, making it possible (though certainly not easy) for certain categories of persons who had lost their citizenship when the national states were created to regain South African citizenship. The government almost immediately declared that the commuter migrants who reside in the national states but work in the Republic, would not be eligible for this restoration. In the ensuing outcry, however, this decision was reversed. The dialectics of this moment in South Africa's present transformation are instructive: what was enabled through legislative flexibility was taken away by administrative fiat, and then made possible again by an ad hoc decision.

6 Of uncivil government: the administration of urban black South Africa

The controls over the movement of African labour which evolved during the course of industrialisation had direct implications for the pattern of African urbanisation and settlement. They profoundly affected the character of urban administration, making it extremely unlikely that government by consent might emerge. They influenced the way the state conceived and defined social services and other amenities appropriate to the condition of blacks living and working in the urban areas. They also had profound effects on the government and politics of rural society in the so-called reserves (later, the homelands).

Indeed, a clear distinction cannot be made between the control and allocation of labour on the one hand and the administration of amenities and services on the other in a situation in which Africans were entitled to be in the urban areas only in order to perform labour services. The official assumption was that all aspects of their lives were to be subordinated to the principle of labour service. In practice, governments could not entirely evade the implications which the continuous settlement of African communities in urban areas raised, including the need to provide services like sanitation and transport, welfare, and so on.

But these issues were not prominent on the agenda either of the central government or of local authorities, and tended to be neglected except in periods of intense crisis. Africans were not represented in parliament or on local bodies. Their political organisations were weak and highly vulnerable to police attack and government proscription. Once again, the official conception of appropriate behaviour, including political behaviour, which flowed out of Stallardism, excluded any stance that was not simply one of subservience. There were few channels of communication with government. Africans were unable to back the representations they made to government by threatening to withdraw support.

Characteristically the changes they won, not always necessarily to the advantage of the groups immediately involved, were achieved by the threat of public disorder, strikes, or community action which might disadvantage white interests or inconvenience the authorities. The phrase, collective bargaining by riot, coined to describe English working-class action during the late eighteenth and early nineteenth centuries, also describes the most significant element in African relations with the South African government.

Thus the effort to develop urban housing on a massive scale was stimulated by the desire to control squatting in the vicinity of major cities after the Second World War. Subsidised bus transport developed only in response to bus boycotts during the same period. The electrification of Soweto began to receive attention only after the 1976 revolt, three-quarters of a century after Africans first settled in the area, and forty years after the establishment of municipal housing there. The labour reforms of the 1970s followed industrial unrest on a scale unmanageable through the use of repression.

Since its initial formulation by Stallard and until the recent past, urban 'native' policy was explicitly built on the premiss that Africans had no political rights in the urban areas, and could never expect to acquire them. They were explicitly denied the right to move freely into and settle in the urban industrial areas. There was an iron logic underlying Stallardism (and, later, Verwoerdism) which Godley softened but did not change.

Stallard asserted that the logical consequence of allowing Africans to settle permanently in the urban areas would be that they should also acquire civil rights within those areas. It was for that reason that he formulated the policy of denying them rights to be permanent urban-dwellers.

The notion that Africans were essentially rural people who must enjoy civil and political rights in the reserves was to have tremendous implications for the position of urban African communities as well as for those living in the rural areas. As we have seen, the Stallard doctrine was not strictly adhered to in government policies relating to urban Africans, and they in fact acquired certain limited forms of rights, which included circumscribed forms of representation on advisory boards, later on community councils, and during the late 1970s and early 1980s on black local authorities, which possessed a limited form of autonomy. (By the time these last-mentioned bodies were established, the government had acknowledged that urban-dwellers had definite rights in urban areas.)

But from the 1920s, when it was first enacted, until the 1970s, by which time the homelands and national states had been created, the Stallard doctrine was followed sufficiently closely to eviscerate the administration of urban African communities of civic content, and to make even the simplest communication between administration and subject, or the least problematic negotiation over the provision of services, extraordinarily complex and ridden with overt conflict. While the alternative and complementary trajectory in urban 'native' policy, initially developed in the Godley report and elaborated by Fagan and most recently by Riekert, was more hospitable to the idea of a restricted form of civic life for urban blacks, it shared with the Stallard doctrine a purely functional view of their position in urban society based essentially on the utility of their labour.

The alternative doctrine differed from 'pure' Stallardism in the extent to which it took cognisance of the needs of some sectors of the economy for skilled workers, and the extent to which it acknowledged the threat of public disorder from a proletariat with no 'stake' in urban society.

Within the terms of such a policy, the financing of services to African communities in the urban areas was and has remained particularly problematic, not only because of the poverty of most of the inhabitants of townships and locations, but also because without home-ownership or local industry or even significant local commerce, there was a meagre revenue base to finance services. Municipalities controlled by white rate-payers and dominated by commercial and industrial interests were reluctant to divert funds to services for African communities. This reluctance lay only partly in the parsimony of local authorities, answerable politically to all-white electorates. (In fact most services in urban African areas were subsidised in one form or another by white-controlled municipal authorities.) It was also a result of the precarious financial base of these local bodies.

Although cities had the legal right to levy taxes on improvements, in practice their revenues were based on rates determined by the unimproved value of land and from the sale of services, as well as from licences, fees and so on. Many services lost money or at best broke even. The result was that even cities with an affluent white citizenry and high property values, like Johannesburg, were constantly strapped for cash.

Indeed, Johannesburg had some very special fiscal burdens to bear as a consequence of its relationship to the mining industry. Mining land, which made up about a fifth of the city's land area, was exempt from rates unless used for non-mining purposes. Moreover, government properties, which occupied extensive areas of cities like Johannesburg, Pretoria and Cape Town, were exempt from rates. Although the government paid grants in lieu of rates, these were seldom adequate compensation for lost revenues.

The consequence was that white local authorities, which before 1971 were largely responsible for providing state housing and other services for blacks in the urban areas, had scarce resources with which to pay for them, and, being answerable to all-white rate-payers, were understandably reluctant to do so for fear of the political repercussions. As will be seen presently, the attempt to develop financially self-sufficient African local authorities during the late 1970s and 1980s was probably a precipitating factor in the disturbances in the urban areas during the early 1980s.

The Natives (Urban Areas) Act of 1923 obliged municipalities to establish a 'Native Revenue Account' for the financial provisioning of services. The intention of a separate account was to prevent municipalities from siphoning off revenues gained from Africans for the benefit of white rate-payers. There were, however, understandably few sources of revenue to be found in the African townships and locations. The inspired solution to this problem was to develop controls (and eventually a monopoly) over the production and sale of traditional African sorghum beer known as *mahau*, and commonly described by whites as 'kaffir beer'.

The extraordinary situation grew up that a major part of funds for services to Africans living in urban areas came from the proceeds of the sale of beer. When the prohibition on the sale of liquor to, and its consumption by, Africans was lifted in 1961, the municipalities (and later the central government) acquired a monopoly over its sale in the townships.

This monopoly was transferred to the Bantu Affairs Administration Boards when they assumed control over the administration of Africans in the urban areas. Of course, beer had been one of the most important lubricants of conviviality in African society, and white-run municipalities could teach Africans nothing in respect of its manufacture.

In order to secure an effective fiscal base, municipalities needed to police closely their controls over beer-brewing. In doing so they came into conflict with a resilient and formidable group of entrepreneurs: the women who made a precarious living, brewing and purveying *mahau* in the townships and in industrial zones. There were riots in Bloemfontein location during the early 1920s and subsequently a series of running battles in other areas too.

These controls were reinforced in 1945, when the municipalities were granted a statutory monopoly over beer-brewing. Significantly, the establishment of the monopoly was achieved simultaneously with the development of a legislative framework that would make possible the improvement of living conditions in urban townships and locations. Napoleon's army marched on its belly; a large proportion of revenues for services for urban Africans in South Africa rested on their consumption of *mahau*.

Municipal control over beer-brewing was intensely resented by Africans. It threatened the livelihoods of the women who brewed it, and forced up the price of beer to consumers. The municipalities set up drinking-halls so bleakly austere that it is a wonder anyone could find recreation in them. Control over brewing represented one more tiresome intrusion into the lives of people already ringed with regulations. Consequently, from the early 1920s onwards there was a series of riots associated with these regulations in many different parts of the country, as well as illicit brewing on a sustained scale. The attempt to control illicit brewing, with its roots in the fiscal problem of servicing urban African settlements, was a major source of conflicts between police and Africans.

It is possible that the municipal interest in brewing was a factor, though not the only one, in the prohibition of liquor to Africans before 1961. This prohibition stimulated the development of a bootlegging industry carried out on a scale and with a degree of sophistication and violence which rivalled the American industry during prohibition in the 1920s. One consequence of prohibition was the development of appalling levels of alcoholism, and sometimes deaths and disease, from the concoctions which were used to lace the precious and precariously available liquor. It was, if anything, an even greater source of conflict with the police than the municipal monopoly over the brewing of *mahau*, with the added twist that policemen sometimes became involved in bootlegging or took bribes from the shebeen owners who were the main purveyors of liquor in the township.

There was yet another twist to the story of government involvement in the liquor trade. After the prohibition on the sale of 'European' liquor to Africans was lifted, the central government turned from control to supply, via the agency of the Bantu Affairs Administration Boards. The Boards became major liquor retailers, the largest in the country.

The financing of services for Africans in urban areas has long been a thorny issue between the central government and local authorities. The central government increasingly tried to pressure industrial interests to pay for African housing and other services, which the latter resisted. During the 1950s, Verwoerd forced the issue by imposing a levy on employers of African labour, thus causing far more resentment within local authorities and white business interests than had the removal of Africans from freehold areas like Sophiatown. Ironically this legislation had been drafted by the Fagan Commission, whose findings were rejected by the Nationalists when they took power in 1948.

Because of their lack of power, the limited forms of African representation in local bodies established from the 1930s seldom generated any substantial political support in urban African communities. From the advisory boards of the 1930s down to the community councils and black urban authorities of the 1980s, such bodies rarely gained the support of more than 10 or 15 per cent of the people entitled to vote for them. In the riots of the 1980s officials and representatives elected to these bodies were frequently attacked, many were murdered, and their property was destroyed.

The conception of the place of Africans in urban society prescribed in segregation and apartheid policy deeply affected the relationships between Africans and the police force and other agencies of law enforcement. Especially in urban African communities, the incidence of serious crimes has always been appallingly high. Soweto can claim some sort of world record for serious crime.

Complaints have been made that the police neglected to protect communities. But it was not simply a matter of negligence. The functions commonly associated with protecting the community against crime, and the relationships between police and community implied in those functions, lay a long way down the police force's list of priorities. In South Africa such protection has never been an unproblematic or contradiction-free function of the police force. This was in part at least a legacy of colonial and republican times, when police functions were barely distinguishable from the quasi-military role of a frontier gendarmerie. The development of police forces in urban areas undoubtedly modified this role in the older towns and cities of the Cape and Natal. But the manifold problems of law enforcement in Johannesburg – 'the university of crime' was Merriman's well-phrased jibe – and the intensification of conflicts on the land, in labour compounds and in other sites of struggle in the process of industrialisation, if anything reinforced the quasi-military character of the police force. Not only were the police used to settle strikes, riots, and other commotions in the urban areas, but their general relationship towards urban Africans was largely shaped by the assumption that Africans were rightless subjects. Any serious modification of a police function that was primarily repressive in character was largely precluded by the logic of Stallardism and Verwoerdism.

The police were mainly concerned with enforcing influx regulations, controlling the liquor trade, and with political repression. Certainly criminal elements were frequently the targets of police action. But this did little to cement a cordial relationship between police and community. Scarcely any element of the black population was secure from the possibility of criminalisation, and crime attracted some of the ablest elements anyway. The use of anti-vagrancy laws and influx controls to control political activities like boycotts and stay-aways which African communities regarded as legitimate has meant that relations with the police were strained at best and, at worst, a state of war. The white opposition press often represented the problem of relations between the police and blacks as though they could be significantly improved with tact, courtesy and respect. But it is important to recognise that the relationship was structurally dictated, in the sense that it derived, at least in the urban areas, from the role prescribed for Africans in the Stallard doctrine, which grew out of migrancy.

From the late 1940s, a new technique of blanket raids evolved which, in the opinion of the editor of the left-wing *Guardian*, 'appears to be, not to trace and trap known criminal gangs, but to conduct what resembles a punitive expedition against the entire local population'.[25] It was a logical development dictated by the conception of the role of Africans in the urban areas. A similar development took place in the rural areas, especially as the crisis on the land intensified. It is dramatically illustrated in the events leading up to the 'incident' at Witzieshoek in 1950. During the 1930s, there was only one white policeman stationed in the reserve. In 1950, after a decade of discontent, a force of police rode into the reserve, and shot on a meeting of tribesmen.

The administration of justice, too, was profoundly affected by the controls over the lives of Africans. The presumption was made in criminal prosecutions under Section 10 (4) of the Natives (Urban Areas) Act of 1945 that the accused was unlawfully in an urban area unless it could be proved otherwise. Swift and summary justice was served in the commissioners' courts which were responsible for prosecuting offenders under the pass laws. Ramarumo Monama's study of the Johannesburg commissioners' courts records that in the six courts he observed over the period of a month, cases took between 30 seconds and 7 minutes to dispose of.[26]

The theory and practice of Stallardism, and Verwoerd's variation on it, had immense implications for the kind and quality of social services which were developed for Africans. The point is often made that per capita the state spends far less on Africans and other blacks than on whites. The difference is not, however, simply a quantitative one. It rests on a different conception of the social rights of different racial groups. Stallardism was crucial in defining and justifying those differences. As we have seen, Stallardism and Verwoerdism linked the right of Africans to live in urban areas to the labour services which they performed. Accordingly, no claims could be entertained from groups whose rights were thus defined to services like unemployment benefits. Similarly the problems of the disabled, the mentally ill, and the other flotsam and jetsam of industrial society tended to be viewed primarily as problems of control, rather than of care. Whatever claims to social services could be acknowledged had to be explicitly linked to labour service.

Harold Wolpe's important paper on cheap labour power in South Africa argued that the kind and quality of social and other services provided for Africans could be explained as a consequence of the migrant labour system, which, in turn, was dictated by the needs of the mines for cheap labour. Under the conditions of migrancy, the subsistence needs of the migrant worker between contracts, and provision for his maintenance during periods of illness, unemployment and old age, could be met in the reserves. So could the subsistence and welfare needs of his children.[27]

While Wolpe's argument opened up an important set of debates about the character of capitalism in South Africa, it did not explain the nature of the social services which, as we have seen, developed in the industrial areas with the explicit purpose of maintaining the labour force, initially the mine labour force, in a fit condition to work. The early history of medical research in South Africa was largely the story of the efforts undertaken to solve the medical problems of African mineworkers. The South African Institute of Medical Research was established before the First World War as a joint project by the government and the Chamber of Mines with this purpose in mind.

The best medical services available to Africans in the country are those for mineworkers. Not surprisingly, the purpose of such service is defined by the needs of the mining industry. A major part of mine hospital services is the treatment of the casualties of mine accidents. The casualty rate in South African mines is much higher than in Britain, Europe or the United States.

From before the turn of the century, conditions in the major industrial centres induced the authorities to intervene, usually by applying slum clearance and sanitary regulations. As in other parts of the world where such regulations have been invoked in the name of public health, both political and economic interests of dominant groups were served by the actions of municipal and central authorities. The fear of contagious disease spreading to whites was an unarticulated but significant theme underlying the segregation policies which developed during the twentieth century.

After the influenza epidemic of 1918, the concern of public health authorities widened to take in the manifold problems of poorly paid and poorly housed African workers in other sectors besides mining.

During the 1930s and 1940s, the state extended its concern with the health of Africans to the rural areas, where hitherto the burden of health care had been borne mainly by church missions, which also provided the overwhelming part of the educational facilities available to Africans. The state health services also attempted to widen the definition of its functions to embrace nutritional and other issues. But the basic purpose behind the broadened scope of health services remained the supply of a healthy labour force. The Department of Public Health reported thus in 1934: 'Apart from any question of humanitarianism, or of our duty to a subordinate race, there is the obvious matter of self interest. Our mines and industries are making increasing demands for cheap native labour. Owing to the poor health and physique of the natives in our own reserves, half of those brought to the examining doctors have to be turned down. For that reason we have had in the past to import some 100 000 natives from our Portuguese neighbours.'[28] These preoccupations by the government obviously reflected the Chamber of Mines' concern to ensure the reproduction of the labour force in the circumstances of deteriorating conditions in the rural areas. During the late 1930s, this concern was also translated, admittedly half-heartedly and ineptly, into plans for rural rehabilitation. Another consequence was the effort to widen the welfare activities of the Health Department. This effort was only partially successful before 1948. After 1948, it was continued, but the doctrine of apartheid subjected every such effort to a host of restrictions and limitations.

One of the consequences of the establishment of the homelands governments and the national states from the 1960s was increasingly to impose welfare functions on the 'homelands' governments.

These impoverished states thus came to bear the obligation to carry a growing burden of providing welfare to the reserve army of the South African industrial labour force, with few of the resources available to metropolitan South Africa. What this means in effect, as John Kane-Berman has pointed out, is that the homelands administrations and national states spend a larger proportion of their much smaller budgets on welfare than the South African government does.[29]

This is particularly onerous in rural communities which have been deliberately planned to hold the economically inactive elements in the society who are most urgently in need of welfare: schoolchildren, the aged, and the unemployed. As Kane-Berman also has pointed out, insult is added to injury by the habit of the South African authorities, the media, and some otherwise impeccable scholars, of referring to grants made by the South African government to these states as a form of international aid. After all, the revenues expended on such disbursements are generated by the economic activities of workers in South African industry, which in-

cludes the migrants who live in the homelands. The imposition of this
function onto the homeland states reflects a continuity between the social
functions of the reserves during the period of early mining capitalism and
the political functions of the present homeland states.

It is a commonplace of radical scholarship that welfare services in
Western capitalist states – education, health, pensions and unemployment
benefits – function in a definite relationship to the requirements of industrial capitalism and of political stability. Such services work partly to create
the conditions for productive labour, and partly to legitimise the social
order and hence help maintain the stability of capitalist societies.

But while social services in South Africa also serve broadly similar
functions, there are crucial differences because of the way in which welfare
developed in South Africa, that make it misleading to compare them with
services in the countries of western Europe and North America. Firstly, the
scale and quality of welfare differ significantly. It was noted earlier that
differences in scale and quality were justified in the ideology of the
dominant social order by reference to the different social rights allocated by
the South African state to various racial groups. These differential notions
of social rights clearly related to the positions in the political economy
occupied by various racial groups, and the differences in the political power
which they could exercise.

As a consequence of the struggles over the first half-century after the
establishment of the mining industry, white workers achieved social rights
comparable to, though less fulsome than, those won by European and
North American workers. Their possession of the franchise, the existence
of a powerful Afrikaner nationalist movement, and their position in the
economy, were no doubt important factors in winning such social rights.

The failure for a general working-class political movement to emerge
that embraced workers of different races, and hence white workers' dependency on the Afrikaner nationalist movement, might also account for the
limited achievements of white workers in respect of welfare services. Like
the European working class during the 1950s and 1960s, white workers
could claim as a right their entitlement to certain social services because
they could base such a right on their membership of civil society, in which
the franchise was the most important qualification, as well as on their ability
to provoke serious civil disturbance. At the same time, ironically, because
they were able to win privileges within a racially bifurcated labour force,
their experienced need for welfare was diminished. A welfare state for
whites failed to emerge, though the need for one was acutely experienced
during the Great Depression and again during the 1980s. But for the most
part, whites relied on the state to give them privileged access to jobs and
bargaining positions.

Rather like monopoly-sector workers in the United States, white workers tended to find it easier to believe that their interests lay in maintaining
the status quo rather than in trying to forge common links with workers who

were poorly unionised, or who were foreigners, or whose organisational powers were poorly developed. But the limitations on the social rights of white workers pale into insignificance compared with the situation of black workers, especially Africans.

African workers had their rights defined by Stallard and Verwoerd in such a way as to exclude membership of the civil society. Accordingly, any rights to welfare were linked solely and exclusively to their role as labourers.

Stallardism has cast a long and sinister shadow over the history of urban African society. Officials giving evidence to a recent select committee correctly traced the source of the problems encountered in urban areas to the establishment and elaboration of this doctrine in the administration of urban areas. Soweto, they argued, was entirely uncoupled from the political process, and its inhabitants were treated as inert objects of administration. Their governance was purely a departmental responsibility. 'The effective government, insofar as it existed, lay not in Soweto, but in Pretoria.' They claimed that the officials who controlled Soweto seldom visited it, and that the laws relating to urban Africans were so complex that no official actually understood them.

The administration of Soweto was grounded on the absolute prohibition established under Stallardism. There were no basic civil rights. The administration was based on rule by force. Soweto was built on the 72-hour immunity in terms of legislation of 1952. In Soweto, one official declared, there was not the vaguest mention of a shadow of a *regstaat* or the shadow of the rule of law. It was the exact opposite.[30]

While it may be true that government policy provided little stimulus to civic virtue among Africans, and in important ways worked to undermine it, political and social life as a consequence achieved an extraordinary momentum outside of the apparatus of controls, and largely in defiance of it. It is a truism of political science that much of the substrate of political life is to be found in the informal structures and processes of communities. But there can be few instances in a developed state of communities comparable to those created by Africans in South Africa's urban areas which exhibit a relationship so tangential to formal administrative structures and procedures, and so indifferent to the political ethos of the dominant classes.

State regimentation and control, low wages, high unemployment and insecurity in getting and keeping jobs and housing, had two partially contradictory effects on urban African communities. On the one hand, they created conditions of personal and social instability, reflected in high rates of infant mortality, alcoholism, crime, mental and physical disability and shortened life expectancy. On the other hand, they generated the conditions for a remarkably original cultural, social and political life, independent from and defiant towards the dominant ethos set by the prevailing political and cultural system.

The fiscal and political problems relating to the administration of Africans living in urban areas had a direct bearing on the intensification of conflicts in these areas after 1976, and especially from the early 1980s. Ironically the severity of this crisis was partly the product of efforts to reform the administrative system by creating autonomous black local authorities, and to 'normalise' their fiscal base. These reforms were instituted as a result of the government's acceptance, implicitly at first, of the permanent presence of a group of Africans enjoying the right to live and work in the urban areas, and of attempts to stabilise the situation in the urban areas by entrenching the position of 'middle class' Africans.

Africans in urban areas had enjoyed some form of representation from 1923 onwards. But until 1977, the bodies on which they sat enjoyed solely advisory powers. The government set up advisory boards in African locations during the 1920s and 1930s. These ought not to be dismissed in retrospect out of hand, for they provided a locus for African political activity, and some significant community leaders (like the Orlando squatter leader James Mpanza) used them as a power base. The ANC, though committed to boycotting racially differential bodies, fought advisory board elections throughout the 1950s; it found these bodies too useful to neglect, notwithstanding their manifest defects. During the 1960s, advisory boards were replaced by Urban Bantu Councils. These too, however, were purely advisory bodies. Until 1971, advisory boards and Urban Bantu Councils advised white local authorities, usually municipalities. In 1971 Bantu (later Black) Affairs Administration Boards, established under the authority of the central government's Bantu Affairs Department, took over the juridical powers of local authorities.

The Boards assumed a wide range of administrative functions. Some of them were performed on an agency basis for central government departments. When new black local authorities with expanded functions and original powers were created from 1977 onwards, the Boards undertook on a service basis the administration of many of these additional functions.

The 1976 riots forced the government to consider measures which might establish its authority in the African communities settled in locations around white cities and towns. In particular, reformist pressure groups, among which the Urban Foundation became the most influential, developed a strategy which aimed at creating property rights for urban Africans, and for upgrading the 'quality of life' in urban African settlements. Among the projects which it helped establish was the plan to provide electricity to Soweto.

These developments required local authorities in urban African areas competent to establish and administer amenities and services and operate capital projects which could transform these areas from dormitories into 'living towns'. The first step in this process was the replacement of the advisory boards and Urban Bantu Councils, neither of which had enjoyed any effective power to influence municipalities or the Administration Boards, by community councils in 1977–8. Before these had been installed, however, they were replaced in 1982 by black local authorities which enjoyed powers roughly comparable to white local authorities. Ironically, these expanded powers intensified some of the contradictions in the administration of urban Africans: the new bodies became charged with some of the functions the Administration Boards had previously operated, including influx control.

These developments also had major financial implications for local authorities in the urban areas, which partly explain the increase in the intensity of conflicts during the early 1980s. However, the financial problems of black local authorities originated in the changes which had begun to take place by the mid-1970s in a system of financing that had changed little since the 1920s.[31]

The 1923 Urban Areas Act had obliged white local authorities to establish a Native Revenue Account for charging services in locations and townships. The intention of this provision was to prevent local authorities from profiteering from supplying services to Africans. At the same time, the Act permitted charges against this account to be met from their General Revenue Account, and in fact it was fairly common for white rate-payers to subsidise services to Africans in urban areas, either directly, or indirectly by providing services at below cost.

For fairly obvious reasons, the revenue bases of the locations and townships themselves were limited. Because few Africans enjoyed the right to own fixed property (and none did in municipal locations) there was no opportunity to charge rates on the value of land. Revenues from rents in municipal and, later, central state housing were held down as far as possible, for few Africans were able to afford economical rents on the wages they earned. Housing for Africans was a major burden for white local authorities. (It was also a burden for white rate-payers, who by subsidising African housing were providing indirect subsidies to employers.) Although it is difficult to generalise for every part of the country over the whole period, it is a safe guess that housing accounts were more likely than not to be in deficit. It was mainly in order to find additional revenues to pay for housing in the African townships that Verwoerd imposed a levy on employers of African labour during the early 1950s.

The major source of subsidy for housing came, however, from the sale of sorghum beer and, after 1961, from liquor. The municipalities established controls over the brewing of sorghum beer, and after 1945 gained a legal monopoly over its production and sale. When the prohibition on the sale of liquor to Africans was lifted in 1961, the municipalities were granted 20 per cent of the profits derived from government sales of liquor to blacks. Although this trade did not provide revenues on the scale of the sales of sorghum, both municipalities and, later, the Administration Boards did extremely well throughout the 1960s and into the 1970s. Most of the Administration Boards inherited healthy surpluses and maintained them. These surpluses went mainly to subsidise black housing and other services.

So despite an inflation rate which crept up, there were no increases in charges in some areas, and small increases in others. In particular, rentals remained fairly static notwithstanding the fact that housing accounts ran up large deficits.

By the mid-1970s, however, the situation had changed quite radically. Most Boards were showing deficits, some of them large ones. By the end of the 1970s the Boards were exhibiting the symptoms of severe crisis. One of the reasons lay in the declining revenues from the sale of sorghum beer. Only the older and less sophisticated Africans were drinking the traditional brew. Although consumption of liquor boomed, the Boards faced stiff competition from private retailers in the white areas. And while the long drinking spree which had financed local government since the 1920s continued, it now coincided with the inevitable hangover.

The problem was exacerbated after 1976 by the heavy investment in capital projects which followed the broad policy of improving facilities and services in the African urban areas. Combined with high inflation rates during the 1970s, local authorities were forced increasingly to put up charges for services. The pressure to do so was reinforced by the growing prevalence in government thinking of the doctrine that direct or indirect subsidies – from employers or the general revenue accounts of white local authorities – should be reduced or eliminated.

The financial crisis was intensified by the government's deepening commitment to privatisation. An assault was launched against the Boards' engagement in liquor dealing, and though the Boards successfully retained this interest, it was clearly under threat. Several inquiries were conducted into the contributions made by employers to the Boards. Again, the outcome was indecisive.

Another element of the fiscal crisis in the black urban areas was the increasing incidence of unemployment which, despite rising wages, imposed a strain on family incomes. According to Jeremy Keenan, nett family wages were declining during the 1970s, notwithstanding rising wages, for two distinct sets of reasons. During economic upswings, inflation outstripped wage increases. During downswings, rising unemployment meant that more people became dependent on the wages of the family breadwinner.[32] With inflation running at between 10 and 16 per cent throughout the decade, there was intense pressure on householders and on local authorities.

These financial issues, and the social, economic and political relationships which underpin them, have a direct bearing on the kind of reforms which began to be discussed after 1976, particularly in the President's Council, and which were incorporated into the 1983 constitution. They will be discussed in greater detail in Chapter 10. But it is worth noting here that if the establishment of regional and metropolitan councils follows the general proposals made during the early 1980s, then the control over the supply of 'physical social capital' in the regions – i.e. water, electrical power and so on – as well as various planning functions, will be located in powerful regional bodies on which local authorities (including black local authorities) will be represented on a proportional basis reflecting both the use of resources and the wealth of the local areas.

It will be argued that the development of these structures reflects two intentions. The first is to rationalise and optimise the costs of production of physical infrastructure and social capital. The second is to legitimise the unequal distribution of access to decision-making in this area in terms of criteria which are not (or need not be) directly linked to considerations of race. The struggles of black communities in the urban areas suggest the nature of some of the pressures which forced this change.

7 Race and the allocation of urban space: segregation and apartheid in the cities

Ethnic and religious ghettos, one-class communities and racially exclusive clauses governing the purchase and occupation of residential property are commonplace features of the cities, towns and villages, and the living space of agricultural communities in many parts of the world. The workings of labour and property markets, and building and planning regulations, and access to housing loans help shape spatial environments in definite relationships to the patterns of class stratification in the community. European, British and American cities provide enough instances of segregation on the basis of race and class to remind us that there are significant continuities and parallels between the effects produced under capitalism on social relationships in the built environment in metropolitan societies and those which developed in South Africa.

The control of social relations in Victorian cities through health regulations, slum clearance and transport and housing policies, provided models for the planners of the physical environment of South African cities after the South African War. These had an important influence on the development of relations between social classes and strata in the urban communities which assembled in the course of industrial development. Several important members of Milner's 'Kindergarten', who shaped the reconstruction of the Transvaal after the South African War and were responsible for pioneering town planning in Johannesburg, had earlier served apprenticeships in London.

Notwithstanding similarities, there were however major differences between spatial zoning in metropolitan societies and in South Africa. South African segregation involved the overt and explicit use of state power to dictate social, political and economic relations between racial groups through the control and allocation of the spatial environment. It was explicitly and intentionally designed to prevent the emergence of a black bourgeoisie; to control the black labour force; and to prevent the emergence of political alliances between black and white workers. The process can be traced from the segregation of classes and strata in particular environments during the first decades of the century down to Verwoerd's attempt to achieve the geographical separation of people on racial lines.

In general, racial segregation worked to control an underclass who were denied access to common political rights and to certain economic opportunities, and who therefore could not be expected to accord legitimacy to the state through the operations of institutions, practices and myths which emphasised common bonds between different classes and communities. Segregation served to consolidate and even extend the repressive labour system on which industrialisation developed in South Africa.

The migrant labour system and the political structures that flowed from it had a deep influence on the development of segregation policy in urban areas, even in respect of those groups which established themselves permanently as part of the urban workforce and population.

The doctrine that Africans had no rights to remain in the urban areas except as labourers also shaped the parameters of their living conditions in the urban areas, and converged neatly with the assumption that those who had achieved such entitlement ought to be made to exercise it as far distant from the 'white' town or city as possible.

It would be a mistake to view segregation in the urban areas simply as an instrument for the repression and control of workers. It also disadvantaged property-owners, entrepreneurs and professionals from the target groups, for whom exclusion and expropriation meant a loss of economic and social opportunities. Such advantages were transferred to whites who were able to gain access to property and opportunities in the areas vacated by blacks.

One particular effect of racial zoning was to proletarianise bourgeois or aspirant bourgeois members of the racial group subject to discrimination, by limiting and sometimes depriving them entirely of access to opportunities to exploit the advantages they might have stood to gain by virtue of their ownership of property. The second characteristic was the degree of outright coercion employed. Both the impoverishment of property-owners and the degree of coercion used against the affected groups are reminiscent of the Nazi policy of forcing Jews into ghettos before the Second World War.

Segregation retarded, though it did not prevent, the emergence of an urban petty bourgeoisie which might have given effective leadership to an African nationalist movement. One of the intentions behind the policy of apartheid was to encourage the development of such a class in the homelands and national states, where its potentialities for a national leadership could be limited and contained.

Racial segregation also worked to conceal and soften class conflicts within white society. White workers gained access to living space in areas from which blacks were excluded and extruded. In this way, inter-class solidarity within white communities was enhanced, especially during periods of intense social dislocation, as during the Second World War, when there was tremendous competition between whites and blacks for housing and jobs.

As white suburbs in most South African cities are fairly strongly linked to class, racial segregation has been important in reinforcing a sense of solidarity in white communities. It thus helped generate a sense of the state's legitimacy in white communities that were subjected to the intense strains of social and economic change.

At the same time, while racial segregation of the urban environment induced some degree of inter-class collaboration between the members of racial groups adversely affected by segregation, it also worked to split and divide communities, by vesting different racial groups with distinct and competing social and economic interests in the built environment.

Like the Immorality Act and the prohibition of 'mixed' marriages, racial zoning served to make racial and ethnic groups the basis of social classes – that is to say, groups that acquired a sense of common identity through sharing elements of collective consumption, services and facilities, which also dictated common mobility opportunities and other 'life chances'. The effect was to concretise race into a lived social reality. Racial zoning also worked to reinforce differences in opportunities available to different racial groups established in other spheres of social action. Comparably, the spatial zoning of racial groups conferred a certain degree of rationality on the separation of amenities and services for different racial groups: transport services, hospitals, schools, recreation, and so on. In turn such segregated facilities reinforced the sense of racial differences.

Although there are numerous variations and combinations, certain themes can be detected in the evolution of racial and class segregation in South African towns and cities. Many of the older South African cities had 'quarters' comparable to the 'native' and 'foreign' quarters in the colonial towns and cities elsewhere in colonial Africa, Asia and America which worked to insulate the *colons* from contact and competition with indigenous peoples and with exotic minorities.

The most famous of these was the old Malay quarter in Cape Town, originally occupied mainly by former slaves, within the city's perimeters and close to its centre. Variations on this pattern developed in small frontier towns and cities, as in Grahamstown, where displaced elements of rural communities settled in Fingo Village. Durban's Indian quarter was yet another variation on this pattern. It became densely settled from late in the nineteenth century by small traders, craftsmen, merchants and workers.

Indians were also assiduous pedlars on the Transvaal highveld, and by early in the twentieth century, many Indian traders were living and trading in central sites on the main streets of Reef towns and cities and small country towns in the Transvaal, where they settled during the last century, often on sites granted by President Kruger. The difficulty they were later to face in acquiring additional land meant that these areas frequently deteriorated into appalling slums. But these sites were crucial to their economic survival.

The distinguishing feature of settlements in these inner-city and main street areas was that non-whites enjoyed the right to freehold ownership, commonly acquired during the nineteenth century. Frequently too, Europeans owned properties in such areas and let slum dwellings to non-whites, as in Doornfontein, near central Johannesburg, which gave white landlords an interest in resisting any efforts at resettlement.

Similar to them in this respect, but different in ethnic and class complexion, were areas like Sophiatown, also a few miles from the centre of Johannesburg, and Alexandra township, some distance away, which were settled mainly by Africans. These areas were dormitory suburbs rather than urban quarters, and they were inhabited by a variety of different racial, occupational and class elements. Landlords in such areas were frequently (in Alexandra predominantly) Africans and Indians. Sophiatown was perhaps the most complex and varied in its class and occupational complexion: professionals, musicians, journalists, gangsters as well as common labourers found a home here.

The encapsulated communities which gradually established themselves in central areas of cities and small towns were to become the targets of systematic state attack during the twentieth century, initially via the mechanisms of health and slum clearance regulations. (These regulations were quite commonly used against whites too: Afrikaner brickmakers in Johannesburg were forced out by such measures, as was a settlement of Indians and Africans in Fordsburg after an outbreak of the plague in 1904.)[33] In Cape Town, a few years earlier, a plague scare, as well as a series of what were termed 'Kaffir outrages', gave impetus to the establishment of segregated locations in the mother city of South Africa and the heartland of South African liberalism.[34] Health and slum clearance measures were commonly used during the 1920s and 1930s to remove workers and their families from the crowded backyards of inner-city slums. These efforts were not always successful, sometimes because of the corruption of municipal officials and councillors by local white landlords, who milked huge profits from inner-city slums and would lose much by their removal. The Doornfontein Stand Owners' Association met regularly in a local hotel and collected money for bribes. The chairman, unable to explain where the money had gone, claimed that he had stolen it! The commission of inquiry drew the droll conclusion that not all the members of the city's Native Affairs Committee had received bribes.[35]

Over the course of the twentieth century, the criteria for exclusion became based more and more explicitly on race. The 1923 Urban Areas Act prohibited the sale of land in urban areas to Africans. The areas in which blacks had previously purchased land thereafter came under continuous siege from white interests. A number of measures to prevent the acquisition of fixed property by Indians were introduced from the end of the First World War. These culminated in the Asiatic Land Tenure and Indian Representation Act of 1946 which provoked the Passive Resistance Campaign and the first United Nations resolution condemning racialism in South Africa. But these laws left many pockets of property in 'white' areas in the hands of non-whites. The most important of them were District Six in Cape Town (as well as the old Malay quarter), Alexandra, Sophiatown and Fordsburg, and the Indian areas of inner Durban. They all became subject to intense removal campaigns during the 1950s and 1960s, as were many of the Indian trading areas of small Transvaal towns and villages.

It was the Group Areas Act of 1950 that was used most systematically to excise these groups (who were often important elements in the commercial life of the cities and more particularly the small towns) from the urban landscape. The Group Areas Act rationalised and consolidated previous legislation which had zoned ownership of fixed property and occupancy rights on racial grounds. It gave the government the power to allocate specific areas for exclusive occupancy and ownership by a particular racial group, to force the 'wrong' group to sell their property to a member of the 'right' group, and to compel tenants to move into areas proclaimed for occupancy by the racial group of which they were members.

It would be difficult to summarise the hardship, personal anxiety and social destruction produced by the Group Areas Act on the communities against which it was directed. Property-owners were the most visibly affected by the Act. In 1951 Indians owned 10 000 acres in Durban, a quarter of the total area of the city, and comprising 13 per cent of its land value. Other non-whites owned a negligible proportion of property in the city. In 1958, it was announced that the intention would be to move 100 000 Africans (mostly tenants, not property-owners), 75 000 Indians, 8 500 'coloureds' and 1 000 whites in the city.

At least one case was reported of an Indian family which had worked a piece of land on the peripheries of Durban as a market garden since the early years of the century, that had to move twice as a result of the Act. Its pathetic story is too long to reproduce here, but the conclusion to the account written for the Natal Indian Congress is worth repeating, both for what it says, and for the insight it gives into the intensity of Congress's hatred of the Act.

Harilall is now fifty years old and has a 30-year mortgage bond ahead of him – a man who until now lived in a freehold home. If he lives to 80 he will be a free man. For the next thirty years his soul and body are mortgaged to the evil spawned by the Group Areas Act and if his sons choose to search for their freedom from the Group Areas Act through the sights of a gun who can blame them?

In the opinion of the Natal Indian Congress, the main purpose of the Group Areas Act was to 'destroy the Indian people in the economic field, make them also a reservoir of cheap labour and coerce them to expatriate from the Union of South Africa'. It was meant to achieve by different methods the results produced on Africans by the Land Acts of 1913 and 1936.[36]

It is difficult to determine which groups were the most severely affected by the Act. Indian property-owners were the most visible among its victims, and its passage wrought a significant change in their political conscious- ness, drawing them into the political struggles conducted by other groups to which they had previously been apathetic or hostile. Indians became prominent in the Defiance Campaign of 1952, and the Indian Congress took part in the meeting at Kliptown in 1955 which approved the Freedom Charter. But other groups, and particularly Africans, who were largely propertyless, were also seriously affected by the Act (as the numbers dislocated in Durban indicate); perhaps Africans were less severely affected by this legislation by the simple fact that so many other controls and proscriptions already affected them that it is difficult to decide its particular effects. One major exception, where urban Africans were severely disadvantaged by Group Areas legislation, was Sophiatown. Sophiatown was important in so many respects that it is worth briefly reviewing the history of its removal. Firstly, although it became very crowded, it was not a slum or a location, but a suburb or, as Lodge put it, an African town.[37] It had originally been intended for white settlement but the Johannesburg municipality established a refuse dump in its vicinity, and whites tended to avoid it. Instead it was settled by a cross-section of South Africa's racial groups, in which Africans were over-represented.

Before the 1923 Act, Africans enjoyed the right to purchase property in the urban areas, and about 800 stands were acquired by Africans. About a hundred stands were owned by Indians. These land-owners were not wealthy; few of them could afford to live off rents. The vast majority of its inhabitants were tenants with jobs in town.

Characteristically, the population of Sophiatown, like other urban freehold settlements of Indians and Africans, more or less doubled during the period between the two World Wars, not by expanding its total area, but as a consequence of land-owners building, or allowing tenants to build, shacks in their backyards. Sophiatown attracted a wide variety of people of every level of wealth and occupation – doctors, lawyers, journalists, ministers of religion, gangsters, artists, musicians as well as day labourers and factory workers. Alongside the rich intellectual and artistic life which it fostered, Sophiatown provided a lively environment for African politicians. The ANC and the Communist Party both had strong followings. Dr Alfred Xuma, the president of the ANC during the Second World War, lived and had his medical practice there.

The gang life of Sophiatown had an exotic glamour, reflected in such names as Gestapo, Berliners, Vultures (a children's gang named after the film *Where No Vultures Fly*) and Americans. The gangs were to become an important element in the resistance against removals. The government announced its plans to remove 'black spots' in the western areas of Johannesburg during February 1950, and Sophiatown property-owners formed an action committee the following year. The national executive of the ANC decided that the issue had wider implications than other removals, and took charge of the organisation of opposition to it. But, it was claimed, the national executive was less militant than local ANC leaders. The most important among these was Robert Resha, who formed a body of 500 'freedom volunteers', and also summoned help from the gangs of Sophiatown.

Different classes or strata were committed in different ways to opposing the removal, and there were obviously some groups who did not have a direct interest in opposing the removals. Indeed, there must have been some people to whom a new house in Meadowlands, while aesthetically dull, would have been preferable to a backyard shack in Sophiatown. On the other hand, the cost of transport to Meadowlands was much higher. Whether or not these matters entered the calculations of the people of Sophiatown, the opposition to the removal was remarkably widely supported, and not simply by land-owners or better-off tenants. Resha's success in summoning assistance from the gangs attests to this. In part the strength of the opposition was also a result of the skill with which the ANC organised the campaign. The removals, which began in 1955, did not happen because the community was apathetic, but because their resistance was crushed by an overwhelming state power.

Surprisingly, some of the communities subjected to the siege managed to survive, albeit in somewhat altered form. Alexandra, for instance, which had been the target of removal attempts from the 1930s onwards, became the site of single-quarter dormitory quarters during the 1960s; but during the late 1970s, it made rapid advances as a quasi-autonomous local authority. During the early 1980s, it stood to benefit from the reconstruction of local authorities under the new constitution by gaining access to revenues generated in the industrial areas of Sandton. Most of the Indians of Fordsburg and Pageview had been removed to distant Lenasia during the 1960s, but significant groups of them retained their right to trade within the municipal area, though most were moved out of 'old' areas and into new bazaars and plazas.

The Group Areas Act of 1950 had a particularly corrosive effect on the aspirations of a nascent bourgeoisie, though it also wreaked havoc on workers of all races who were affected. The Act forced the sale of property by members of one designated racial group to another. It thus arbitrarily inflated or deflated property values, created conditions of crowding and uncertainty, sometimes lasting for generations, and induced intense personal misery and social tensions. Together with the Population Registration Act of 1950, which defined and classified the people of South Africa in racial categories, the Group Areas Act was a crucial instrument in the routinised, bureaucratic organisation of spatial relationships in South Africa along racist lines.

A different direction pursued in urban segregation policy by the South African state concerned the housing of African workers employed in secondary industry. New townships began to be constructed from the end of the First World War, and were developed on a massive scale after the Second World War. They came increasingly under the control of the central government during the 1950s and 1960s, and jurisdiction was wholly transferred in 1971.

During the earlier period, these municipal housing projects were developed to resettle the inhabitants of inner-city slums on sites distant from the cities. Thus the establishment of Orlando during the 1930s was undertaken to rehouse people living in Doornfontein. Notwithstanding the permanency of the physical structures, and the increasing entrenchment of family communities in them, the old Stallard doctrine persisted in its new Verwoerdian garb until the late 1970s. That doctrine justified the close controls imposed over the townships built for African workers and their families, including their surveillance by the police for pass offences. Although they were not physically, politically or socially identical to the labour compounds built to house migrant workers, something of the same spirit pervaded their construction; their occupants were there simply because they worked in industry.

The motives for urban segregation varied considerably between the different classes, strata and interests of the white community. It reflected the determination of municipalities and central government to control the African urban population. In those situations where segregation was most systematically pursued – Johannesburg is perhaps the best example – the police and the military were able to isolate these areas in periods of insurrection. By contrast, the spatial reorganisation of Cape Town and its environment along racial lines lagged behind the less liberal, more efficient reorganisation of the PWV, which early in its history as an industrial area adopted segregationist principles in planning. As a consequence, during the 1980s, even a ride in Cape Town from the airport to the city had all the excitement of a drive through guerrilla country. Segregation also reflected the struggles of white workers to achieve salubrious housing. Because many of the inner-city quarters, as well as such areas as Sophiatown, were potentially lucrative sources of income to interests like building contractors, estate agents and property speculators, such activities could whet the appetites of a variety of small and medium-size entrepreneurs. Sophiatown condensed all of these aspirations, for it was rebuilt as 'Triomf' (Triumph), initially a suburb for white workers.

Segregation did not, however, serve only the narrow interests of white workers and small entrepreneurs, though it is certainly the case that the benefits it delivered to them were important in securing their political allegiance to parties pushing segregation policy. It became instrumental in constituting urban South Africa as the physical and spatial as well as the political domain of white South Africa.

The segregation of urban areas along racial lines had by the mid-1970s created racially distinctive urban enclaves – white fortresses with distantly situated black residential and business satellites. This pattern was most successfully established in the urban areas of the Transvaal and the Orange Free State. During the early 1980s, there were many informal breaches of the Group Areas Act, and blacks settled illegally in the central flatlands of

Johannesburg and other cities, which in this respect came to resemble the occupancy patterns of North American and European cities. The prohibition on blacks trading in central business districts was removed during 1986. There were calls too for the repeal of the Group Areas Act. Aside from security considerations which might impede such a move, it is important to note that nearly three-quarters of a century of urban growth in South Africa was shaped by racial zoning, and this feature is likely to characterise the dominant pattern of property-ownership, occupancy, economic activity and social relations, unless strong measures are taken to change the situation.

The reforms which were introduced in local and regional government after the passage of the 1983 constitution are based on the principle that local authorities in black areas must enjoy the same status as those established in white areas. They were intended also to enjoy representation on the regional services councils in proportion to their use of the services controlled by the councils. But aside from any bias in favour of more affluent (i.e. white) areas in terms of this machinery, racially constituted communities were envisaged in the constitution as the basis of local authorities. In that sense, residential segregation on racial lines was the cornerstone of the government's reforms in local and regional affairs.

Segregation and apartheid policies affected the structures of African politics in a number of important ways. Distance between residence and workplace, exclusion from common rights in the urban areas, and social isolation made for conditions of intense anomie, extreme exploitation and discomfort among urban blacks, but these conditions also forged a political agenda and a set of methods which, in the absence of effective institutions, gave shape and structure and distinctive forms of consciousness to African political life in the urban areas. Segregation and apartheid made possible the development of alliances between classes, or, to put the point in another way, reduced the differences in interests between property-owners, entrepreneurs, clerks, schoolteachers and professionals on the one hand, and the great body of manual labourers on the other. In the struggle to resist the removal of Sophiatown, the alliance even extended to include criminal elements when the ANC used street gangs to help organise the resistance.

The structures of segregation and apartheid created the framework for a range of quite specific political instruments, of which the transport boycott and the stay-away provide two variations. The transport boycotts which emerged during the 1940s, and evolved into movements with great potential support, were the direct consequences of a policy which forced the poorest elements of the workforce to live at a distance from the workplace, and, unusually, if not uniquely, transport costs became a crucial issue in the politics of black workers. Perhaps more interestingly, the transport boycott provided a dynamic link between the politics of the workplace and the politics of communities.[38]

The second feature of the transport boycotts was the facility with which

African entrepreneurs had a direct interest in and became involved in their organisation. During the 1920s, African entrepreneurs opened up the transport industry to the often distant areas in which the majority of African urban-dwellers were forced to reside. During the 1930s and 1940s they were squeezed out of this field by white transport operators, who entered an intimate relationship with local transportation boards, the statutory bodies set up to issue transport licences. Once the white operators had established control over the field, they pushed fares up. Although there were other issues, the commonest cause of boycotts was fare increases.

Before 1945, African entrepreneurs were involved in organising boycotts. In 1945, a monopoly was established over bus transport in Johannesburg in direct response to a great boycott by African township-dwellers. Moreover, boycotts (not only transport boycotts) were responses to the segregationist policies in the sense that the isolation and distance of African settlements from the 'white city' provided a basis for concerted community action which would have been difficult to generate in racially mixed areas. The first transport boycott of which this writer is aware took place in 1940. They have never ceased since then. Significantly, the boycott of white-owned businesses became during the late 1970s and early 1980s one of the most important weapons in the political struggles of black communities, particularly so because of the repression of political organisations, and the difficulties which Africans have faced in organising strikes.

Bus boycotts provide an important though by no means unique instance of a non-institutionalised form of direct political action which generated its own momentum, methods and processes. Because of the severe limits imposed on institutionalised action by Africans, especially from the early 1960s, these activities were important in shaping African politics.

The boycotts were shaped by the several separate but intersecting relationships in which urban Africans found themselves. As workers, their wages lay at or below subsistence. As the objects of segregation policy, they were forced to live long distances from the workplace, and accordingly paid a higher proportion of their wages on transport than British or European workers. As members of the poorest strata in the urban workforce, this placed an additional strain on wages that were already stretched to the limit. As people without political rights, they were unable to organise effective pressure groups through legitimate political channels, either as consumers or as potential transporters. These general interests often overlapped with the specific interests of small African entrepreneurs who had managed to enter the transport business, usually but not always on a small scale. They sometimes found themselves vulnerable to the pressures which rival white transporters, enjoying access to the government agencies regulating transportation, were able to bring to bear in order to squeeze them out. So boycotts provided a common focus for alliances between the variety of groups and interests which made up the urban African community.

Secondly, under certain circumstances, boycotts achieved an extraordinary impact on government, attracting not only repression, but also attempts to reorganise transport services. Thirdly, they influenced other forms of collective action, including those adopted by the ANC and the PAC.

The earliest boycotts took place in urban working-class communities located a long way from the workplace in big industrial cities. But as industries became relocated in the border areas and long-distance commuting developed, bitter boycotts have taken place in the homelands states. The conflicts have been intensified by the stake which clients of the new elites in the homelands acquired in road transportation. Here attention will be focussed on the bus boycotts which took place in Alexandra township, near Johannesburg, from the 1940s to the late 1960s.

The domicile of increasing numbers of Africans in locations situated a long distance from the workplace made transportation a field of keen activity among small entrepreneurs, who found the modest outlays, high returns, and, before the thirties, absence of significant controls, attractive. A host of taxis, transport clubs, and even rickshaws, plied the long distances between places like Kliptown and Alexandra, and the city. By the late 1920s, small bus companies, usually owner-driven, had entered the field. Fares dropped by about three-quarters during the period ending in 1939. Cheap transport and low rentals made Alexandra a viable dormitory for African workers, and partly account for the rapid increase in its population during the 1930s. These conditions began to change from the late 1930s. The Motor Transportation Act was passed in 1930 in order to protect the railways from competition from motorised transport. But it was also intended to regulate road transportation. R. G. Balloi, an African entrepreneur who later became treasurer general of the African National Congress, ran buses and taxis from Alexandra to the city. He described the change in the following terms: 'At that time there was no control. Each and every owner could just run as he wished. This system made it difficult for European bus owners to operate. . . . In 1931, the Transportation Act was enforced. . . . It compelled all owners to work and operate according to one timetable and a stipulated fare. This was done in order to do away with competition.'

By the beginning of the Second World War, white entrepreneurs had achieved sufficient control over transport between Johannesburg and Alexandra to risk putting up fares. There were three boycotts during the war, culminating in the great boycott of 1945, which saw the establishment of the Public Utility Transport Corporation (Putco), which enjoyed a government subsidy. The boycott of 1957 brought major forces into play, exposing cleavages between different interests and strategies in African politics. These included rivalries within the ANC, as well as between the ANC and the Liberal Party, for some members of which the boycott offered an opportunity to drive for support in Alexandra.

The boycotts proved great schools in political strategies and tactics. The recurrent choice which faced the leaders thrown up in the boycott movements was to decide when to accept the offers that came from the authorities or white business, or, more usually, a concert of both. The townships and locations provided a forum in which these issues could be debated with remarkable vigour and subtlety, far more so than industrial sites. In the context of the highly authoritarian administration of urban government, this counted for something.

They also brought into play a range of political and economic interests which might otherwise have lain dormant. The bus boycotts of the war years attracted potential transporters, the ANC, and a variety of white leftists (including Trotskyites). The great boycott of 1957 brought to the fore rivalries between the ANC's established leadership and a group calling itself the 'African-minded bloc' as well as between the ANC and the Liberal Party, which sought the opportunity to gain a following there. The boycotts of buses in the national states during the 1970s and 1980s exhibited intense conflicts between workers and bus companies owned by the political elites of the national states.

The efficacy of the boycott as a political weapon should not, however, be exaggerated. At bottom, the momentum of the boycott was provided by the willingness of people living in a particular community to walk to and from work each day, up to ten miles sometimes, faced by official harassment. Some of the boycotts might last for months. They certainly helped build political structures which had not been there before, but often at the cost of exhausting the individual participants.

The stay-away, attempted with many variations and with varying success, approximated to the model of the political general strike, in that issues, like wages or conditions of work, were linked on one hand to community issues and on the other to broader political issues. Their specific momentum and organisational forms were derived from the fact that they were organised in the location or township. The combination of distance, exclusion and isolation, which had developed over the course of nearly three generations of urban segregation, gave this political method its specific form. One of the stay-aways organised by the schoolchildren in Soweto during 1976 was highly effective, and in 1984 stay-aways were remarkably successful.

8 Apartheid in the countryside: politics and government in the homelands and national states

By the end of the nineteenth century, the African tribes of South Africa had lost their independence. But the forms of tribal power and much of its substance remained in a variety of institutions. There were many variations in the structure of authority between different tribes, ranging from the 'consensual' structures of the Mpondo polity on the eastern borders of the Cape, where political authority resided in clan chieftaincies, to the more highly centralised and authoritarian societies of the Zulu, Swazi and Sotho, where power was concentrated in extensive kingdoms.

Variations in political structure also reflected differences in the mode of incorporation of traditional authorities into colonial political society. The colonial power tried to reduce the powers of traditional authorities along the border areas of the eastern Cape, where chiefs had stoked the fires of frontier wars for half a century, as they reacted to the penetration of their domains by white settlers. It should be noted, however, that although the dominance of the colonial power was ultimately secured in the eastern Cape and the Transkei on the basis of its military strength, it was only in one of nine territories that it was secured directly by conquest.

In other areas, by way of contrast, treaties between the chief of a tribe and a colonial or republican political power might provide the basis for maintaining a limited tribal autonomy. Thus the chiefs of the Bapedi tribe at Witzieshoek were descended from Mo-Paulus Mopeli, a half-brother of the Basotho king, Moshoeshoe. Mopeli had timeously made a separate peace with the Free State burghers during the wars of the 1850s and 1860s, and had been granted land on the eastern Free State border with the Basotho kingdom. Mourning the passing of the old days, his successor, Charles Mopeli, recalled how in earlier times, when problems arose, he would ride to Bloemfontein to consult with his friend, the president of the Orange Free State.

The colonial and treaty state which was widely established by the end of the nineteenth century was no idyll. At worst, it was as brutal and exploitative as any other of the structures installed during the course of European colonisation in Africa. The establishment of colonial government over Africans marked the terminal phase of effective political independence. But it did not strip tribalism of an authentic political identity in the way in which post-Union 'native administration' did. Nor did the attempts to codify and regularise African customary law, as in the Natal Native Code.

Both forms of colonial hegemony left large elements of an indigenous culture intact. This culture provided a framework of attitudes, interests and institutions which were exploited by successive governments in the resurrection of tribal forms to justify segregation and apartheid. The remnants of these cultures also provided a structure which sustained various forms of resistance and rebellion.

The pre-Union efforts to reconstruct the chieftainship as an instrument of colonial rule did, however, have the effect of undermining chiefly authority, for they imposed an unresolvable contradiction on the chieftaincy. The most important base of chiefly power in pre-colonial society had lain in the role of the chief in distributing land and cattle. However, the shortage of both land and cattle which appeared from before the turn of the century, and even much earlier, made it increasingly difficult for the chief to make just or rational allocations.[39]

By the 1920s, the migrant labour system which had been set in motion by the Glen Grey Act and reinforced by the 1913 Land Act was beginning to destroy the economic self-sufficiency of the reserves. The juridical destruction of the last remnants of tribal political autonomy, undermined by the evisceration of the reserve economy, was achieved through the reorganisation of tribal government after the Union of 1910 created a centralised administration in South Africa.

The South Africa Act of 1909 conferred on the Governor-General the powers hitherto exercised by colonial governors in their capacity as supreme chiefs of African tribes. In 1927, the Natives Administration Act consolidated these powers, and vested them in the Minister of Native Affairs. Aside from the solemn absurdity of vesting the formal authority of supreme chieftainship over Zulu and Xhosa in a British peer, and the effective power in an Afrikaner cabinet minister, these Acts completed the subordination of traditional chiefly power to the central government, though some of their judicial powers were preserved, and it was not until the Bantu Authorities Act of 1951 that traditional chiefs (as distinct from appointed chiefs and headmen, who had suffered this fate in 1927) were reduced to the position of an element in the bureaucratic hierarchy.[40]

The 1927 Act consolidated a plethora of statutes dating from colonial times, and established a uniform system of administration in most parts of the Union. (In a few areas, special arrangements were maintained.) A chief native commissioner was appointed to administer all Africans in the Union. Under his authority, a hierarchy of native commissioners and superintendents was elaborated.

The native commissioners were given the power to recognise, appoint, and depose chiefs, and to prescribe their duties, powers and privileges. A limitation was placed on judicial proceedings by members of tribes against the chiefs. Powers were conferred on the Governor-General to define the area of a tribe, to change, divide, and amalgamate tribes, to constitute new tribes, and to remove a tribe or portion of it 'as necessity or good government' might require.

He also assumed the power to revoke land grants. Land registration and tenure were devolved onto the native commissioner. Native commissioners also assumed criminal and, with certain limitations, civil jurisdiction. African chiefs occupied a rather ambiguous position in the chain of command. Traditional chiefs preserved some of their independence, though enjoyed few powers. Appointed chiefs were little different in their relationship to the administration from headmen. African headmen represented the bottom rung of this hierarchy. In effect, they came to occupy a poorly paid echelon in, but not of, the Native Affairs Department.

In the Transkei, in common with many other areas, the smallest administrative units were the 'locations' (sometimes referred to as villages), over which the headmen had control. No attempt was made to ensure that the boundaries of these units, or the districts in which they were grouped, coincided with the boundaries of the chiefly authority. The effect was not to eviscerate the powers of the chief completely, but rather to preserve elements of chiefly authority, especially in the traditional courts, which formed the lowest rung of the judicial hierarchy and where many matters were settled without reference to the white magistrates or native commissioners.

Throughout the country, African chiefs became subordinated within a hierarchy controlled by a government bureaucracy, the establishment of which no African was entitled to enter, and which was answerable to a political leader elected to a parliament in which no African had the right to sit. In effect, the forms of 'traditional rule' were used to justify the administration of rural Africans through a bureaucratic absolutism scarcely less authoritarian than the administration of urban Africans.

Officials in the Native Affairs Department were often sympathetic to the problems of the people who were in effect their subjects. Some of them organised markets for cattle, in which Africans would get a better price than they might have unaided, or made representations to the central authorities which might modify or ameliorate conditions. But as a system, the administration of Africans (which might more accurately be described as control rather than administration) institutionalised authoritarian rule in a stable, bureaucratic form, which had not previously existed, even late during colonial times. Moreover, as members of a state department which was closely involved in the apparatus of controls that operated the migrant labour system, there was an inherent contradiction in these interventions in the economy of the reserves. It is likely that the main beneficiaries were a small class of cattle-owners. These interventions probably worked to reinforce the stratification of rural society into a class of property-holders and a rural proletariat.

From before the Second World War the reserves became sites of intense conflicts, between chiefs on the one hand and tribesmen on the other, or, when chiefs accepted the responsibility of leading the resistance, between them and the state administration. Sometimes, the leading families of a tribe were split between collaborators with the state and opponents of its policy. The government used increasing repression in trying to carry out its policies. During the earlier period, roughly up to the 1930s and 1940s, administrative functions were expected to be carried out through the 'traditional' structures of the African rural community, the extended family and the tribal authorities. But these structures corroded in reaction to the failure of local economies, and in consequence tribal authorities failed to maintain even limited authority over many elements in the society or limited autonomy in the face of the encroaching state power. These conflicts were intensified after the passage of the Land Act of 1936, which provided for 'betterment' schemes that included cattle-culling and limitations on ploughing.

In order to try to control the situation, the central government assumed increasingly direct control over the administration of the rural areas. In effect the political institutions of the reserves (and later the homelands) became increasingly subordinated to the dictates of a bureaucratically structured, highly centralised government, workable only through arbitrary measures. As it came under attack, in Pondoland, in the Transkei, in Witzieshoek, in Sekhukuniland, to name a few sites of serious conflict, the native commissioners would summon the support of armed police and sometimes military power.

When 'traditional forms' of African government are cited to explain the authoritarian structures of contemporary political rule in the homelands and the national states (or a variety of other real and imagined characteristics of contemporary African political life), it is sometimes easy to overlook the fact that those traditions were effectively obliterated for more than half a century by the system of centralised and bureaucratically organised power which the Act of 1927 brought into existence, and that that system in turn replaced the eviscerated semi-autonomous structures which a century of conquest and treaty had left. More simply, the predominant traditions which the 'independent' homelands states inherited were not derived from pre-colonial African states or polities, nor even from the treaty and conquest states instituted by colonial rule. Both of these forms preserved considerable areas of local authority and autonomy.

These efforts to centralise power through the subordination of traditional authorities did not end experiments in limited forms of indirect representation, which culminated in the formation of the Natives' Representative Council and the establishment of the system of Natives' Representatives in the Union parliament during the late 1930s. But the indirect method of election to the Council barely modified the authoritarian tendencies in 'native administration'. Its purely advisory functions and limited base forced it into a peripheral role for the bare decade during which it existed. All the same, it was a significant development, and attracted the attention of a variety of political groups.

The NRC and the system of Natives' Representatives in parliament was instituted under the Representation of Natives Act of 1936, which also removed African voters in the Cape from the common roll. As a form of compensation, Cape African voters were entitled to vote for three white members of the House of Assembly. The African electorate for the NRC was also entitled, along with Cape African voters, to elect four white members of the Senate.

There were thus three quite distinct elections: those for the members of the NRC itself, and those held for members of the Union Senate, and those held during general elections in which Cape African voters elected the Natives' Representatives in the House of Assembly. The NRC elections were also held in two stages; in the first stage, voters cast their ballot for electoral committees which in turn elected the Representatives. Three elections were held to the NRC, in 1937, 1942, and 1948.

Despite the strict limitations on the powers and effectiveness of the Council, many of the most prominent figures in African politics took part in them, including important African communists like Edwin Mofutsanyana. Some of the most exceptional members of parliament were people like Margaret Ballinger, J. D. Rheinallt-Jones, and Hyman Basner, elected under the system. Ironically, most of the leaders of the campaign against the 1936 Acts stood for election to the Council in 1937, and won. The notable white communist, Hyman Basner, was defeated in the Senate elections in 1937, but elected in 1942. (He had in the meantime left the party, but this had no bearing on his chances.) Two prominent leaders, A. W. G. Champion, and the former president-general of the ANC, Josiah Gumede, were defeated in NRC elections.[41]

With all its serious limitations, the Natives' Representative Council nevertheless stands out as one of the political institutions established during the late 1930s which drew the attention, if not the support, of political groups that enjoyed a genuine base in African society. It was one of the few institutions created by the South African government which did not simply reproduce the structures of bureaucratic controls over the lives of Africans. The Council adjourned after the 1946 miners' strike. It never met again.

The principle that Africans should enjoy their rights in the reserves, or, as they came to be known, the homelands, was radically reinforced with the accession to power of the National Party in 1948. The central plank in the policy of apartheid was that separate, self-governing states would be formed in the reserves. An explicit undertaking was made by the government that these areas could and would be developed into economically self-sufficient units. To this end a commission of inquiry was appointed under the chairmanship of the agronomist Professor F. R. Tomlinson. Its report was published in 19 volumes in 1955. Its main conclusion was that the reserves could be made economically viable at a cost of 104 486 000 pounds sterling over the next decade.[42] The government promptly published a white paper in which it refused to accept such a massive financial obligation.

Yet though it shrugged off the financial obligations, the government had already lain the foundations for the political structures of apartheid in the Bantu Authorities Act of 1951, which abolished the representative system set up in 1936.

The Bantu Authorities Act was the most important instrument of the Nationalist government in establishing the basis for the apartheid system in the countryside. It completed the process of incorporating the chieftaincies into a bureaucratic hierarchy which had begun with the Act of 1927. The chiefs became the key elements in the apartheid political system in the reserves. The Bantu Authorities Act expanded the judicial and administrative powers of the chiefs. It became common for headmen to charge a fee for allocating land and to expect to receive gifts in exchange for favours. Chiefs imposed levies on the recipients of social services. Their power to appoint teachers supplied them with a crucial means of disciplining a profession which was ever a potential source of opposition to traditional authorities and the government.

The powers of chiefs were massively expanded in the Transkei under Proclamation 400 of 1960, the emergency regulations introduced there to stifle the popular resistance against Bantu Authorities that began during the mid-1950s and reached its height in the Pondoland uprising during 1960–1. Proclamation 400 could be used to punish individuals considered to undermine chiefly authority. A common punishment for persons accused of this charge was to move them out of the area and to demolish their huts. It thus became a helpful instrument reinforcing chiefly powers.

Chiefs also used Proclamation 400 to prevent the opposition Democratic Party from holding meetings, thus strengthening the bond between chiefs and the Transkei National Independence Party. They were able to enhance their influence directly over voters through their occupation of the post of electoral officer in 23 out of 26 constituencies in the Transkei. This office entitled them to record the preferences of illiterate voters, a not inconsiderable power in a community with an illiteracy rate of around 60 per cent. Prospective TNIP candidates in the 1973 elections in Transkei found themselves facing committees consisting of the heads and members of local tribal authorities. Any prospective candidate with a reputation of hostility towards chiefs had little chance of success.[43]

The corollary of the principle that Africans were permitted to be in the urban and industrial areas solely to provide labour services was that they were to enjoy civil and political rights in the reserves, which later became elaborated in the form of citizenship rights in independent states. This implied also that those functions of capitalist states concerned with the administration of welfare – the maintenance of the family, education, health care, care of the aged – were properly to be located in the reserves and their succeeding forms.

The principle meant too that unemployed and migrant workers during periods between contracts were to remain in the homelands, and that African communities in the 'white' urban and rural areas of South Africa deemed to be redundant or superfluous were also to be relocated in the homelands. Thus the homelands states became charged with the functions which some theorists of the state have labelled legitimation functions and social control functions. In 1959, the Promotion of Bantu Self-Government Act was passed, which established the machinery necessary to propel the reserves towards political independence. The Transkei Constitution Act of 1963 replaced the old Transkei Territorial Authority with a legislative assembly competent to make laws. The Bantu Homelands Citizenship Act of 1970 provided that every black would become a citizen of the territorial authority area to which he was attached by birth, domicile or cultural affiliation. Finally, the Bantu Homelands Constitution Act of 1971 empowered the government to grant self-government to a homeland. Roger Southall has made the point similar to that made by Dugard, cited earlier in this study, that 'independence represented an attempt by the South African regime to externalise its race relations into the international arena, and to impose structures of political domination (through the willing cooperation of black "sellouts" or stooges headed by Matanzima) upon the unwilling mass of South African blacks.'[44]

A number of claims were made on behalf of these states, intended to provide them with some legitimacy in South Africa and (with very little success) internationally. These claims were cast in the language and rhetoric of post-1918 notions of nationalism (about the time that the Afrikaner nationalist movement was taking shape). They were also cast in the language of traditionalism, as befitted a political order in which chiefs played a central part; and moreover, somewhat diversely, in the language in which African nationalist movements elsewhere on the sub-continent expressed their demands for independence.

Typically each homeland was led by an individual who could plausibly claim some relationship with a traditional royal or at least chiefly family. However, the efficient principle governing the selection of the homelands leaders seems to have been their willingness and ability to establish Bantu Authorities. Lucas Mangope, the first president of Bophuthatswana, appealed to the Minister of Bantu Administration to 'lead us and we shall try to crawl'.[45] Kaiser Matanzima had been a minor chief who was promoted to the position of paramount chief of Emigrant Tembuland because of his support for Bantu Authorities, and his ability to impose them on the territory despite massive opposition.

For the fact of the matter was that in most places where they were installed, Bantu Authorities, and the rehabilitation, improvement and betterment schemes in agriculture which accompanied them, were immensely unpopular, even more unpopular than the schemes introduced under the 1936 Land Act. These schemes unsettled the people, for they could be used to force people to resettle in order to improve the efficiency of agricultural production. Provision was also made for 'community labour' – a polite euphemism for forced labour. Many of the projects undertaken with 'community labour' turned out to be cheaper than the Tomlinson Commission had anticipated. Both in the Transkei and in the western Transvaal, there were massive upheavals during the 1950s. Several attempts were made on Matanzima's life. During its entire history as an apartheid state, since the mid-1950s, the people of the Transkei have lived under a state of emergency in one form or another.

The Pondoland revolt was a rebellious response by Mpondo tribesmen to the imposition of Bantu Authorities in their area. The revolt was organised in a movement which bore the name Ikongo (Congress) and was led by a group known simply as Intaba – the Hill. It opened hostilities during March 1960, with the killing of one Saul Mabude, a supporter of Bantu Authorities, and thereafter a series of attacks on other supporters of the Authorities. One of the casualties of the violence was Vukaibante Sigcau, brother of Botha Sigcau, the paramount chief of East Pondoland, who enjoyed the support of the South African government.

The attacks on chiefs were conducted with such systematic thoroughness that some chiefs repudiated Bantu Authorities, and the majority of chiefs in the region fled. The Hill assumed the character of a provisional government, instituting courts and an administration. The courts were used to put pressure on people who continued to serve Bantu Authorities, and to try police informers.

The government delivered a massive blow to the resistance in June 1960, when a force of policemen armed with sten guns fired on a meeting at Ngquza Hill in the Flagstaff district, killing between 11 and 30 people.

Five thousand people were arrested, over five hundred were put on trial, and 21 were hanged. The Hill tried to finance the defence of people put on trial through a general levy and, most ingeniously, by appeals to white traders. These latter might be counted as among the most conservative elements in white South Africa, and not likely to support willingly the resistance. But the appeal for assistance placed them under intense pressure, for if they were known not to give financial aid, they were liable to face a consumer boycott. In fact they were placed in a very difficult position, for if it became known to the authorities that they had given money to the Hill they were likely to lose their trader's licence.

True to the rhetoric of post-colonial nationalism, the homelands states all have parties with names that include one or more words like 'Independence', 'People's', 'National', and 'Democratic'. Yet they were caricatures of even the least reconstructed African nationalist movements elsewhere on the sub-continent. Without exception, they were poorly organised and inefficient, with low memberships, relying on traditional structures, chiefs, headmen and councils, for recruitment and organisation.

But, aside from reinforcing the bias towards the status quo, the reliance on chiefly authority also underscored the contradictions in the position of the chief: in the Transkei, for instance, chiefs were not allowed to serve on party committees, in order to protect them from political exposure. Indeed many of these parties were virtually one-man, or one-family, affairs. The Matanzima brothers commanded the Transkei. The Sebe family dominated nominations in the Ciskei. The Sebes were clearly not even a very happy family: the president of Ciskei got rid of his brother from the cabinet and put him in prison for plotting a coup. Nor was it only the government parties that suffered from these weaknesses. The opposition party in Transkei, the Democratic Party, was more often at war with itself than with the government, and for a number of years had *no* dues-paying members. The homelands parties were riven with internal divisions, some of which revealed the formalistic character of the parties. For instance, there was a split in the Bophuthatswana National Party during 1973–4, precipitated by Mangope's attempt to expel the deputy leader, Chief H. Maseloane, from the party. Maseloane successfully appealed to the Supreme Court to reinstate him, whereupon Mangope resigned from the BNP and established a new party, the Bophuthatswana Democratic Party. Not surprisingly, D. A. Kotze concluded that the main differences between various groups in the Bophuthatswana legislature concerned tactics, not principle.[46]

In Southall's opinion, the Transkei National Independence Party was inseparable from the structure of the chieftainship under Bantu Authorities, and was controlled by local chiefs. In one district, the chief made membership of the TNIP a condition of the right to graze on common land. This intimate relationship goes some way to explaining the poor level of participation in rural areas. In the urban areas, however, there is greater scope for the rank-and-file membership to engage in political activity. In more recent times, parties have acquired new leverage from their control over development agencies.

The exception to the general rule that political parties in homelands and national states were small and limited in their political reach is provided by Inkatha, the Zulu political movement formed by Chief Gatsha Buthelezi.[47] Inkatha was established during the 1920s as a Zulu cultural association. (The term symbolises the unity of the Zulu community.) It was resuscitated during the mid-1970s, enjoying an initial membership of 30 000. Within a few years, this membership had soared to 300 000. Southall suggests that Buthelezi modelled Inkatha on the form of a mass movement in order to counteract efforts by the South African government to prevent him from assuming a commanding position in KwaZulu. The government intended to establish the Zulu king, the pliant Goodwill, at the centre of KwaZulu politics, not the exceptionally able and highly critical Buthelezi. Through Inkatha, Buthelezi was able to resist pressure to move KwaZulu towards the status of a national state as well as to generate considerable prestige nationally and internationally. The massive increase in membership of

Inkatha could be explained by the difficulties which non-members face in securing employment in the educational system and civil service, and by the strength of the movement's support among chiefs, particularly in the rural areas. The KwaZulu Legislative Authority even publicly announced that membership was a consideration when assessing the chances of civil servants for promotion. But this does not satisfactorily explain the strength of the movement in the countryside, nor indeed why the movement also has a strong membership in the urban areas, including the Witwatersrand, where it would be implausible to believe that Inkatha could coerce people to join because of its control over the administration. It is also difficult to understand why Chief Gatsha Buthelezi, who resuscitated the movement, was able to build a mass party rapidly and effectively, in marked contrast with other movements and parties established within the framework of the apartheid system.

Shula Marks has offered a penetrating and sophisticated interpretation of Zulu politics that goes behind the structures currently in place to the historical transformations which made possible the development of this form of ethnic nationalism. With the decline of the powers of the traditional chiefs under the impact of capitalist development and ensuing social dislocation, one of the few ways in which people could express their resentment towards whites was in affirmations of loyalty to the Zulu royal family. This was strongly supported by South African administrators, who were concerned that the Zulu might be won over by radical political forces. But ethnic nationalism also offered opportunities to Zulu landowners and professionals. These considerations do not, however, explain why Buthelezi was able to mobilise ethnic sentiment *against* King Goodwill. Marks argues that Buthelezi, the nephew of Solomon kaDinuzulu, the son of the last king, Dinuzulu, was able to do so because of the weakness and ineffectuality of Goodwill.[48]

Notwithstanding the mass support it is capable of generating, the overt hostility which its leader displays towards the South African government, and his flirtatious, though complex, relationship with the ANC, Inkatha has pursued essentially conservative political and social objectives. It has been active in promoting the interests of a Zulu petty bourgeoisie. Unlike the governments in other homelands and national states, which contented themselves with repressing trade unions, Inkatha in 1986 launched a trade union, whose general secretary is a businessman, in order to win workers away from unions based on shop-floor organisations associated in the Congress of South African Trade Unions.

Inkatha members have frequently been involved in violent confrontations with opponents, including students and trade unionists, though it would be difficult to show or prove that Inkatha violence was undertaken at the prompting of the leadership. Unlike in many ways the political formations in other homelands and national states, Inkatha is, like them, trapped in the structures of the apartheid state.

Independence in the homelands intensified the stratification of society in the rural areas of South Africa. Three main groups in the homelands, aside from the chiefs (whose interests were represented in at least two of them), benefited from independence. The first was a numerically small, but massively important, bourgeoisie (or comprador) class, whose wealth was directly and immediately related to the key positions it occupied in the political and governmental system of apartheid, as well as to the terms of the transfer of power. This wealth was largely acquired as the immediate effect of the efforts to which the South African authorities went to make it possible (and cheap) for the political leaders of the homelands to acquire farms and other property, for example by converting low-rental or free leaseholds on property into ownership.

The ease with which the political leaders of the homelands became the central elements in a new property-owning class in the homelands might be seen as one token of the importance which the South African government attached to the leadership, and a guarantee of its continued loyalty to the system of apartheid. It was also facilitated by the leverage which their positions in government gave them in respect of access to licences, contracts and information, all of which were extremely valuable in the context of development projects, building programmes and the other activities stimulated by independence, and the attendant need it generated for airports, public buildings, housing for civil servants, and so on.

The Matanzima brothers, Kaiser and George, respectively prime minister and minister of justice in the Transkei during the 1970s and early 1980s, were perhaps the most prominent representatives of this class. Interestingly, the Matanzimas and other members of the cabinet purchased much of the agricultural property they acquired during the 1960s from the Bantu Trust at prices considerably lower than the Trust had paid for the farms. The Matanzima brothers also became major shareholders in a number of hotels, again purchased from the Bantu Trust on very favourable terms. The price of shares acquired by a number of Transkei's political leaders in companies controlling hotels has held up well, as very often these hotels enjoy a local monopoly over liquor licences. Transkeian beaches are exceptionally beautiful. A repackaged tourist industry there, including the inevitable casino, strip joint and soft-porn movie palace, tailors neatly in with the economic interests of Transkei's political class. Other members of the TNIP leadership have similarly ascended into the ranks of the bourgeoisie via profitable deals with the Bantu Trust and the Transkei Development Corporation.

The second group of beneficiaries of independence in the homelands was a much more numerous class of petty-bourgeois traders and business operators, who acquired, via loans from the homelands development corporations, the properties and businesses of departed white traders. As in the case of the embourgeoisement of the political leadership of the homelands, the development corporations were crucial in providing the facilities for transferring the assets of white business to their black successors.

The political skill of the South African leadership – Verwoerd, in the case of the Transkei – was indispensable in securing the assent, albeit reluctantly, of white traders to leave the territory and surrender their businesses to a successor class of African businessmen. Traders were the only group of whites in the Transkei whose material stake was so important that they were prepared to provoke a backlash. The other whites there – public servants and public employees and a scattering of people living in the urban areas – were less intransigent because they could relocate with relative ease in 'white' South Africa.

White traders in the Transkei also enjoyed the support of the United Party, whose local MP was a formidable representative of their interests. Although a large proportion of the white traders were English-speaking, they were otherwise typical of the conservatism on which the Nationalist government relied for its support. They thus constituted a potentially dangerous threat to the government. Verwoerd managed to get their consent, and to undermine the United Party, by pursuing a strategy which in effect decreased the assets of the traders the longer they delayed selling out. In 1960, he told them that their time there was running out. In response to the outrage which this evoked from them, he adopted a more placatory tone but made it clear that he was not prepared to revise the government's policy. The only issue which the government was prepared to discuss was the scale of compensation. It soon became obvious that the longer white traders prevaricated, the smaller the compensation would become.

The transfer of assets was accomplished through the purchase of white-owned businesses by the Bantu Investment Corporation (before 1965) and the Xhosa Development Corporation. The Corporation might run a business for some time before selling it to an African purchaser with a loan, also provided by the Corporation. The XDC in addition established a wholesaling business from which African businessmen could obtain credit. One of the significant issues raised by this was the vested interest which the black petty bourgeoisie acquired in a racial definition of Transkeian nationality, for it virtually forced whites out of the territory. The transfer of property, so smoothly effected, strengthened the political structures of the homelands states by giving the new African trading class a stake in the political order.

Aside from white traders, the element which lost most from independence was the peasantry. The defeat of the Mpondo rebellion in 1960 ended the organised resistance to Bantu Authorities. It also entrenched the political class led by the Matanzima brothers firmly in power, and reinforced the position of the chiefs as the subaltern class of the emerging national states. The defeat also deprived the peasantry of any power to act effectively in the defence of its interests. This class, and the migrant workers who represented the most important element in its economically active workforce, were seriously disadvantaged by the establishment of the homelands states in the Transkei and elsewhere. The peasantry found themselves subject to the weight of the obligations imposed on it to perform 'community labour' services and the repressive controls wielded by the chiefly class, whose powers and privileges had been stiffened and invigorated. The peasantry was also disadvantaged by the massive increase in the weight of taxation levied on it.

Yet the new political structures of the national states, as well as escalating unemployment in metropolitan South Africa, made it increasingly difficult for able-bodied men to take the route of migrant labour which for three-quarters of a century past had made it possible for the peasantry to survive. Moreover, from the late 1960s and early 1970s, conditions in some areas were so bad that families adopted the hazardous strategy of squatting in the urban areas, as they had done during the 1940s.

All of this would suggest that the apartheid system was working to reinforce and entrench the political system of white domination. But there is another side to the issue. The resurgence of working-class action from the early 1970s and the emergence of a powerful union movement were initiated by the strikes that broke out among a labour force in which migrant workers were becoming an increasingly significant and increasingly vocal element. The great strides which the union movement made during the decade after the strikes of 1971–2 must in part be explained by the strength of its support among migrant workers. The national states, especially Transkei, Ciskei and Bophuthatswana, have acted with a degree of force amounting to brutality against trade unionists. Yet the movement has continued to receive vigorous support from migrant workers and workers in the border industries inside the national states. Moreover, this movement became intercalated with a number of other forces and processes which reflected its rural base. From being an important auxiliary power in South Africa's political defence system, the national states may turn out to be one of the weakest links in the chain of control.

9 Movement and organisation in the politics of the underclasses

The history of African politics in South Africa during the twentieth century was largely shaped by three developments. The first was the destruction of the African peasantry from the 1890s onwards. The second included the circumstances of industrialisation and urbanisation, including the pass laws and influx control, the restrictions on Africans' access to land, jobs and services, and the repression and coercion of the labour force in all sectors of the economy. Thirdly, African politics were affected by the government's efforts to develop segregated political institutions as an alternative to the principle of common rights and institutions established in the Cape during colonial times. The policy of segregation undercut existing rights by a slow attrition. The policy of apartheid which followed after 1948 required the total extirpation of those rights.

While the effects of these processes were manifold, one consequence was that alliances between different class interests in African society were frequently facilitated by the *racial* form of repression and exploitation. The members of the embryonic African middle classes were frequently subjected to the same hazards, indignities and discriminations as the working class. The salaries of schoolteachers and clerks were often not much better than workers' wages. African entrepreneurs were scarcely distinguishable from the working class. While these 'petty bourgeois' elements sometimes tried to win privileges for themselves, they were also increasingly forced to enter alliances with working-class groups. As has been noted, repressive racial policies tended to compress divergencies in class interests, and to give credibility to ethnic or nationalist claims. But racist policies also worked to fragment and diffuse African political life. The denial to Africans of rights that could give them access to national or regional levels of government, combined with the severity of repression, poor communications, and impoverished living conditions, made it extraordinarily difficult for African political groups to establish or maintain links between different regions and organisations.

The political life of Africans was perforcedly carried on in a myriad of small-scale transactions, confrontations and conflicts, often generating a momentum over wide areas of the country and stirring large groups of people into action. These small-scale conflicts often energised political movements, reviving dormant associations or giving rise to new ones. The institutional nexus of political action was frequently created in organisations that are not commonly thought of as political: in religious sects, burial societies, gangs, including prison gangs, or spontaneous groupings of individuals affected by particular issues, and gathered into more or less impromptu joint activities.

But larger processes can be seen to have been at work in these diverse activities. Tom Lodge, the historian of post-war African politics, has pointed out that Africans made two kinds of responses to capitalist development in South Africa. The first expressed adherence to the 'ideal of a racially integrated society' which rejected the 'tenets of romantic nationalism: emphasis on linguistic, racial, cultural or religious identity. . . . The second tendency has been the obverse of the first.'[49] The first response was exemplified in the development of the African National Congress. 'It was the logical outcome of capitalism, urbanisation and industrialisation: the development of political organisations motivated by the class interests of different groups engaged in different ways with the operation of a modern industrial economy.' The Pan-Africanist Congress, on the other hand, was 'representative of . . . those movements which in one way or another are fuelled by the impulse to resist the social implications of a developing capitalist economy.'[50]

With Union began the destruction of political rights which had been established on a limited property but colour-blind basis during colonial times. Although provision had been made for an African franchise in colonial Natal, in practice only a handful of Africans enjoyed the vote there. In the Cape, the only colony where a significant number of Africans enjoyed the franchise, they had held the balance of electoral power in half-a-dozen constituencies. The South Africa Act of 1909, which laid the constitutional framework of Union, prevented blacks from sitting in parliament. Although it maintained the existing franchise rights of Africans and other blacks in the Cape and Natal, the South Africa Act also set out a procedure for changing the franchise. Above all, the Act entrenched the exclusive white franchise which had been established in the Transvaal and the Orange Free State.

The South African Native National Congress, the forerunner of the African National Congress, was formed in 1912. Its founders realised that the political position of Africans in South Africa was likely to deteriorate after Union with the dilution of the Cape liberal tradition. Its leaders consisted mainly of representatives of the tiny professional class of Africans that had begun to emerge, many of them from Transkeian and Ciskeian families which had succeeded as peasant farmers during the last few decades of the nineteenth century. Among their numbers were prominent journalists like Sol Plaatje, and lawyers like Pixley ka Izaka Seme. They resolved to institute campaigns of 'peaceful propaganda' rather than try to influence policy and administration indirectly through their connexions with sympathetic and important whites on whom they had previously relied.

During its formative years, the ANC (as the SANNC was renamed in 1923) was dominated by conservatives who continued to rely on 'peaceful propaganda' to achieve its ends. The conservatism of the SANNC/ANC during the earlier period reflected the influence of a liberal tradition reaching back to the mid-nineteenth century, as well as the interests of the middle-class professionals who dominated the organisation at that stage. For instance, the SANNC abandoned a campaign against the pass laws when the war broke out in 1914, and instead it offered to recruit African volunteers for service. The ANC offered to do so again at the beginning of the Second World War. These gestures were not the signs of supine acquiescence, but an affirmation of African claims to rightful membership of one of the community of states incorporated in the British Empire and Commonwealth.

The petitions and deputations by Africans to the British government in London before Union and at the end of the First World War were other expressions of those claims. John Dube expressed the affirmation of these principles when he spoke of the 'sense of common justice and love of freedom so innate in the British character'. All the same, these principles imposed certain implicit limits on African political action.

But from before the end of the First World War the social and political changes brought about by wartime industrialisation in South Africa faced this conservative leadership with a radical challenge. For the first time, a class of unemployed urban workers appeared on the scene. Industrial action by African workers opened up new avenues for political organisation. Their emergence challenged the conservative consensus presided over by the Congress, articulating conflicts which had not been present on the surface of African politics a decade earlier. New political organisations, specifically the Industrial and Commercial Workers' Union and the Communist Party of South Africa, came onto the scene during the 1920s as rivals to the Congress's position as the leading expression of African political opinion.

These two organisations were specifically responses to the strains and tempo of industrialisation; the Congress was not. The Congress leadership responded in different ways to this challenge. In 1917, the executive which had previously been dominated by men from the Cape was taken over by leaders from the Transvaal, where the harsh trekker doctrine of no equality in church or state shaped different reactions from those of Africans brought up under the influence of the liberal traditions in the Cape. In 1918, these new leaders organised a campaign demanding a minimum wage of a shilling a day. In the same year, the SANNC supported municipal workers in Johannesburg in their epic strike, and in 1919 launched an anti-pass campaign. In 1920, the organisation came out in support of the mineworkers' strike.

In part this new militancy in the SANNC was also the consequence of the deteriorating position of middle-class Africans who, like workers, were disadvantaged by poor services and fixed wages. The apparent radicalism of Congress met with considerable criticism from the Cape leaders. Sol Plaatje was disturbed by the militancy exhibited during the miners' strike. D. D. T. Jabavu complained about the emergence of 'bolshevism' among Africans. So, although some of the groups to which the SANNC looked for support were radicalised by industrialisation, urbanisation and rapidly rising prices, the more conservative elements of its leadership demonstrated their hostility to socialist ideas.

Government policy during the early 1920s exacerbated tensions between different classes and strata in African society. As we have seen, the Natives (Urban Areas) Act of 1923 rested on the premiss that Africans could not expect to enjoy the right to live permanently in the urban areas. But it also provided for housing and other services which were obviously crucial to Africans who had achieved a foothold in urban areas if they were to win for themselves a viable existence. Even the policy of segregation provided some limited benefits to African traders in the segregated areas who were protected in some measure from the more powerful white trading interests. Moreover, first-class accommodation was made available to Africans on the railways; while clearly this was not a significant route to embourgeoisement, it made segregation a little more palatable to middle-class Africans. Such considerations explain why elements of the leadership began to demand some differentiation between the 'educated and civilised' (like themselves) and 'those who had yet to reach that stage'. This demand corresponded remarkably well with the sort of policy being shaped in terms of the Natives (Urban Areas) Act of 1923. At the same time, the inauguration of the Joint Council of Europeans and Non-Europeans, the forerunner of the Institute of Race Relations, which laid the basis for an inter-racial consensus, offered political distractions that tempted many middle-class leaders.

The Industrial and Commercial Workers' Union (ICU) brought an entirely new set of issues to the fore. Led by Clements Kadalie, who was a former mineworker from Nyasaland, it spread rapidly among the Cape urban proletariat. Kadalie established links with the Cape unions, but did not build up a systematic organisation. His main support came, however, from farm labourers. During the 1920s, white farmers, exposed to the strains of commercialisation, in turn brought extreme pressure to bear on African farm labourers. They reduced the access of labour tenants to land, and tried to destroy the remaining independence of rural squatters on the farms in order to force them completely into the position of wage labour. In retaliation, African farmworkers absconded, refused to work and mutilated animals.

The ICU promised to form companies which would acquire land for African ownership and occupation, and to negotiate with farmers over wages and conditions of work. It seemed to offer farmworkers a solution to their problems, and they joined the movement in their thousands. By 1927, it had acquired 100 000 members. Kadalie generated a new language and a new style of political organisation among Africans. But for all his imagination and flair, he could not offer either industrial labourers or farmworkers anything tangible. As one member bitterly remarked, 'It all ended up in speeches.'[51] By the end of the 1920s, the ICU was a spent force. It nevertheless had a significant impact on African activity and political organisation.

The rapid growth of the ICU during the 1920s attracted the attention of the Communist Party, formed in 1921. The party had initially concentrated on recruiting support among white workers, but after the Rand Rebellion of 1922, it turned its attention to Africans. The mass membership of the ICU offered an attractive potential recruiting ground. The ICU leadership resented this attention, especially as communist members tried to reorganise into industrial branches a movement whose main strength lay in the countryside. By the mid-1920s, there were marked tensions between the two bodies. The communists were expelled from the ICU, and turned directly to forming industrial unions and recruiting African members.

The interest of the communists also stimulated the intervention of white liberals in African politics and union affairs. The Joint Council movement itself was partly a response to the threat of a radicalised proletariat in the cities. The prospect of a communist take-over of the ICU resulted in William Ballinger, a Scottish trade unionist, coming to the country at the invitation of the liberal novelist Ethelreda Lewis to establish a non-communist African union movement.

By the mid-1920s, the ANC was disillusioned with the politics of collaborating with segregationist policy and, indeed, with the stately style of conducting political affairs which characterised the Cape leadership. Their disillusionment was partly precipitated by the election of the Pact government in 1924, and specifically by the four 'Native Bills' which Hertzog introduced in 1926. These bills, which were withdrawn and later reintroduced in 1936, included one removing African voters to a separate roll and another amending the 1913 Land Act. The ANC joined the ICU in demonstrating against the bills. In 1927, Josiah Gumede was elected to the presidency, and he subsequently tried to build the movement on the basis of branch membership, and actively recruited for members among Cape farmworkers. These innovations in organisation and leadership showed some of the impact of the ICU on African politics. Ideologically, Gumede was influenced by Marcus Garvey on the one hand, and by communism on the other.

During the early 1930s, African politics reached its nadir, as did trade unionism and left-wing politics generally. Many factors contributed to the decline: political repression, economic depression and unemployment, the demise of white working-class militancy, the embourgeoisement of the (white) Labour Party and bureaucratisation of the labour movement. The ANC also re-entered a period of conservatism. Characteristic of this mood of retreat after the stirring 1920s was the attempt by Pixley ka Izaka Seme to reconcile educated Africans with tribalism, and his courting of traditional chiefs. He also created a climate of opinion in which self-help movements and savings organisations replaced labour militancy.

The passage of the two 'Native' Acts of 1936 stimulated attempts to revive African resistance, and during the following decades there was an intense struggle against many of the measures introduced under the new legislation. The All-African Convention was formed to protest against the passage of the Acts. But while the Convention assembled a very wide spread of interests – perhaps the largest single protest hitherto in African politics – it did not produce a definite political strategy or organisational innovations.

The outbreak of the Second World War coincided with (and partly precipitated) a remarkable revival in African politics. Even before the war, the crisis on the land, exacerbated by the 1936 Acts, was forcing Africans in many areas of the countryside to move to the cities at an increasing rate. It also marked the beginnings of a period of rebellion in the countryside, partly in response to the radical deterioration of conditions there and partly against the measures introduced under the 1936 Trust and Lands Act, like cattle-culling and limitations on cultivation imposed under the government's 'betterment schemes'. In Free State and northern Transvaal reserves there were ominous rumblings as local communities refused to comply with government regulations. The Regent of the Batloaka tribe in the Orange Free State was fined in 1942 for refusing to participate in a betterment scheme. In the northern Transvaal aircraft of the South African Air Force bombed villagers into submitting to restrictions on ploughing. These rumblings were the first signs of the storms of rebellion which swept through the countryside during the 1950s.

A series of savage droughts early during the war seriously affected production in the reserves and on white farms. By the beginning of the war the new marketing and subsidy schemes introduced during the mid-1930s were starting to take effect. They worsened the position of African labour, and pushed up the costs of food, not only in the urban areas but in the countryside too.

All of these impulses accelerated African urbanisation and intensified the political struggles on the land and in mining and manufacturing industry over the widest imaginable array of issues: over wages, access to land, transport, housing and other community issues. The immigrants to the urban areas found wages low (especially for unskilled workers – skilled workers were relatively well-paid). Food and other necessities were expensive. Housing was likewise expensive and difficult to find. Conditions in all urban areas were overcrowded. Infant mortality rates were extremely high.

There were three consequential changes in the form and agenda of African political activity: the revival of working-class action in the workplace, culminating in the mineworkers' strike of 1946; the emergence, with few pre-war precedents, of direct action in urban communities, like transport boycotts and squatter movements; and the emergence of an Africanist Youth League in the ANC, which precipitated a crisis in its leadership and set it on a new and more vigorous course of action. The cumulative effect was to change the relations and attitudes of politically aware Africans to the institutions and relationships which characterised the power structures of white politics.

There was an increase in strike activity by Africans which lasted until about 1948. Most African unions were affiliated to the Council for Non-European Trade Unions, formed early during the war with communist support. CNETU claimed an affiliated membership of 158 000, including 40 per cent of Africans employed in commerce and manufacturing.

The major episode following this season of African working-class turbulence was the African miners' strike of August 1946. The strike came as the climax to a series of strikes and riots on the mines, precipitated by a combination of low wages, dangerous working conditions, poor rations and poor living conditions. Mineworkers felt perhaps more acutely than other workers the erosion of their pay packets and the increasing strains they faced in meeting their responsibilities to maintain families in the reserves as the reserve economies declined. The cash wages of mineworkers declined from 2s. 6d. per shift in 1890 to 2s. 0d. in 1942. Although there had been strikes before, including the industry-wide strike of 1920, African mineworkers were extraordinarily difficult to organise, housed as they were in compounds located on private property, and subject to close surveillance by the mine managements who frequently summoned the police to maintain control.

The strike was largely organised by the African Mineworkers' Union, formed in 1942. Led by Gaur Radebe, the secretary for mines of the Transvaal African Congress and a member of the Communist Party, AMWU was a significant instance of the political forms evolving in the African workforce, and of the array of forces which were constituted within it.

Despite police intimidation, AMWU was remarkably successful in bringing attention to the grievances of mineworkers. It successfully put pressure on the government to appoint a commission of inquiry into the industry. In 1944, the commission reported. It acknowledged that the reserves no longer supplemented the wages of migrant workers, and recommended that they should be paid wages comparable to those paid in manufacturing industry. The government in fact subsidised a small increase, which the Union dismissed as inadequate. Nevertheless, the Union stifled calls for a strike. (Generally, unions dominated or strongly influenced by communists were reluctant to strike during the war.)

By the end of the war, however, the Union was stirred to action by the deteriorating situation of miners. It demanded a wage of 10s. a day, family housing, paid leave gratuities, and the repeal of War Measure 145, which prohibited strikes by Africans. The Union was rebuffed in its approaches to the Chamber of Mines. CNETU resolved to support a strike, and a mass meeting of mineworkers held early in August took the decision to strike.

On 12 August, 50 000 workers stayed in their compounds. Within two days, police armed with batons were entering the compounds. On one mine, the workers tried to hold a sit-down strike and were driven 'stope by stope, level by level' to the surface. In all, 73 000 workers went on strike, and 16 000 policemen were used against them. Photographs of some of their encounters look like battle scenes. Production stopped on ten mines and was seriously affected on many others. Leaders of the Union were tried under war regulations, and all the members of the national executive of the Communist Party were put on trial for sedition. The failure of the strike led to deep disillusionment with strikes as a weapon and with CNETU and the Communist Party; 27 unions disaffiliated from the Union. Nonetheless, the strike had profound consequences for African politics in South Africa.

Dan O'Meara has described the strike as a watershed in South African history.[52] The strike reinforced the strength of radical groups in the ANC. It brought to a head the slowly growing impatience of politically aware Africans with the Natives' Representative Council.

The Council had been offered as a compensation in return for the removal of Cape African voters from the common roll in 1936. In the first Council election before the war, mainly middle-class and conservative Africans were elected. The Council quickly earned the reputation of being a talking-shop. In the 1942 elections, however, more radical groups were elected. The miners' strike was the last straw. During the strike, the Council resolved to adjourn in protest. Paul Mosaka, leader of the African Democratic Party, described it as a 'toy telephone, an apparatus which cannot transmit sound'. The adjournment of the Council was a symptom of African disillusionment with the failure of the government to respond to African demands. It was never to meet again. In 1947, the leading members of the Council rejected an offer by Smuts to enlarge the Council and extend its powers, because the offer failed to meet their demand that Africans should be recognised as citizens of South Africa. The demise of the Council marked, in effect, the terminal stages of a long, if faltering, tradition of colonial liberalism in South Africa. (It was not until the 1950s that the tradition was finally destroyed with the accession to power of the National Party and the introduction of apartheid, reflecting the ascendancy of a tradition in Afrikaner nationalism based on neo-Fichtean conceptions of race, which profoundly transformed the whole character of political discourse in South Africa.)

The Second World War had lifted African hopes of a change in their situation, but the government refused to acknowledge the validity of claims to common rights or access to government. The publication of the Atlantic Charter in 1943 stimulated African aspirations to equality. A document entitled *African Claims in South Africa* called for the acceptance of the main principles of the Charter in South Africa, and formulated a Bill of Rights. This Bill demanded the abolition of racial discrimination, freedom of movement and residence, equal rights with respect to property, occupation, and pay, free and compulsory education, state assistance to African farmers, welfare and social security for all. This Bill of Rights, a prototype of the Freedom Charter which was presented at Kliptown a decade later, revealed important changes in African opinion towards an explicit rejection of racism as the basis for political rights, including citizenship. It registered the impact of the movement against colonialism spreading throughout Asia and Africa. Smuts refused to take any notice of it.

These developments were accompanied by organisational and ideological shifts in the ANC which culminated in the formation of the ANC Youth League. The Youth League was strongly influenced by the puritanical and populistic ideas of Anton Lembede, who provided the intellectual base for Africanism. Lembede asserted: 'Moral degradation is assuming alarming dimensions . . . [and] manifests itself in such abnormal and pathological phenomena as a loss of self-confidence, inferiority complex, a feeling of frustration, the worship of whiteness, foreign leaders and ideologies. All these are symptoms of a pathological state of mind.'[53]

Although it was not until the establishment of the Pan-Africanist Congress in 1959 that Lembede's ideas fully received organisational expression, Lembede's emphasis on the importance of indigenous leadership and national self-determination gave point to a number of issues existing between the Youth League and the ANC leadership. The League complained of the ANC's tendency to yield before oppression, to accept European condescension and regard foreign ideas as superior.

The contrasting vigour and directness of Africanist slogans like 'The leaders of the Africans must come out of their own loins' or 'Africa is a black man's country' struck a response especially among less educated and rural people. Moreover, the Africanists in the League were, as Lodge puts it, imaginative in their reactions to the 'social eruptions around them'.[54] They were sensitive to the possibilities offered by direct popular action – riots, boycotts, strikes, civil disturbance, and acts of disobedience. In the climate of intense social upheaval and political repression of wartime South Africa, their populist, anti-liberal stance drew a great deal of support.

Dr A. B. Xuma, who became president of the ANC in 1940, was favourably impressed by the young Africanists in the League, even though their organisational styles reflected different ideological assumptions and inclinations. He also disagreed with their strategy of refusing to participate in government institutions, like advisory boards and Natives' Representative Council elections.

In 1949, the ANC launched the Programme of Action, perhaps the boldest and most defiant policy hitherto adopted in its history. The Programme of Action placed the struggle for national freedom, political independence and self-determination at the head of the political agenda of the ANC. White leadership and segregation were rejected. The ANC was beginning to experiment with new political strategies partly based on the recent experiences by Africans of direct political action, and partly influenced by events elsewhere in colonial societies. These new strategies included the boycott of all discriminatory political institutions, strikes, civil disobedience and non-cooperation. In 1949, also, Dr James Moroka was elected president; he was more sympathetic towards militant tactics than was his predecessor, as were the most important Youth Leaguers now emerging towards national leadership in the ANC – Nelson Mandela, Oliver Tambo and Walter Sisulu.

Until after the Second World War, African political organisations worked on the assumption that peaceful protest and representation rather than direct confrontation or challenge were both desirable and necessary means for improving the position of Africans (or significant groups of Africans) in the society. No doubt this policy was based on a realistic recognition that in direct confrontation with the repressive forces of the state, Africans would lose out. It was approved by liberal whites sympathetic towards the political aspirations of Africans. From 1948, this strategy found less and less support among significant African political leaders. During the 1950s the ANC and its allies were increasingly committed to the course of confrontation as it came to stand more determinedly against the whole set of social, economic and political institutions constituting the apparatus of white domination.

The Programme of Action, which was launched during the early 1950s, was a measure of the determination by African political groups to challenge the whole basis of white rule by conducting systematic campaigns against the laws on which white rule was based. Perforcedly, however, it was a challenge which they had to carry out by peaceful means; for ultimately, like the strategies of peaceful protest and representation which it succeeded, it was based on a moral appeal to whites. Such campaigns do not invariably fail, but their success is based on the sense of a shared moral universe with those in positions of power.

This campaign culminated in two developments. The first was the Defiance Campaign of 1952. Organised under the joint aegis of the ANC and the South African Indian Congress, thousands of African and Indian volunteers defied regulations zoning public places like railway waiting-rooms for the exclusive use of particular racial groups. It was a convincing expression of political cooperation in a campaign of passive resistance against racial laws, not only involving Africans and Indians, but also white liberals (the Liberal Party was to be formed in 1953) and leftists, who formed the Congress of Democrats in the same year. The alliance of African and Indian movements was an important consequence of the Durban race riots of 1949 in which Africans killed a number of Indians and destroyed their property.

Aside from its significance for inter-racial cooperation against apartheid, the Defiance Campaign was the prelude to the transformation of the ANC into a mass organisation. After the campaign, its membership reached 100 000. It nevertheless continued to exhibit certain organisational weaknesses, partly no doubt because of the poverty both of its members and of the groups among whom they worked, long hours, poor transport, and a highly organised structure of state repression and police harassment. Undoubtedly, too, the lack of an appropriate institutional framework (such as the franchise created for white political groups, forcing them to organise for elections) made it difficult for the ANC to develop a commitment to working from house to house, or to develop local branches.

In 1953, anticipating that the ANC might be banned, Nelson Mandela proposed that a system of cells, zones and wards should be established which could operate clandestinely, but the 'M Plan', as it became known, was only put into effect in a few areas. In 1955, the national executive complained that the ANC continued to concentrate on mass meetings to the neglect of other organisational methods. The present writer recalls the excitement and camaraderie of those hot dusty meetings, held during the late 1950s on open land in freehold areas around Johannesburg, invariably named 'Freedom Square'; but like the excitement generated by the ICU during the 1920s, it all ended in speeches.

A major impediment to the progress of African political organisation was the weight of repression which the government was prepared to bring to bear on it. For most of the twentieth century, this repression had taken the form of police action against individuals under a variety of statutes, such as Section 29 of the Natives (Urban Areas) Act of 1923, which made provision for the removal from an urban area of a person deemed to be 'idle and dissolute'. The crime of sedition could be used in serious confrontations such as the miners' strike of 1946. Statutory control over meetings was provided in the Riotous Assemblies Act of 1930. The pass laws and influx controls; the prohibition on the sale of 'European' liquor to Africans and the protection of the municipal monopoly over the brewing of *mahau*; the common law of trespass; municipal licensing laws: these and myriad others could be used to justify police raids into townships and locations, and hence the disruption of the political life of African communities.

While the state authorities continued after 1948 to control African political activity through devices such as these inherited from previous governments, the Suppression of Communism Act, passed in 1950, introduced a major innovation in political repression. This Act, which was used immediately to proscribe the Communist Party and seize its assets, could be used against individuals and organisations who were deemed to further the aims and objectives of communism. The latter could be proscribed and their assets seized. The former might be named, banned, prevented from attending meetings, prevented from meeting other banned persons, restricted to particular magisterial districts, or banished to specific areas. These controls in effect placed the victim under a sentence of civic death.

In terms of later legislation modelled on the 1950 Act, persons might also be placed under house arrest.

Despite its name, the main purpose of this and other legislation which followed it was intended to control the political activities of blacks, usually members of the African National Congress and the Pan-Africanist Congress, the South African Indian Congress, and members of the Congress of Democrats (white) and the Liberal Party, who were seriously engaged in political action against apartheid.

The opposition to apartheid which emerged during the 1950s included a wide variety of competing and opposed elements. They were frequently unable to agree about political purpose, beyond the need to change the racial basis of admission to civic and social rights in South Africa. The government reacted in 1956 by putting its leaders on trial for high treason, and shortly after their release and the cataclysmic events of Sharpeville and Langa, it took the even more extreme action of banning the ANC and the PAC in 1960.

It was only with the Defiance Campaign of 1952 that the ANC joined in efforts to mobilise mass opposition to the apartheid policy, and likewise it was only at the Kliptown conference of 1955, that a coherent political manifesto enunciating an alternative to racial domination emerged in the Freedom Charter.

The Defiance Campaign created a mass movement, but it did not articulate a clear ideological position, nor did the Congress's organisation sustain the enthusiasm generated by the campaign. In an effort to consolidate these developments, the ANC embarked on a Programme of Economic Advancement. The Programme demanded the end of the job colour bar, the removal of restrictions on trading rights, the fixing of a minimum wage, and the entrenchment of trade union rights. The culmination of the Programme was even more far-reaching: at a conference in August 1953 Professor Z. K. Matthews, a leading conservative in Congress, proposed calling a 'national convention' which would draw up a 'Freedom Charter for the Democratic South Africa of the future'.[55]

The idea which grew out of that proposal during the next year was that the Charter would flow from discussions held by committees set up in villages and townships throughout the country. These would in turn send delegates to the national convention. The convention was to be a great assembly which would thrash out the design for a democratic South Africa. 'The Charter', claimed *Advance*, 'will emerge from countless discussions among the people themselves. It will truly be, in every sense of the word, the charter of ordinary men and women.'[56]

Not surprisingly, the intention to engage the indirect participation of every village and location in formulating the Charter was unsuccessful. It proved difficult to set up the local committees which were meant to elect delegates to the national convention, and Congress officials undertook to canvass local opinion. There were other impediments too: many Congress leaders were banned, which effectively neutralised even the most determined of them. Congress's energies were diverted by its efforts to counter the emergent apartheid state, and particularly the removal of Sophiatown and the introduction of Bantu Education. An intrinsic problem lay in the parochialism and myopia of many of the ordinary folk. It was also claimed in the ANC that the Congress of Democrats had appropriated the direction of the campaign. Its white, uncommonly well-educated and politically experienced members had obvious advantages over many Africans in Congress.

The Congress of the People was nevertheless an impressive gathering. Three thousand delegates of all races and political positions attended the meeting at Kliptown near Johannesburg. Its business was conducted in a ceremonial manner which transformed it into a moving piece of political theatre. The Charter itself was couched in poetic language. The method of its presentation made it all the more impressive. It was read out clause by clause, accompanied by speeches, a show of hands and applause. But the dramatic finale was a raid by policemen armed with sten guns who occupied the platform, seized documents and dismissed the delegates. The material seized at the Kliptown Congress of the People provided much of the evidence on which the treason trial of 1956–60 was based.

The treason trial ended in acquittal for the accused. But aside from the terrible political, financial and emotional burdens which it imposed on the individuals concerned, on their families, and the organisations which they represented, the trial also marked the intensification of the government's assault on the extra-parliamentary opposition.

In turn, African political groups and movements intensified their efforts against racial laws. A new factor in the situation which contributed to this process was the split in the ANC and the formation of the Pan-Africanist Congress in 1959. The establishment of the PAC signified an important movement in African nationalism away from the radical non-racism which had been espoused with more or less emphasis in the Congress movement over the previous decade or so.

The leadership of the ANC encouraged political cooperation between different racial groups, albeit organised in racially exclusive bodies, and not without some resentments against whites. But such resentments were held within the boundaries of a common commitment between the different organisations in the Congress movement to a non-racial political and social order. The overriding ideological objective was to eliminate racism. The Pan-Africanists emphasised the primacy of populist aspirations and the paramountcy of ethnic nationalism. In Congress, the ideological objective was to destroy white (and other) racism. In the PAC, overt anti-white racism was avoided, but it sometimes lay ill-concealed beneath the surface of affirmations that the supreme political allegiance of all, irrespective of skin colour, who lived in Africa was towards Africa. These differences between the ANC and the PAC were not superficial; they corresponded to the different modes of incorporation into capitalist society of various strata in the African community. They were reflected in the differences between the leading figures in the movement and the dominant groups in the ANC; the leading Africanists originated mainly in the rural areas of the Transvaal and the Orange Free State, their qualifications and career achievements were relatively modest, and they enjoyed limited contact with whites. These differences also became significant in the ways in which the two organisations came to terms with the problem of using violence as a political instrument.

By the late 1950s and early 1960s, when the position of Africans in South Africa had become an international *cause célèbre*, the die was virtually cast in favour of direct confrontation. Albert Luthuli was the last ANC leader who represented African political claims as a desire to share power with whites in South Africa. Many Western leaders clung obdurately to the hope of peaceful change, long after most South African liberals had given up such hopes. In 1961, President Kennedy applauded Luthuli on the occasion of his receiving the Nobel Peace Prize for 'working for change through peaceful means'.

But if he intended to express the hope that South African blacks would continue with the politics of passive resistance he had misjudged the change that was taking place in African politics and in white society. Great changes were occurring elsewhere in Africa; the 1960s was the decade of decolonisation. By the early 1960s, Portugal was gearing up to face the strains of the guerrilla wars which were to destroy its colonial empire in Africa. It was difficult to believe that South Africa's blacks, who included the most sophisticated proletariat with the longest experience of modern political organisation in the sub-continent, would continue indefinitely with a political strategy which drew such a bitter return of increased repression.

This does not mean, as the government claimed from the mid-1950s, that the ANC was launched on a path of violent confrontation with the state, let alone that it had embarked on a race war against all whites. Undoubtedly there were elements in the ANC and the PAC which entertained sanguinary dreams of confronting whites in a pitched battle: such dreams were partially realised in the Poqo uprising at Paarl in 1962. But Poqo represented the extreme flank of that element present in both organisations (though more strongly in the PAC than the ANC) that tried to resist the implications of capitalist development. It was not the predominant element.

Such fantasies were of course not the exclusive property of African migrant workers who formed a significant constituent of Poqo; they were shared by the least reconstructed elements among white Afrikaners, with the telling difference that whites imagined themselves as the victims, not the perpetrators, of such violence. In both cases, these fantasies had their roots in the recollection of an Arcadian 'idyll turned to nightmare' (in Hannah Arendt's phrase) under the impact of colonial capitalism. But it was not the dominant ideological figure of either African or Afrikaner nationalism.

The direct confrontation which precipitated the banning of the ANC and the PAC followed the pattern of earlier campaigns against apartheid legislation. Both the ANC and the PAC resolved in December 1959 to embark upon a campaign aimed at eliminating the pass laws. Both campaigns were characteristically protests against these laws. They were not intended to precipitate a more generalised resistance. The ANC's Anti-Pass Planning Council announced a diary of prayer meetings and street processions. Only in Natal did it seek to use the strike as a weapon in this campaign. The PAC campaign was probably on the whole announced in more militant terms than the ANC. But its campaign was focussed narrowly on the specific issue of the pass laws, and was conducted with caution and decorum.

As it turned out, the PAC's campaign precipitated the crisis that was to lead to the state of emergency and the banning of the Congress movements. Although in general the PAC had rather a poor organisation in most parts of the country, it was strong in two areas, the Cape Peninsula and the southern Transvaal, which exhibited certain similarities: a high proportion of migrant workers, a high level of governmental disruption of daily life, and the weak presence of the ANC. It was in these areas that the two episodes which provoked the state of emergency took place.

The PAC announced that its campaign would begin on 21 March. Its organisation was particularly good in the townships and locations around Vereeniging in the southern Transvaal, and processions to police stations in these areas were well attended. Some were dispersed by low-flying Sabre jet fighter planes. The crowd that gathered outside the police station at Sharpeville refused to disperse, and the police declined to arrest a group of PAC supporters who presented themselves. The crowd swelled, and the police became jittery. As usual in such affairs, it is difficult to know what brought about the tragedy; it is thought that a policeman was pushed over, and the relatively inexperienced policemen fired into the crowd in a panic. Most of the bullets were in the backs of the victims. In all, 69 people died, and 180 were wounded. A general strike followed in the area.

In Cape Town, the main event was a march by 30 000 people, mainly from Langa, the main residential area for Africans outside Cape Town, on 30 March. It was that march, not Sharpeville, that provided the immediate pretext for the government's decision to impose the state of emergency. A number of demonstrations took place in and around Cape Town from 21 March.

The Sharpeville crisis did not, as some have argued, present African nationalists, liberals and communists with a political opportunity which they failed to seize. Rather, it forced them to reconsider, and ultimately to reject, both the political objective of participation in and the reform of existing political institutions, and the political means – demonstrations, protests, boycotts, and other essentially non-violent strategies – which had characterised their political struggles for the previous half-century.

The banning of the ANC had a cataclysmic effect on the organisation; it was affected far more profoundly than the Communist Party had been a decade earlier. The CPSA had a coherent organisation. It had debated the matter of going underground during the late 1940s. It was the heir to a tradition of clandestine and conspiratorial politics, though the conditions in South Africa were far less severe than those which had shaped Lenin's party and the German Communist Party. (Indeed, members of the Communist Party continued to be active politically throughout the 1950s, sometimes through their influence over organisations like the South African Congress of Democrats, and had a considerable effect on the conduct of oppositional politics in South Africa.)

The ANC had few of the organisational resources requisite for its reconstruction as an effective clandestine movement. It had never developed an electoral machinery; such machinery was otiose in circumstances in which Africans were unenfranchised. The only elections in which prominent Congress figures had participated were for the indirectly elected seats on the Natives' Representative Council. They had stood as individuals rather than as members of Congress. Congress had worked for the most part as a popular movement, organising demonstrations, rallies, campaigns, boycotts, and other such open activities. During the last decade of its legal existence it had become a mass movement. But that did not equip it for the activity of a clandestine, let alone revolutionary, movement. Indeed, this structure made the transition to a clandestine form of organisation even more difficult to accomplish, for it involved the delicate business of encapsulating an open set of associations and relationships in closed ones.

True, this problem was anticipated in Mandela's enunciation of the 'M Plan' to reorganise the movement on the basis of wards and blocks, but within three years of the ANC's banning, Mandela was imprisoned for life. After the Rivonia trial, there was little left of a domestic political organisation. The ANC made its way into clandestine politics by the hardest route possible, the route of exile politics. For most of the 1960s and into the 1970s, this was effectively confined to establishing offices in European capitals. Until the mid-1970s, this meant extraordinarily long lines of communication. As Tom Lodge has suggested, the movement was obliged to concentrate on an informal kind of diplomacy, subject to all kinds of compromises and inhibitions, and its leadership were forced into the restrictive role of stateless leaders of states.

However, despite these disadvantages, the movement not only survived for nearly a quarter of a century of clandestine existence; it managed to increase its political support within the country, as well as achieve international respectability. While it would be premature to attempt an explanation, part of the reason undoubtedly lies in the calibre of the leadership which went into exile and into jail; the limitations of alternative kinds of political organisations and movements, internally and externally; and, not least, the failure of the government to generate political institutions that could rival the promise of the ANC to accomplish the liberation of black South Africans.

The banning of the ANC and the PAC also forced them and other political organisations to contemplate the prospect of the use of violence. In December 1961, representatives of the ANC and PAC, as well as African members of the Progressive Party and of the Liberal Party, met in Orlando to discuss strategies of non-violent action. In March 1962, another conference was held in Pietermaritzburg, which called for a campaign of mass non-cooperation. The campaign was expected to begin with a strike, and then to unfold with attacks on Bantu Authorities, boycotts and withdrawal from participation in school committees and advisory boards. Both phases of the campaign were abysmal failures. Their failure made it fairly obvious not only to the leaders of the ANC and the PAC, but also to militants associated with other groups and parties, including the Liberal Party, that there was no future for non-violent mass action, and that the use of force now needed to be considered.

Among Africans, the recognition of the necessity for violence did not, however, follow simply from the failure of non-violent mass action. It also had a source in the frustration and hatred which many Africans held for whites. It was never a problem for any movement to find volunteers for dangerous expeditions.

Both the ANC and the PAC formed armed wings in 1961. Both were strongly influenced by the mood of frustration among Africans. But there were significant differences in the way the two organisations approached the question of violence, which reflected the ideological and material differences between them. The armed wing of the ANC, Umkonto we Sizwe (The Spear of the Nation), admitted non-Africans to membership, as well as members of the Communist Party. The movement to establish it was taken reluctantly, if Mandela's account at his trial is accepted, in order to 'canalise and control the feelings of our people' and to prevent the outbreak of terrorism. Similar arguments were used subsequently to justify the use of sabotage: Umkonto stated that it intended to sabotage economic installations in order to give the government the opportunity to change its policies, and thereby avoid the extremes of civil war. From the end of 1961, there were something like 200 attacks on installations. But, contrary to the policy of avoiding endangering lives, many attacks on installations also put lives at risk. Moreover, there were many attacks on policemen, 'collaborators' and 'informers'. Nonetheless, the involvement of individuals could plausibly be explained as a consequence of breaches of discipline or the desire for personal revenge by individuals, rather than the intentions of Umkonto's leaders.

The PAC's conception of the coming revolution was simple. It would take the form of attacks on police stations and the mass killing of whites, whom Potlake Leballo termed 'the forces of darkness'.[57]

The uprising at Paarl in November 1962 provides the most important instance of the efforts to put such ideas into practice. Some 250 men armed with pangas and axes marched from the location to the town, made an abortive attack on the police station, and then killed two whites and wounded two others. Five of them were killed. The rest were hunted down, and later put on trial.

Lodge's analysis of this uprising suggests some of the factors which underlay Poqo's tragically simple aspiration to overturn the social and political order in South Africa in a single heroic gesture. Most of the participants were migrants who lived in barracks without their families. Paarl had previously endorsed out to the Transkei the wives of workers who could not show that they had lived there for at least fifteen years. The influx controls were severely applied. To make matters worse, they were administered by a corrupt director who sold passes and made pass offenders work on his private farm.

It is not impossible that members of the ANC might have used violence in the past (and might do so in the future) in order to act on such motives as were evident in the episode at Paarl. However, such motives received little explicit or implicit support in the ideological configurations which predominated in the Congress movement.

The proscription of the ANC and the PAC in 1960 had a profound effect on the politics of the organisations, which were increasingly dictated by international circumstances and the prospects for developing a base for insurrection in South Africa itself. It was only from the early-to-mid 1970s that they were able to establish bases in adjacent territories, though Lesotho had earlier permitted both organisations to operate from its territory, and the PAC established its headquarters there. But for the intervening fifteen years or so, the lines of communication were impossibly long, and the organisational problems extremely difficult.

The ANC and the PAC experienced similar difficulties, but the PAC was less able to cope with them, and its experience in exile has proved almost fatal to the movement. There were disputes between different factions in the movement. (One of these led to the dynamiting of the house of the leader, Potlake Leballo.) There were misappropriations of funds, suspensions, expulsions, and ideological witch-hunts. The decision which was taken in 1967 to intensify guerrilla activity resulted in a series of frustrating and often abortive training projects in half-a-dozen African countries. There was a lack of discipline in the organisation which led to the explusion of individuals from African countries, and the Organisation of African Unity withdrew its support from the movement because of its internal problems. There were a number of disastrous alliances (including one with Unita), and for a time the CIA provided the movement with financial aid. In part these problems stemmed from the lack of movement during the decade and a half in which the South African government commanded the region without challenge, and the ANC experienced such problems too. But they were certainly exacerbated in the PAC by an organisational style and ideological direction which had characterised the movement since its inception. The PAC was marked by organisational weaknesses which were linked to its spontaneism. Another expression of this spontaneism was the assumption that the revolution would take the form of a single, spontaneous act of insurrection. Indeed, Leballo planned just such an uprising in 1962, but spoiled the effect by announcing it in a press conference!

Perhaps the signal achievements of the PAC consisted in getting South Africa expelled from the United Nations General Assembly, and getting the OAU to accept its document arguing South Africa's illegal status.

The ANC went through similar problems, but survived them in better condition. The major ideological divisions which it underwent concerned the place of communists in the movement. There was only one serious episode of this sort, and it was resolved without major trauma. The chronic organisational problems associated with exile politics arose too, in the form of a leadership isolated from its followers, including followers-in-exile. These problems were recognised and some attempts made to solve them at the conference held at Morogoro in 1969. The emergence of Tambo and Mandela to positions of leadership during the late 1950s was fortunate for the movement, for both straddled the centre of the movement. Both, too, enjoyed considerable authority, not the least because of the diplomatic skills which they commanded.

During the early 1970s, the pattern of sabotage carried out in the country suggested that the ANC had developed an internal organisational network. Both this network, and the external movement, were immensely strengthened in the aftermath of the 1976 uprising in Soweto.

By the late 1970s the ANC had come to enjoy as much prestige among Africans in South Africa as it had before it was banned (if not more). It must be unusual for a man imprisoned over a quarter of a century ago to command the popular respect and admiration which Mandela does. Because of this, it is often assumed that the ANC is the heir apparent to the post-liberation South African state. It is also assumed that movements like the United Democratic Front (UDF), and the union movement which congregated under the banner of the Congress of South African Trade Unions (COSATU), are organisationally and ideologically continuous with the ANC. Yet there are serious structural, social and political differences between them. The UDF and COSATU are essentially the products of the transformations of the 1970s (which the ANC, of course, helped to bring about). Of the elder statesmen of the ANC, Mandela has spent the past quarter of a century in prison, and Tambo has spent it engaged in diplomatic life. Neither of these experiences is likely to provide the preparation requisite for re-entry into South African public life, except perhaps as figureheads. There are younger men in the ANC who could supply a competent leadership. Some of them were educated abroad and have spent their adult lives out of the country. Such problems are not negligible. Since 1976, the organisation has been invigorated by the exiles who left South Africa after the Soweto uprising, and also, in the opinion of experts on the movement, the development of a strong clandestine organisation in the country.

10 Revolution and reform: the emergent forces

The spectre of revolution has long haunted white South Africa. Its upper and middle classes have enjoyed the perilous benefits of one of the highest standards of living in the world in a sub-continent that includes some of the poorest people in Africa. White workers, though poorer, less powerful, and certainly less well-provided with welfare services than comparable European or North American workers, constituted a privileged stratum in the workforce, with an even more immediate stake in racial privileges than the middle and upper classes.

From the mid-1970s, the issues debated interminably for the past quarter of a century took on a new urgency as regional, international and domestic crises compounded one other. These crises impelled government policy to move simultaneously in two directions. On the one hand, the state's repressive apparatus was strengthened, and both military and police acquired expanded powers and resources. On the other, efforts were made to remodel political institutions, increase economic and educational opportunities for blacks, and institutionalise relations between capital and labour, in order to generate some legitimacy for the social order. While there were many disagreements within the political class about the most effective way in which to achieve some consent for the regime among the underclasses, there was little disagreement about the objective to be pursued: stability and order in a period of economic restructuring and social change. It was increasingly recognised among white political leaders that there would have to be changes in the political institutions of apartheid if the social order was to survive.

As noted in Chapter 4, the centre of gravity in white political opinion shifted significantly in the process, from an avowed and dogmatic determination to resist all changes at any cost, to support for institutional changes controlled by a powerful, highly centralised state in which security had a top priority. Political rhetoric changed markedly over the decade of the 1970s, from evoking visions of last-ditch struggles by a brave minority determined to concede nothing to black demands, to a far more complex set of strategies.

As the costs in blood and treasure of such intransigence became more and more apparent, such sanguinary imagery was replaced by grim warnings to profit from the experiences of unreconstructed colonialism elsewhere on the continent. From the early 1970s, government spokesmen, military men, newspaper editors, members of parliament, trade unionists, and church and university leaders, swelled a chorus calling for 'change', a chorus punctuated by hysterical tremoli during the seasons of riot in 1976, 1980, 1984 and 1985–6.

The mood for adjustments had in fact been set as early as 1966, when Vorster succeeded Verwoerd as prime minister. By the mid-1970s, the call for change had become a central figure in the political discourse, and from 1974 all general elections have been fought around the issue. The terms of the debate about reform which emerged during the 1960s were set mainly by the issues raised by the Progressive Party in parliament and by corporate business interests outside. Although the themes set by these groups have been taken up by some Africans, the latter have not been prominent in formulating the issues.

Radical groups bore hardly any role in formulating the agenda for reforms, for a variety of reasons. Not least important among these was the heavy weight of state repression bearing down on them. The proscription of the SACP, the ANC, the PAC, and the black consciousness movements demonstrated the stifling limits to political activity for such groups that wished to continue to work openly. Almost as important as the silencing of a radical voice from significant political institutions was the general hostility of the South African media, particularly the state-controlled broadcasting services and the pro-government newspapers. Even the English-speaking press opposed to government policy pursued a militant anti-communism which inhibited the emergence of a genuine debate on alternative priorities in formulating policies on the political economy.

The most important group on which white South African radicals were represented, that contributed something to generating a public debate around the problems of change in South Africa, was the Study Project of Christianity in Apartheid Society. Established in 1969, it published a dozen major reports, based on a hundred preparatory papers. The Project declared that: 'the South African social system is in urgent need of radical change . . . . The aim must be to re-allocate power so that the black majority can exercise an effective role in the decision-making processes of the society and a more equitable share of the land's resources.' It added that the 'white oligarchy . . . will increasingly have to respond to black initiatives'.[58]

Despite its recognition of the need for African political participation, the Spro-cas debate, characteristic of liberal debates of the time, was dominated by whites. Moreover, there was a contradiction between the Project's stated purpose of seeking fundamental change and the concern to reduce the levels of 'conflict' which those changes would inevitably incur. For instance one of the reports argued that the 'greatest hope for peaceful change in South Africa lies in the possibility of there being opportunities . . . for blacks to exert constructive pressure on whites and within white-controlled institutions. In South Africa, the latent potential for ultimate violence can only be dissipated by institutionalised and regulated "conflict", in the course of which blacks can press for specific rights and improvements . . . .Organised and regulated bargaining between blacks and whites . . . will provide the greatest guarantee of reasonable stability for South Africa in the long run.'[59] This might indeed be true, but it substituted the goal of 'reasonable stability' for 'radical change'.

Secondly, the author of the report made the large presumption that 'white-dominated' political institutions were flexible enough to black pressures to make their entry into such institutions possible and worth the effort. He also accepted that these institutions would offer scope for real change, and not simply for the continued maintenance of white domination via institutions into which blacks had been coopted. Thirdly, the report overlooked the political violence on which the political system rested.

In various parts of the Project the preference was expressed for a form of liberal pluralism in which political affiliations cut across the lines of race, ethnicity and language, within a political structure which guaranteed the rights of individuals or of groups against arbitrary actions by the state. However desirable such a political order might be thought to be, it is unlikely that anything approximating to it might come about in South Africa (or indeed in any part of the contemporary world). Perhaps more important, this conception of a future political and social order for South Africa formulated a political myth which was inherently incapable of sustaining *any* kind of meaningful change. (It is possible that some of the members of the commission, like Richard Turner, the brilliant scholar and author of *The Eye of the Needle,* who was assassinated in 1978, would have taken a fairly critical view of the anti-revolutionary bias in much of the Project's work. But he was certainly in a minority.)

Spro-cas deserves attention for several reasons. It was a coherent and sustained effort by some of the most imaginative liberals in the country to try to formulate a strategy for reform. Secondly, its reports marked the outside limits to which whites were prepared to go in elaborating a strategy for change. Liberals were under pressure and harassment by the government – Peter Randall, the Spro-cas director, had a banning order imposed on him. Thirdly, the ideas running through the commission have subsequently, in a curious and quite typically South African way, been diluted into the orthodoxy of the reform movement which overtook government thinking during the late 1970s.[60]

Although more radical opinions have percolated into the domestic political discourse of white South Africans via the access enjoyed by such organisations as the ANC and SWAPO to international bodies and to the international press, they have been seen as part of the problem, rather than meaningful contributors to its resolution, by many progressive reformers, as well as by the government and its supporters. This may in part have been an effect of the constraints placed on political participation as much as any matter of principle or of interest on the part of white critics of the regime. It is true that some groups working within the parameters of the political system have appreciated the importance of dialogue with the radicals. But their motives have been to generate the conditions for a conservative consensus. Even those groups which envisage transcending such a consensus have had to proceed very cautiously in entering such dialogue for fear of alienating their political support among whites. The problem underscores the limitations facing groups attempting to work 'within' a system which is based on the principle of exclusion. That principle has constrained the strategies and tactics of groups working within the system, even though they found the principle restrictive and offensive.

But there were also issues of principle and interest, as well as of strategy, which limited the scope and penetration of the reformist critique. Cumulatively, these dictated that the reform movement was dominated by a liberal critique of apartheid, inhospitable to a radical critique of 'racial capitalism', and that it became in essence an effort to reform rather than to eliminate apartheid (including the apparatus of homelands states and segregated institutions). Reformism was also heavily influenced by the new conservatism in Britain and the United States, placing heavy emphasis on the therapeutic effects attributed in that doctrine to privatisation. In many ways, it reflected corporate ideology in South Africa and outside, and was influenced by the rapprochement between government and business. The parameters of the problem of reform were set by a liberal business establishment whose criticisms of apartheid had been dismissed by the Nationalists during the Verwoerd era, often with derision, as subversive to the survival of whites in South Africa. Although it cannot be assumed that the reform movement was dictated by the transformation of the structure of the political economy, it can hardly have been accidental that it coincided with marked transformations in the structure of big business, and in the relationships between big business and the state.

The main political expression of political reformism until the 1970s was the Progressive (later Progressive Reform and later still Progressive Federal) Party. The Progressives' access to and contact with African opinion were limited both by external circumstances and by party policy. The proscription of organisations like the ANC and the PAC meant that there was no effective African political leadership with whom they might openly make contact. Their own efforts to recruit a 'moderate' African membership were circumscribed by the party's opposition to the universal franchise. Party policy rested on property and educational qualifications, which meant it had little appeal to the broad mass of Africans, and its African members were drawn mainly from an aspirant petty bourgeoisie in the urban areas. Even this restricted contact was destroyed by the Prohibition of Political Interference Act of 1968.

The kinds of organisations that had served from the 1920s onwards to provide a medium for inter-racial political contacts, like the Joint Council movement established during the 1920s, no longer had any real constituency in white politics, while the vital quasi-official contacts which white liberals enjoyed with government ceased after 1948. These factors probably influenced the agenda for reform constructed by white critics during the 1960s and 1970s, which percolated into the programme for reform formulated by *verligte* Nationalists in and close to government from the middle-to-late 1970s. The critique of apartheid developed from within the political class was largely based on the assumptions that apartheid impeded the development of the economy and that it endangered the stability of the social order. The reception of this brand of progressive reformism into official political discourses was by no means an easy process. Part of the reason for this lay precisely in the scarcely concealed dislike among reformers for white workers, protected against the worst effects of capitalism by racial privileges in the workplace (though there were few statutory protections by the 1970s) and, more important, in access to housing and education, and by their right of free movement.

The progress of the 'reform from above'

The progress of the reform movement, by no means coherent or irreversible, may be traced in three phases, which correspond in part to the arenas in which they were enacted, and in part to the historical sequence in which they have taken place. The first phase consists of the changes which took place in the issues within as well as between parliamentary political parties. The redistribution of electoral support between opposition parties was a significant feature of the process. The emergence of a division between *verligtes* and *verkramptes* in the National Party, and the successive purges by the National Party of its 'right' wing, the demise of the United Party, and the alliance between the Progressives and the 'Young Turk' faction of the United Party, who together formed the Progressive Reform, later Progressive Federal, Party, were some of the moments in this phase.

The significance of these realignments was not that the National Party might be defeated at the polls, though as noted in Chapter 4, the elections of the early 1970s were the most vigorously contested since 1953. Rather, they clarified the debate between white liberals and conservatives, and laid the basis for a reconstruction of the party system which diminished the significance of 'grassroots' opinion as a serious impediment within the National Party to a reformulation of apartheid policy. The change in the lines of the debate projected the discourse between liberals and conservatives into the heart of parliamentary debate. While the significance of this phase of the process ought not to be minimised, the limitations on any attempt to liberalise state policy or institutions via party-legislative structures were obvious. The debate seriously threatened the authority of the National Party among its supporters, and induced a degree of irresolution which reduced the capacity of the government to generate any appropriate reform strategies within the parliamentary arena. On this terrain the reform movement degenerated rapidly into the trivia of style, timing and personal rivalries.

The reform movement entered its second phase of policy reformulation some time during the mid-1970s. This phase was shaped by the failure to achieve any significant advance via party-parliamentary discourse, and was probably accelerated by the strikes of the early 1970s and by the popular struggles which began with the schoolchildren's revolt in Soweto in 1976. The second phase took the form of attempts to reconstruct state policy through a variety of ad hoc devices available internally to the state, of which commissions of inquiry, particularly those orchestrated by experts, became favourite instruments.

It is perhaps less the use of expertise in the commission of inquiry than the fields in which it was applied that was novel in this development. Expertise had hitherto been used in areas like banking, agricultural credit, local government financing or road transportation. The use of 'labour relations' experts was a telling attempt to shift state intervention in the area of labour control from coercion to 'scientific' management. The relative success of the Wiehahn Commission (compared with the failure of the Riekert Commission to come up with a solution to the problem of urbanisation) enhanced the reputation and political authority of putatively neutral experts, and coincided with the reconstruction of the Human Sciences Research Council as an instrument of reform during the late 1970s and early 1980s.

The government also tried to shape a new policy via consultative committees involving business leaders and the well-publicised but essentially ad hoc Carlton and Good Hope conferences between government and business. Conflicts between purportedly progressive ministers and conservative civil servants began to be reported. Ministers could represent the impediments to change as a consequence of bureaucratic inertia and intransigence rather than of policy or political structure. Like the first phase, the phase of reformulating state policy via ad hoc devices was constrained within close limits.

One of its important effects, however, was to shift the emphasis towards technicist solutions in which state experts were accorded a leading role. To take one example, the Human Sciences Research Council (HSRC), previously a somewhat conservative body with rather limited powers and functions, was vigorously reorganised and armed with widened functions. It undertook research projects, notably in the educational field, which served as a basis for the changes in the educational system from the early 1980s. It also undertook surveys of public opinion which were used to justify changes in petty apartheid.

These piecemeal and reversible efforts to introduce changes within the interstices of the party-legislative-bureaucratic structures were preludes to the third phase of state reconstruction, the origins of which symbolically coincided with (though historically it preceded) P. W. Botha's accession to the premiership in 1978. Its significant moments may be marked in developments such as the disbandment of the Senate, the establishment of the President's Council, the reorganisation of the public service, the expansion of the Prime Minister's Office, the reformulation of the functions of the Human Sciences Research Council, the moves towards reconstructing local and regional government, and the creation of new representative institutions in central government. Some of these developments have their roots in older structures; others are quite novel. Cumulatively they point to a profound shift in the state's structure. They culminated in the new constitution of 1983, which had been ratified in the referendum of 1982.

The new constitution is not only extremely complex; it is also a framework the substantial contents of which are not likely to emerge fully in the course of a decade or so. The discussion that follows is in no sense an attempt to analyse the full implications of this massive transformation. It is aimed, rather, at elucidating the logic of the 'reform from above' and its relevance to the process of liberalisation. The main features of the innovation are the establishment of an executive presidency, elected by a college of MPs, which absorbs the premiership; two new parliamentary assemblies, the House of Representatives (for coloureds) and the House of Delegates (for Indians), in addition to the existing, whites-only House of Assembly; and the President's Council in place of the Senate.

The constitution distinguished between 'general affairs', matters common to different racial groups, and 'own affairs', which were particular to each racial group, or, in the phrase used in the constitution, concerning its way of life, culture, traditions, and customs. 'General affairs' were to be administered by a multiracial cabinet; 'own affairs' by three racially homogeneous Ministers' councils. The State President had the sole power to decide whether a matter was a 'general' or an 'own' affair, and his decision could not be adjudicated upon in any court of law. While this *diktat* undoubtedly saved the government from the prospect of having to engage in much tiresome litigation, it does not solve the political and administrative problems which are likely to emerge. A health matter would be a 'general affair' if it concerned more than one racial group, but an 'own affair' if it were peculiar to one racial group.

The 1983 constitution is difficult to understand. But several things are clear about the general form of government which it proposes. The executive president enjoys wide powers, and is not directly or immediately answerable to any elected body. His office is powerful, too, in the sense of the expertise, opinion and intelligence available to it, via bodies such as the HSRC and the military, as well as the appointed President's Council which replaced the indirectly elected Senate.

Elected legislative bodies were weakened; the notion of the sovereignty of parliament was all but abandoned. The establishment of parliamentary representation for Indians and coloureds in separate legislatures in 1984 did not so much express a broadening of the basis of consent as a multiplication of racially defined constituencies represented in the legislatures. Given the conflicts of interest among the groups represented separately, as well as the procedural obstacles standing in the way of combinations between oppositional groups in the three assemblies, it is difficult to envisage how the new arrangement could provide a basis for political alliances except those initiated by the government itself, even since the recent lifting of the Prohibition of Political Interference Act.

The discussion of the process would, however, be incomplete and misleading if it were simply to suggest that the new constitution was intended to intensify the coercive and repressive powers of the state. On the contrary, while these powers are likely to be enhanced by the changes, the signal feature of the 'new dispensation' lies in the attempt to develop consensual and non-repressive structures. The new constitution (precisely as the government claimed) created an institutional basis for a consensus (on terms dictated by the government) between the groups represented in the central institutions of the state. There were, of course, limits to that consensus, and few options were available to groups whose interests cannot gain expression via these institutions. Yet even here it is interesting that the constitution established a base for meeting the practical grievances of groups, like urban Africans, while denying them the same kind of representation offered to Indians and coloureds.

The new constitution substituted corporatist forms of representation for electoral ones, both at the national level (in the President's Council) and in the regional services councils which took over functions from the provincial councils and local authorities. The effect of these developments might be to insulate broad state policy-making from the party-legislative arena, thus isolating Botha's reform movement from the intense and damaging conflicts which were the feature of the early phase of liberalisation. The new forms of representation also give some idea of the way in which the new constitution might create administrative forms that could rationalise state interventions in the production and development of infrastructure, and insulate these too from popular pressures.

The reconstruction of local and regional government, though far from completely formulated, seemed likely to centralise control over the infrastructure and major services, and to devolve issues of purely local concern onto local authorities based on racially defined communities. The plan contemplates the upgrading of black local authorities to the same status as white ones. The apparent tendency is to give all urban communities similar local government institutions, but also to reduce the control of any local authority over 'hard' services, and indeed to eliminate their direct control over such services. The first phase in this reconstruction took place when the elected provincial councils were phased out in mid-1986. The Administrators of the four provinces remained, however, and were vested with powers crucial to the operation of the regional services councils which were to take over many of the functions both of the local authorities and of the provincial administrations. The absence of any direct electoral access from local communities to the regional services councils confirms that regional government will reinforce the authoritarian tendencies of the central government.

The Committee for Economic Affairs and the Constitutional Committee of the President's Council proposed a 'functionally dual' system of metropolitan, regional, and local government, which distinguished between 'hard' and 'soft' services. 'Hard' services were defined as those 'merely welfare and business services' that do not 'necessarily have to be rendered by a governmental institution' and include many elements of social capital services, e.g. roads, land usage, passenger transport and transport planning, water, electrical power, sewerage, airports, health services, and other planning and infrastructural services.[61] These would be controlled by regional services councils.

'Soft' services, on the other hand, were defined as those services distinguished by the committee as 'community-sensitive' or 'culturally-sensitive' services which could be controlled at the lowest level of local authorities – swimming pools, streets, pavements, community halls, residential areas, housing, beaches, schools, and so on. The distinction between 'hard' and 'soft' services is analogous to the the distinction drawn in the 1983 constitution between 'general' and 'own' affairs. Translating these terms into the language of contemporary critical political sociology (for instance, into the language employed by James O'Connor or Claus Offe) suggests that state interventions concerned with accumulation functions are located in the regional services councils, while legitimising structures will be situated in the local authorities.

Local authorities would be entitled to cast votes on a regional services council in a proportion equivalent to their use of the services administered by the council. No local authority would be entitled to more than 50 per cent of the votes on the regional services councils. The consumption of services in industrial areas and central business districts would be excluded from the calculation of voting strengths, and this would reduce, but not eliminate, the bias in voting towards affluent, white local authorities. Even so, this would mean that the big users of regional services would predominate in the regional services councils.[62]

The Local Government Bodies Franchise Act of 1984 conferred the municipal franchise on a number of 'juristic persons' that included companies, deceased estates, and trusts. Directors, shareholders, employees, trustees and executors would be entitled to cast votes in every ward in which the juristic person owned rateable property above a certain value. This bias towards the over-representation of property suggests that the poorer elements of communities which acquire political rights in local authorities, will be under-represented in them. Although white local authorities would be likely to be more influential than black ones on the regional services councils, they have been stripped of many of their most important functions. Not surprisingly, there has been considerable resistance from a number of municipalities which are reluctant to lose control over services. At present, local politicians enjoy a power base in white working-class and petty-bourgeois support.

The state's control over 'hard' services (of which private capital is the major user) would be largely immune from access by popular interests. Control over 'soft functions' – mainly elements of collective consumption – would be accessible to community interests. The weighting of the municipal franchise by additional votes is likely to ensure that a suburban petty bourgeoisie rather than the working class would predominate in the politics of collective consumption. (This predominance is not new but in the future it is likely to be secured through more formal mechanisms.) The system is likely to reinforce and perpetuate conflicts within these classes and strata. Moreover, as residential segregation is likely to continue to be maintained on the basis of racial considerations, conflicts over resources will probably continue to take the form of racial conflicts at these levels. Given the tendency towards the 'deracialisation' of state discourses, these conflicts are certain to be judged as the expression of archaic prejudices.

Organised industry and commerce have been highly critical of the new system, partly because the financial base of the regional services councils will include revenues raised from levies on employers and vendors. The dislike which business has for levies is understandable. But aside from that the new system holds certain advantages for big business. The direct enfranchisement of the owners of property in local authorities may or may not be electorally significant, but its political symbolism as an affirmation of a belief in capital can scarcely be exaggerated. Moreover the kinds of services which will be carried out in the regional services councils include important interventions by the state in the production process. It is vitally important to capital that such services should be supplied on a regular basis at stable minimal prices. The criteria by which these are to be managed emphasise that technical rationality will predominate over popular demands in their allocation and management. The committees of the President's Council which drafted much of the legislation decided an issue like the optimum size of cities in accordance with the recommendations of a group of consulting engineers, who based their findings on the cost-effectiveness of services.

The new system was developed in part in order to resolve problems in the development of local authorities in black urban areas. Under the new system, black local authorities will have the same status as any others. The regional services councils were empowered to redistribute their revenues in order to equalise the standards of services of different local authorities. It is possible that such redistributions will be used to control the escalating costs of rents and services imposed by black local authorities which has been an important cause of popular action, including attacks on the persons and properties of local councillors, in the urban areas during the past decade or so. It is also possible that the principle of cost-effectiveness on which the regional services councils are based will dampen the rising costs of services in these areas.

In brief, the establishment of this machinery could be seen as a way of addressing some of the practical grievances of Africans living in the urban areas, as well as putting in place the structures which will be needed to manage the massive wave of urbanisation that is being predicted for the next few decades. However, it is by no means clear that these measures will provide a basis for generating legitimacy for the state among urban Africans, or substantially modifying the overall structures of power in the society as a whole. The problem with these proposals is that they represent efforts to reform the institutions of local and regional government in the absence of any effort to address the key issues in South Africa's current crisis: the absence of common political rights at the national level, the racial basis of existing rights, and the authoritarian controls over political organisation and action.

Forces in the revolution

In the wake of Sharpeville and the proscription of the ANC and PAC, Africans' belief in the possibility of a liberal solution to racial conflict in South Africa was deeply shaken. The decision by the ANC to engage in armed struggle during the mid-1960s, the involvement of many young white liberals in sabotage, and the voluntary liquidation of the Liberal Party in 1968 after the passage of the Prohibition of Political Interference Act, were other signs that the space for non-violent action available to political forces seriously committed to opposing racial domination in South Africa had shrunk drastically.

Yet for more than a decade there were few opportunities available for blacks to do anything to change the situation, by force or by any other means. During the strange twilight decade which ended in the mid-1970s, whatever legitimacy white authorities and white-dominated political institutions had previously enjoyed visibly collapsed. But during that decade blacks lacked the power to resist government policy, let alone confront the state with force.

One of the expressions of this unresolved crisis was the emergence of the black consciousness movement, which registered both the collapse of any significant belief among Africans in the possibility of a liberal resolution to the South African crisis, *and* their inability directly to confront the state with violence. The leading organisation in the black consciousness movement was the South African Students' Organisation (SASO), formed in 1968 after Steve Biko and Gerald Rey had broken with the multiracial but white-dominated National Union of South African Students (NUSAS), deliberately, it is said, by challenging white students to join him in defying the pass laws.

The various organisations which identified themselves with the black consciousness movement expressly rejected liberalism, including multi-racial associations with whites. (Despite an Africanist tinge in its rhetoric, the black consciousness movement was genuinely committed to multiracialism with respect to other black groups, one of its many differences with the PAC.)

The second feature of the movement was the militancy of its commitment to liberation, combined with a critique of capitalist institutions. Notwithstanding this militancy, it deliberately eschewed the use of violence as a method of achieving liberation. The movement purposely and explicitly worked in the open, relying on a process of 'conscientisation' to contribute to liberation. The movement's espousal of 'psychologism' – its assumption that conscientisation towards psychological liberation was the key to freedom – was a symptom of its impotency in the face of state power.[63] The black consciousness movement contributed in important ways to changing Africans' perceptions of themselves and of whites. Undoubtedly in the long run, this will turn out to be no less important in the rehabilitation of Africans' sense of self than the notion of négritude did elsewhere.[64] Politically, too, it may have provided a focus for the Soweto student rebellion of 1976. But the precise way in which it contributed to the development of revolutionary struggle was by no means clear. Sam Nolutshungu observed that while the members of the black consciousness movement confidently saw the possibility of armed struggle, 'none of their expectations amounted to clearly formulated policies, clearly communicated by organisations to their following'.[65] Nor would it seem that any policy for covert action by the black consciousness movement was formulated, let alone one that might realistically be termed a revolutionary strategy.

The non-violent but trenchant militancy of the movement found expression in an extremely potent language, as well as in expressions of open admiration for liberation movements elsewhere in the sub-continent.

As white fears deepened into hysteria after Frelimo took power in Mozambique, the police took action against SASO. Many of its leaders were put on trial for crimes against the state and sentenced to long terms of imprisonment. And, deepest blow of all, Steve Biko, one of the most attractive and creative black political leaders to have emerged in a generation, died in police custody, in an incident which continues to resonate in the country and internationally.

Two developments during the early and mid-1970s overlapped with the black consciousness movement, but achieved a greater impact on African political organisation, and on the response of the state. The first was the emergence of the union movement; the second the schoolchildren's revolt which began in Soweto in 1976.

Black working-class action and organisation underwent a twenty-year depression, roughly from the early 1950s until the early 1970s, for reasons very similar to the depression experienced by other political organisations.

Many unionists were banned under the Suppression of Communism Act. Africans were extruded from the definition of employee, and thus were statutorily excluded from the process of industrial negotiation. A whole array of legislation could be used to control workers. Workers were vulnerable to being dismissed, especially migrant workers on contract. Wages were low. African unions were poverty-stricken, their officers underpaid and hampered in other ways by the general net of controls which lay over Africans.

In 1953, the Native Labour (Settlement of Disputes) Act was passed, which provided a basis for segregated in-plant bargaining and conciliation procedures. They were not very effective in giving black workers any say in negotiations with employers, but so heavily did repression lie on working-class movements and organisations that they endured with remarkable success as the sole form of direct negotiation available to African workers. Strikes could be declared illegal in essential industries, but even outside of these, strike action declined after 1948, and remained at a low level until the early 1970s.

One of the reasons for this was that the Suppression of Communism Act could be used to harass trade unionists, particularly left-wingers. The most militant unionists to emerge during and after the Second World War were leftists. Symptomatic also of the weakness of black working-class action was the system of parallel unions whereby African interests were communicated to employers and government via white-controlled unions. The South African Trade Union Council (later the Trade Union Council of South Africa – TUCSA) was instrumental in establishing this system, excluding African unions from direct affiliation.

The parallel union system led to a split in the union movement. The South African Congress of Trade Unions was established on the basis of 19 unions which rejected parallelism. SACTU took an explicitly political position in support of the other elements of the Congress movement, and attended the Congress of the People at Kliptown. A number of its leaders were put on trial for treason. SACTU's experience of the state's backlash against 'political' unionism was not lost on the unions that emerged during the 1970s, many of which took an extremely cautious stance towards overtly becoming identified with political movements.

The strikes that broke out during the early 1970s initiated a period of development in the black unions on a scale and of a momentum which surpassed all previous revivals of working-class action and organisation. It attested to a remarkable change in the potential strength of black workers. In Durban, more than 100 000 workers marched through the industrial areas of the city early in 1973. The number of workers involved in strikes declined radically between 1974 and 1980, partly because of the recession of those years, but then rose markedly, reaching 200 000 in 1983.[66] There were two consequences of this increase in worker action. First was the establishment of a number of unions and federations of unions organising primarily, though not solely, among African workers, which took a stand in opposition to parallel unions. Secondly, government and the major industrial interests took active steps to institutionalise black workers' organisations through a system of recognition, bargaining procedures, and the creation of an industrial court.

The strongest support for the new unions came from migrant workers rather than workers permanently settled in the urban areas and enjoying Section 10 rights, who were the most privileged groups among blacks in the workforce. The strength of support the unions received from among migrant workers corroborates the argument made in Chapter 8 that the homelands and national states may have begun to fail in their function as a buttress of the South African political economy.

A study by Ari Sitas of metal-workers on the east Rand suggests the general forces at work in the new union movement, as well as documents in fascinating detail the world views of the migrant workers who made up the predominant support of the movement. Although the statistical picture is not entirely clear, the majority of workers, at least 80 per cent in many cases, in the small-to-average metal factory on the east Rand were migrant workers. They were not, however, commonly recent migrants from the rural areas. Some of the workers interviewed by Sitas had been working on contract for more than 30 years. Aside from the juridical status imposed on them by the apartheid system, they were no less 'permanent' elements in the industrial labour force of the Witwatersrand than people enjoying permanent rights to live in the urban areas. Nevertheless, their juridical exclusion from permanent rights deeply constrained their choice of jobs and the wages which they could expect to earn.

The migrant workforce presented a combination of potentially explosive features: long experience of industrial work, and exclusion from even the few rights which permanent workers enjoyed. This latter feature probably accounts for the heavy reliance of east Rand foundries, and presumably other industries which needed workers to do particularly dangerous and unpleasant jobs, on migrant workers. The workers themselves saw this feature very clearly: 'We get lower jobs than township people. In those places where workers are gently treated we are not wanted. We are only needed in those places where there is rough work.'[67] In Sitas's interviews, the migrant workers allude constantly to the differences between themselves and 'township' workers, enjoying rights to reside permanently in the urban areas. According to Sitas, the strength of migrant support for unions arose from four causes: their awareness of poor wages; the great difficulty they would have in changing the job to which they were tied by their contracts; the arduous conditions of their work; and the transformation of the hostels in which they lived into sites for the mobilisation of worker consciousness. As an organiser of the Metal and Allied Workers' Union put it, 'they preach unionism to each other the whole night.'[68] The important thing to note is that almost every one of these factors for facilitating worker consciousness could a decade or so earlier have been cited as a source of worker, particularly migrant worker, passivity in earlier years.

It may be, as Keenan has argued, that the extremity of the controls over and exploitation of migrant workers 'provided a ready and fertile ground for the organisation of the migrant workforce and . . . underlay the militancy of its response'.[69] But if so, it is difficult to understand which factors had changed from the highly repressive period of the 1950s and the 1960s. Possibly it was the intensification of the problems of migrant workers (such as, for instance, the deterioration in the economic condition of the homelands) combined with changes in the political environment – internationally, in the region, and locally – which led to the reinvigoration of their movements. It should be recalled that similar forces in earlier times underlay the emergence of militant action by migrant workers – for instance, in the mineworkers' strike of 1946.

Another feature of this trade-union consciousness, Sitas argued, was that it reflected a unitary consciousness and not, as older theories of migrancy had sometimes claimed, the split ideology of 'men of two worlds'. The men in his sample all had links with the rural areas. One had land and family in Transkei, and had recently built a homestead there. Another, a Zulu royalist, who had a large allotment in KwaZulu which supported two wives and eighteen children, aspired to become a prosperous peasant cultivator. Others were landless people from the homelands, or from European-owned farms in Natal which they had been forced to leave during the drives against rural squatters during the 1960s. Despite these diverse backgrounds, all subscribed to a militant, populist workerism which rested in the last resort on notions of popular justice: 'Our life is not human without justice . . . . But without law everything breaks down and brother kills brother. That is why we get together and we control each other. The union makes the people's law because they make us see the truth.'[70]

Since the 1950s and 1960s, if not earlier, migrant workers living in urban African areas have shown antagonism towards the communities of permanent urban-dwellers in which their hostels were located. There had been a terrible riot in Soweto during the 1950s in which hostel workers attacked people living permanently in Soweto. During the 1976 students' uprising in Soweto, migrant workers living in hostels in the area went on a rampage against students, with fatal consequences. Such activity suggests the importance of the cleavages which have been established and reinforced by the migrant labour system, expressed in this instance in the antagonism of migrants towards relatively privileged groups in urban society: the outsiders' anger turned against the insiders. Sitas's study showed quite markedly how conscious migrant workers were of the easier lives led by those who enjoyed Section 10 rights. According to one of the migrant workers interviewed by Sitas, 'Township workers have been corrupted by rich whites and blacks, by teachers and bad priests. They don't believe in the brotherhood of workers.'[71] Thirdly, some, though not all, of the unions and other worker movements were closely linked to community organisations, and hence had access to a range of political weapons which lay outside those available in the workplace. Thus in a strike called by meat workers in the Cape in 1980, community organisers called for a consumer boycott of red meat. Similarly strikers in two manufacturing companies called for consumer boycotts of the companies' products, sweets in the one case (1980–1) and pasta (1979) in the other. Conversely, workers might strike over community issues. The leader of the Port Elizabeth Civic Organisation (PEBCO), Thozamile Botha, was called to task by the Ford motor company, by whom he was employed, for spending too much time on community affairs. When he resigned, the entire workforce of 700 at one plant walked out in protest. On the other hand the most important federation of trade unions to emerge during the 1970s, the Federation of South African Trade Unions (FOSATU), deliberately set itself against such involvement in community politics.

The development of a powerful workers' movement organised through unions stimulated immense interest among government and the business community in labour issues during the late 1970s. The first step in this direction was to amend the 1953 legislation in order to make it possible for liaison committees to be established. These consisted of nominees of employers and of a group, not less than 50 per cent, of workers elected by the African workforce. The chairman could be appointed by the employer, an arrangement which may explain why they were so popular with management. Within two years of their establishment, there were 1 751 liaison committees in existence round the country. Similarly, works committees were established at a phenomenal rate: from 24 in 1973 to 239 in 1975.

In 1981, the South African parliament passed the Labour Relations Amendment Act. This law accorded African unions rights to negotiate, subject to their registration. It drew widespread criticism from unions, which centred on four matters: the exclusion of farmworkers and domestics from its application; the very wide controls it conferred on the state; its prohibition on unions engaging in political activities; and its prohibition on unions providing support for illegal strikers. Notwithstanding these controls, the legislation provided some space for union activity, of which they took advantage. But it also made for divisions, or potential divisions, between different unions.

The issue of registration created considerable conflict within the union movement. FOSATU opted for registration, despite the powerful arguments made against such a move. FOSATU's role in the new movement departed quite radically from the old SACTU line and from the position adopted in some of the independent unions. It tried to keep out of community issues and indeed any political issues which did not bear directly on labour, and to remain independent from political organisations. It did so mindful of the risks of laying itself open to attack by the state. It also developed and sustained a commitment to shopfloor democracy.

FOSATU's strategy was dictated by the consideration that it could win political as well as narrowly economic advantages for the workforce by making 'critical use' of the state's registration system.[72] In line with this strategy, FOSATU made its acceptance of registration conditional upon the state's accepting its non-racial character.

The Congress of South African Trade Unions (COSATU) was formed in November 1985, adopting a far more overtly political stance than FOSATU, and FOSATU affiliated to it.

The emergence of the new union movement raises the question of the long-term political implications of the South African working-class movement. The answers to this question which have begun to surface range from the argument that African workers demonstrate revolutionary consciousness to the one that the unions are in no position to develop a revolutionary programme.[73] Whichever of these arguments turns out to be true, there is little doubt that black workers achieved considerable political significance during the 1970s. It is likely that this significance will be increased under any successor state. A nice illustration of union opinion of union power in a post-white rule future was given by a shop steward interviewed by Swilling who said: ' . . . we can put Mandela as the Prime Minister . . . but [he] must be controlled by the workers. . . .'[74]

The re-emergence of a union movement with a non-racial membership, based on a strong shopfloor organisation may reinforce tendencies in African political movements, consciousness and organisation, towards the radical non-racialism which had by the 1950s become dominant in the African National Congress. On the other hand, the problems faced by the migrant labour force, locked into the political structures of the homelands and the national states, render them vulnerable to repression and counter-mobilisation. Inkatha established a union on May Day of 1986, the United Workers' Union of South Africa (UWUSA), directly as a rival to COSATU. The general secretary is a prominent businessman and former member of the KwaZulu Legislative Authority. The union does not seem to have a viable shopfloor base. Nevertheless, it might provide a pretext to coerce workers from KwaZulu from joining unions affiliated to COSATU.

The second instance of the re-emergence of an African political presence during the 1970s after more than a decade of quiescence was the student movement, which became visible on the streets of Soweto on 16 June 1976, and which has subsequently scarcely been absent from newspapers and television screens.[75] For all the differences between the student movement and the workers' movement which had reappeared a few years earlier, there were certain common features. Firstly, like the workers' movement, the student movement expressed the revival of opposition to apartheid which had emerged during the 1950s, and which had been crushed after Sharpeville.

The specific issue that had precipitated the earlier rebellion was the introduction of Bantu Education and its imposition on primary, secondary and tertiary institutions. Bantu Education directly expressed the role which the Nationalist government had in mind for Africans in South Africa. They could not expect to enjoy an education which would give them equality with whites. They were to be given an education which fitted them for life in the reserves, on the farms, and in a predominantly migrant, unskilled labour force. Those who secured rights to live in the urban areas could never expect their right to entitle them to live there permanently.

In pursuit of this policy, the government took direct control over existing schools, many of which were run by missionaries, locating its administration in the hands of the Native Affairs Department. A long protest followed. It was organised by a variety of groups, including the ANC and the Congress of Democrats (which operated the African Education Movement), teachers' associations, and parents.

Although the opposition to Bantu Education was widespread, it was difficult to sustain as an effective movement. It generally took two forms, along with sporadic and localised attacks on schools. The first was the boycott; the second was an alternative form of schooling. In fact the struggle against Bantu Education never really entirely ceased, especially in the universities set up in terms of the Extension of University Education Act of 1959, which forced the 'open' universities to close their doors to black students, and under the authority of which new ethnically pure universities were established. The students at these institutions continued throughout the 1960s to express their protests against the conditions they found. Black consciousness found a ready response from students in the homelands universities.

However, this opposition was isolated and fragmented. Part of the reason lay in the simple brutality with which the authorities dealt with campus and classroom disturbances. But another factor that explains the difficulty of generating opposition to apartheid through opposition to the educational system was the mood of hopelessness among Africans who had reached adulthood around the time of Sharpeville, and their despair that they could secure any significant change through political action, and that therefore any hope for change would need to be pursued 'within the system'.

During the 1960s, black parents saw the main hope of upward mobility for their children to lie in the chances they could get of a better job, the most important route to which lay via the educational system. This aspiration provided the basis for passive acquiescence and consent in Bantu Education. One of the questions a sample of workers were asked in a survey conducted by Eddie Webster and Judson Kuzwayo was whether the respondent would like his son or daughter to do his job. More than three quarters of the sample said no. Some 60 per cent of this group (i.e. 45 per cent of the sample) said they wanted their children to have non-manual jobs. Some of them specified one of the professions.[76]

Both for that and other reasons, educated Africans enjoyed tremendous prestige, especially in urban African communities. (A poignant indicator of this prestige was an advertisement for some domestic comestible which used to appear in magazines with a large African circulation. In this ad, a group of African graduates, wearing full academic regalia, would be featured sitting around the dinner table.) Concomitantly, there was during that decade or decade and a half a tremendous expansion in the scale of educational services provided for Africans, both in the homelands and in the urban areas.

This expansion was most noticeable at the primary level and in the homelands, but it was also significant at secondary school levels and in the urban areas. Moreover, there was a significant improvement in the rate of African matriculation although it remained appallingly low by comparison with whites. The number of African children at school increased more than two-and-a-half times over the period 1955–75. Whereas less than 1 per cent of pupils enrolling in primary school in 1958 reached Form V (the matriculation year), nearly 2 per cent of those enrolling five years later did so.[77]

However, in the changed economic circumstances of the early 1970s, it is likely that the perceptions which parents held of the educational system as an escalator which would carry their children out of the working class became less easy to transmit to children. There was a significant change in the prospects facing school-leavers in the conditions of the economic downturn which began during the early 1970s. The generation of black youths who took part in the Soweto uprising were perhaps the most politically aware and most highly educated group to have appeared in Johannesburg's satellite city. But their prospects of getting jobs that were commensurate with their educational qualifications deteriorated quite radically. The significance which their parents had attached to education, and which was one of the instruments for maintaining their acquiescence in 'the system', had withered away.

The revolt was precipitated by the Bantu Education Department's attempt to enforce an edict that Afrikaans was to be used as a medium of instruction in black schools. Twenty-thousand students appeared on the streets of Soweto on 16 June to protest against the edict. A child was killed by a policeman's bullet. The schools were closed, but the revolt spread across the Transvaal, and by August Cape Town's locations were engaged. The edict concerning the use of Afrikaans was withdrawn in July, but this was no longer the only or major issue, and the attacks on schools continued. So did attacks on public libraries. A solemn proceduralism sometimes accompanied the destruction of property. Thus a group of students held a debate to decide whether a particular library building was a place of learning or a piece of white man's property.

Aside from their campaign against apartheid education, students conducted attacks on shebeens, the drinking-holes which stood as symbols of black subjugation through alchohol. ('Less liquor, better education'; 'We want more schools, not beerhalls', were slogans seen by Kane-Berman.) They also became increasingly hostile to the police, not only because of the way the police represented the whole apparatus of repression, but specifically because of the ferocity of the state's counter-offensive. By May 1977, 618 people had died, mostly at the hands of the police. The police conducted raid after raid into the townships. Children of all ages were killed and injured in raids which were horrifying in their casual and indiscriminate character. (It could be argued that official, or possibly vigilante, violence was intentionally indiscriminate in order to terrorise the people.)

The significance of the Soweto uprising, and of the other uprisings which have followed it, did not however lie in the physical confrontation between youths and the police, though these attest to the courage they showed. The uprising was not an unarmed struggle. It was primarily a political campaign organised in and around the schools by pupils who sought to overthrow the system of apartheid. This campaign was organised by the blandly named, but formidable Soweto Students' Representative Council (which soon inspired numerous similar imitators).

Before considering the way in which it worked, and the issues which it raised, it is necessary to touch on the central mechanisms through which the revolt was articulated. The most important one was the collapse of parents' authority over their children and the children's assumption of political authority in the family. The children labelled their parents collaborators and tools of the system. From accepting their parents' pragmatic or apathetic acceptance of the system, the children turned to issuing instructions to their parents concerning strikes, stay-aways and boycotts. In effect, the SSRC acquired cadres of activists posted in every family in Soweto with school-going children.

As early as May 1976, Orlando West Junior School elected a representative committee, and the SSRC was established in July. This committee rapidly asserted its control over a vast area of Soweto's political life. It organised three stay-aways during 1976. Those held in August and September were largely successful, with absenteeism in Johannesburg's black workforce ranging between 60 and 75 per cent. The November stay-away was abortive. The SSRC organised protests against shebeens; against the Administration Board's increases in rents and rates; against Christmas parties, and even against Christmas cards. Above all it kept children out of school: by the end of 1977, some 27 000 pupils had not returned to school. During 1977, it tried to extend its interest beyond these local issues, and in April issued pamphlets demanding the abolition of the homelands, lower transport costs, and higher wages.

The children's revolt and the SSRC had a remarkable effect on Soweto's political organisation. Within a few months new organisations had appeared there: the Committee of Ten; the Black Parents' Association; the Teachers' Action Committee; the Azanian People's Organisation.

Similar organisations were established elsewhere.

Yet as Philip Frankel argues, the episode was a rebellion, not a revolution, and there were serious limitations inherent in the attempt to mobilise mass action among people without rights against the might of the state's repressive armoury. However, as he points out, even in this respect, the uprising was important, for it finally put paid to the idea that significant changes could be brought about through such mass action. Instead, attention turned to more 'subversive and specialised modes of political struggle'.[78]

It is easier to describe than to explain the phenomenon. As with other developments during the early-to-middle 1970s, the successes of the anti-colonial struggles in the adjacent territories of the country had a demonstration effect on the black people of South Africa. The fact that the efforts of black South Africans to hasten the process by directly confronting the power of the state was premature was a measure of the vastly more difficult obstacles which faced the struggle in the country, and not of the absence of a revolutionary mood. On the other hand, the tradition of open mass political action gained force with the establishment of the United Democratic Front in early 1983. The UDF was a broad popular front for the large variety of associations which sprang into existence after the banning of the black consciousness movements. At its inception the UDF had 85 affiliated associations; a year later they had increased to 500. The movement did not have strong links with the unions. Its largest group of constituents consisted of student and youth movements, and civic, women's and political movements. Its ideas are correspondingly diffuse.[79] The emergence of the UDF undoubtedly signified the transformation of black politics that followed the revolt of 1976. But it is not clear how its emergence will have affected politics in South Africa.

By the mid-1970s, after the collapse of the Portuguese colonial empire, armed struggle had become a much more likely possibility than it had at the beginning of the decade. As decolonisation on South Africa's periphery proceeded, and the rhythm of resistance in the country intensified, the internal oppposition increasingly embraced the idea of armed liberation as a feasible strategy.

The difficulties confronting the organisation of political opposition to apartheid within the country threw the onus of organising the liberation struggle, including armed struggle, squarely onto the shoulders of the liberation movements, particularly those abroad, and specifically the African National Congress. But one of the most important questions which need to be addressed does not concern the military capacity of the ANC, or even its power to mobilise political support and alliances. In both these areas, the ANC has exhibited a considerable though not limitless capacity. Rather, the central problem lies in how the ANC, either singly or in the variety of alliances which it might conceivably enter in attempting to take power, will cope with the issues that have been raised in the decade since about 1976.

The political consequences of the reforms introduced by the state since the late 1970s, and the two movements which have expressed the reinvigoration of black politics – the labour movement and the student movement – all raise questions about the political stategies which could become available to any successor regime, or indeed to any alternative government to the present one.

Manifest contradictions emerged between the union movement on the one hand, and movements, like the student movement and its successors, which strengthened the privileges, intentionally or not, of urban Africans. Such developments reinforced the cleavages between groups that were the social and political representatives of the two major elements in African society – the migrant labour force (and behind it the most repressed element of the homelands and the national states), and the young relatively well-educated urbanites who became major targets of reformist strategies. These contradictions are unlikely to prevent the collapse of the present regime, but they almost certainly pose very serious problems to any that is likely to follow.

The ANC has reiterated the principle inscribed in the Freedom Charter that 'The People Shall Govern'. In doing so, it has raised expectations that an ANC government would introduce some form of majority rule. But the social bases and political direction of the two movements which were reviewed earlier, as well as the reformist strategy which the government has developed, all suggest that it is highly likely that the movements will reinforce the deep conflicts and contradictions in South Africa. There is an historic irony in this situation, for such contradictions existed within the ANC for most of its history as an open organisation.

Before pursuing the matter, it is worth recalling that during the 1950s the state was challenged on two fronts – labour and education – and responded by crushing its opponents. The 1970s saw the renewal of those challenges. Now whatever the outcome of the conflicts, it is fairly certain that oppositional forces are much stronger than their precursors a quarter of a century earlier.

There was, however, a third site of struggle during the 1950s – the countryside. Although there have been rumblings and stirrings there too during the 1970s, the question needs to be asked what possibilities exist for rural revolution, and what its instruments might be. A plausible answer might be that the weapon of rural revolt is armed struggle, which might assume a variety of forms. The armed struggle carried on by the ANC might hold out the hope or the expectation among a half-starved peasantry that their pressing need for land will be met by a future Congress government.

But there are several other possible forms of 'armed struggle', which include vigilante terror and local feuding over land and cattle, as well as the coercion exercised via political movements such as Inkatha. These possibilities raise the question of further conflicts and contradictions among the array of interests in the countryside that will arise to welcome a government based on majority rule. The migrant workforce is in some sense the alter ego of the proletarianised peasantry, and part of the union movement might find its way to aligning itself with other groups in the homelands and national states. But it is improbable that Africans living permanently in the cities are likely to do so.

It is possible that efforts to democratise politics in South Africa could reinforce such cleavages as these, and even introduce others, as new expectations emerged and perhaps old ones resurfaced. To a very considerable degree, these cleavages were created under the policy of apartheid. But it would be over-optimistic to imagine these cleavages disappearing, even with the demise of apartheid under a system of majority rule. Southall's study of class formation in Transkei, which was summarised in Chapter 8, provided telling evidence of the emergence of a group whose privileges would not disappear except, perhaps, under the impact of a regime as ruthlessly egalitarian as, say, Khmer Rouge in Cambodia during the 1970s. There is little to suggest that there might emerge a comparable phenomenon in South Africa.

It was more likely that the divisions between urban 'insiders' and rural 'outsiders', between skilled and unskilled workers, and between the well-educated and the poorly educated, would contribute to creating and reinforcing political divisions within black society even after an African leadership had taken power. It was also probable that the longer the moment of its accession to power was delayed, the more difficult it would be for that leadership to reverse the process. Since 1978, and perhaps even earlier, the major strategy underlying state reform had the effect of increasing class divisions in African society. This was achieved not simply by a Verwoerdian strategy of divide and rule based on apartheid (though the maintenance of apartheid institutions despite their oft-advertised impending demise has reinforced such cleavages).

Perhaps more significant in the long run, these divisions were also reinforced by the very reforms introduced by the government, including the policy of privatisation, which would remove from state control potential levers for a future policy aimed at securing greater equality between different groups of blacks.

In the minds of many whites, fear of revolution converged with the fear of black majority rule. In their opinion, the accession of such a political organisation as the ANC was to be resisted because it inevitably would bring about a system of black majority rule. This argument rested on a crude and unreflecting theory of racial determinacy in politics. The possibility of a democratic political order in which white and black class, cultural, regional, occupational and sectoral interests might emerge to modify a simple racial polarisation was largely excluded from view. One significant feature of the argument was its ahistorical character. It was formulated long before the ANC decided to engage in armed struggle. Indeed, it shaped the predilection of South African governments for using coercion rather than negotiation in dealing with blacks, a predilection that contributed in major part to the escalation in conflicts which preceded the banning of the ANC and the PAC.

The argument ignored the strength, both actual and potential, of class conflicts to fracture the unity of present and future political formations among Africans. The discussion of the homelands and national states in Chapter 8 suggested that many Africans and other blacks have acquired a stake in racial and tribal definitions of nationality. While they might be persuaded or coerced to trade these for a political identity which discriminated against whites, it is difficult to envisage a reconstruction that eliminated the extremely sharp cleavages which have developed around class, region and education.

Given the carefully constructed strategies intended to defend a modified version of the status quo, the problem which a revolutionary or radical reformist movement would have to face is not solely bound up with the fact that the present regime presents formidable difficulties to any project to capture state power. Even if this extraordinarily difficult prospect were to be accomplished, a range of fundamental problems would remain in order to bring about a new political regime that was not a complex form of neo-colonialism. It is that set of issues which need urgently to be addressed.

References

1 H. Adam, *Modernizing Racial Domination* (Berkeley, California, 1971), Chapter 3.

2 The following works represent some of the efforts to specify the relations between the state and dominant class interests: B. Bozzoli, *The Political Nature of a Ruling Class*; S. Clarke, 'Capital, fractions of capital and the state: neo-Marxist analyses of South Africa', *Capital and Class*, 5, Summer 1978; S. Greenberg, *Race and State in Capitalist Development*; F. A. Johnstone, *Class, Race and Gold*; D. O'Meara, *Volkskapitalisme: Class, Capital and Ideology in the Development of Afrikaner Nationalism, 1934–1948.*

3 D. Yudelman, *The Emergence of Modern South Africa* (Westport, 1983 and Cape Town, 1984).

4 T. Karis, 'United States policy', in G. Carter and P. O'Meara (eds), *Southern Africa: The Continuing Crisis* (London, 1979), pp. 314–15.

5 S. Trapido, 'South Africa in a comparative study of industrialisation', *Journal of Development Studies*, 3, 1971. Trapido's paper adapted Barrington Moore's study to the South African case. Cf. Barrington Moore, *The Social Origins of Dictatorship and Democracy* (London, 1966).

6 The most influential application of Rostow's theory to South Africa was M. C. O'Dowd's paper, 'The stages of economic growth and the future of South Africa', in L. Schlemmer and E. Webster (eds), *Change, Reform and Growth in South Africa* (Johannesburg, 1978).

7 J. A. Lombard, *The Role of Mining in the South African Economy* (Pretoria, 1980).

8 Trapido, 'South Africa in a comparative study of industrialisation'.

9 C. Bundy, *The Rise and Fall of the South African Peasantry* (London, 1979).

10 S. Marks and S. Trapido, 'Lord Milner and the South African state', in P. Bonner (ed), *Working Papers in Southern African Studies*, vol. 2 (Johannesburg, 1981).

11 C. van Onselen, 'The Main Reef Road into the working class; proletarianisation, unemployment and class consciousness amongst Johannesburg's Afrikaner poor, 1890-1914', in his *Studies in the Social and Economic History of the Witwatersrand, 1886-1914*, vol. 2, *New Nineveh* (Johannesburg, 1982).

12 B. A. Cox and C. M. Rogerson, 'The corporate power elite in South

Africa', *Political Geography Quarterly*, 4, 3 (July 1985), 219–34.

13   M. Morris, 'The development of capitalism in South African agriculture: class struggle in the countryside', *Economy and Society*, 3, 3 (1976).

14   H. Bradford, 'Lynch law and labourers: the ICU in Umvoti, 1927-1928', unpublished paper presented to the African Studies Institute, University of the Witwatersrand, n.d.

15   D. O'Meara, *Volkskapitalisme: Class, Capital and Ideology in the Development of Afrikaner Nationalism, 1934–1948*, (Johannesburg, 1983), especially Chapter 13.

16   Trapido, 'South Africa in a comparative study of industrialisation'.

17   The statistics in this section are mostly taken from D. Hindson, *The Pass System and the Formation of an Urban African Proletariat in South Africa: A Critique of the Cheap Labour-Power Thesis*, D.Phil. thesis, University of Sussex, 1983.

18   A. W. Stadler, 'The 1974 general election in South Africa', *African Affairs*, 74, 295 (April 1975).

19   P. B. Rich, 'Administrative ideology, urban social control and the origins of apartheid theory', *Journal of African Studies*, 7, 2, (1980). The most systematic study of influx controls is D. C. Hindson, *The Pass System and the Formation of an Urban African Proletariat in South Africa: A Critique of the Cheap Labour-Power Thesis*, D.Phil. thesis, University of Sussex, 1983.

20   Hindson, *The Pass System, passim.*

21   C. Coker, 'Retreat into the future: the United States, South Africa, and human rights, 1976–8', *Journal of Modern African Studies*, 18, 3 (1980), 509–24.

22   J. Dugard, 'South Africa's "independent" homelands: an exercise in denationalisation', *Denver Journal of International Law and Policy*, 10, 1 (1980), 11–36.

23   Hindson, *The Pass System*, p. 307.

24   Cf. A. W. Stadler, 'Birds in the cornfield: squatter movements in Johannesburg, 1944–1947', *Journal of Southern African Studies*, 6, 1 (October 1979).

25   T. Lodge, *Black Politics in South Africa since 1945* (London, 1983), p. 35.

26   R. Monama, *Is This Justice? A Study of the Johannesburg Commissioners' ('Pass') Courts*, Centre of Applied Legal Studies occasional papers', 4, Witwatersrand, 1983, appendix A.

27   H. Wolpe, 'Capitalism and cheap labour power: from segregation to apartheid', *Economy and Society*, 6, 4 (1972).

28   U.G. 40–1934, Department of Health *Report*, p. 83.

29   J. Kane-Berman, 'Fiscal Apartheid', in A. W. Stadler (ed), *The Creation and Distribution of Wealth*, The 1984 Senate Special Lectures, University of the Witwatersrand (Johannesburg, 1985).

30   S.C. 10–1982, Report of the Select Committee on the Constitution, p. 10.

31   See S. Becker and R. Humphries, *From Control to Confusion: The Changing Role of Administration Boards in South Africa, 1971–1983*, (Pietermaritzburg and Grahamstown, 1985.)

32   J. Keenan, 'The effect of the 1978–1982 industrial cycle on Soweto houshold incomes and poverty levels', in E. A. Kraayenbrink (ed), *Studies on Urbanisation in South Africa* (Johannesburg, 1984).

33   Cf. C. van Onselen, 'The Main Reef Road into the working class', pp. 111–21.

34   C. Saunders, 'The creation of Ndabeni: urban segregation, social control and African resistance', History workshop, Witwatersrand University, 1978.

35   Johannesburg Public Health and Native Affairs Departments, *Report of the Commission of Inquiry*, 1935.

36   S. Bhana and B. Pachai (eds), *A Documentary History of Indian South Africans* (Cape Town, 1984), pp. 214–21.

37   The account which follows is based on Lodge, *Black Politics in South Africa since 1945*, Chapter 4.

38   Cf. A. W. Stadler, 'A long way to walk: bus boycotts in Alexandra, 1940–1945', in P. Bonner (ed), *Working Papers in Southern African Studies*, vol. 2 (Johannesburg, 1981); A. W. Stadler, 'The politics of subsistence: community struggles in wartime Johannesburg', in D. Hindson (ed), *Working Papers in Southern African Studies*, vol. 3 (Johannesburg, 1983); and T. Lodge, '"We are being punished because we are poor": the bus boycotts of Evaton and Alexandra, 1955–1957', in his *Black Politics in South Africa since 1945*, Chapter 7.

39   See, for instance, S. Marks, *Reluctant Rebellion: The 1906–1908 Disturbances in Natal* (Oxford, 1970), p. 41.

40   Cf. W. D. Hammond-Tooke, *Command or Consensus: The Development of Transkeian Local Government* (Cape Town, 1975), for a detailed exposition of these processes.

41   This account is largely drawn from Miriam Roth's paper, 'Domination by consent: elections under the Representation of Natives Act, 1937–1948', presented to the African Studies Seminar, University of the Witwatersrand, August 1983.

42   Fortunately there is a 211-page summary, U.G. 61–1955, *Summary of the Report of the Commission for the Socio-Economic Development of the Bantu Areas within the Union of South Africa*.

43   D. A. Kotze, *African Politics in South Africa, 1964–1974* (London, 1975), p. 129.

44   R. Southall, *South Africa's Transkei: The Political Economy of an 'Independent' Bantustan* (London, 1982), p. 4.

45   Cited in Lodge, *Black Politics in South Africa*, p. 278.

46   Kotze, *African Politics*, p. 194.

47   This account is taken from R. Southall, 'Buthelezi, Inkatha and the politics of compromise', *African Affairs*, 80 (1981), 443–81.

48   S. Marks, *The Ambiguities of Dependence in South Africa: Class, Nationalism, and the State in Twentieth-Century Natal* (Johannesburg, 1986), pp. 111–14.

49   T. Lodge, *Insurrectionism in South Africa: The Pan-Africanist Congress and the Poqo Movement, 1959–1965*, D.Phil. thesis, University of York, 1984, p. 2. More generally, see Lodge's *Black Politics in South Africa since 1945*.

50   Lodge, *Insurrectionism in South Africa*, p. 110.

51   *Ibid.*, p. 24.

52   D. O'Meara, 'The 1946 African mineworkers' strike in the political economy of South Africa', *Journal of Commonwealth and Comparative Politics*, 13, 2 (July 1976), 146-73.

53   Lodge, *Black Politics in South Africa*, p. 21.

54   Lodge, *Insurrectionism in South Africa*, p. 52.

55   Lodge, *Black Politics in South Africa*, p. 69.

56   *Ibid.*, p. 70.

57   *Ibid.*, p. 247. The following account is based on *ibid.*, pp 246–55.

58   P. Randall, *A Taste of Power* (Johannesburg, 1973), p. 6.

59   L. Schlemmer, 'Strategies for change', in P. Randall (ed), *Towards Social Change* (Johannesburg, 1971), p. 161.

60   Cf. A. W. Stadler, 'Anxious radicals: Spro-cas and the apartheid society', *Journal of Southern African Studies*, 2, 1 (October 1975).

61   They are listed in Schedule 2 of the Regional Services Council Act, 109 of 1985.

62   This discussion is based mainly on recommendations 11–18 of the Joint Report of the Committee for Economic Affairs and the Constitutional Committee of the President's Council on Local and Regional Management Systems in the Republic of South Africa, PC 2/1982, pp. 128–9, and the legislation introduced subsequent to its report.

63   I am indebted to Mark Swilling for a discussion on this point. The more general analysis of black consciousness is derived from S. Nolutshungu, *Changing South Africa* (Manchester, 1982, and Cape Town, 1983), Part III.

64   Cf. N. C. Manganyi, *Being-Black-in-the-World* (Johannesburg, 1973).

65   Nolutshungu, *Changing South Africa*, p. 179.

66   Cf E. Webster, 'Organisational trends, achievements and potential of the labour movement in the post-Wiehahn period'. I was unable to see the published version of this paper in Werner Pushkra (ed), *Black Trade Unions in South Africa: The Core of a Democratic Opposition?* (Bonn, 1986).

67   A. Sitas, *African Worker Responses on the East Rand to Changes in the Metal Industry, 1960–1980*, Ph.D. thesis, University of the Witwatersrand, 1983, p. 414.

68   *Ibid.*, p. 415.

69   J. Keenan, 'Migrants awake – the 1980 Johannesburg municipality

strike', *South African Labour Bulletin*, 6, 7 (May 1981), 11.

70   Sitas, *African Worker Responses*, p. 434.

71   *Ibid.*, p. 413

72   R. Fine, F. de Clerq and D. Innes, 'Trade unions and the state: the question of legality', *South African Labour Bulletin*, 7 (1981), 39–68.

73   The various positions are set out in Roger Southall's review article: 'South African labour studies', *South African Labour Bulletin*, 9, (1984), 88–114.

74   M. Swilling, *The Politics of Working Class Strategies in Germiston*, Honours dissertation, University of the Witwatersrand, 1983, p. 149.

75   There is a large literature on the Soweto revolt. I have relied mainly on three sources: J. Kane-Berman, *Soweto: Black Revolt, White Reaction* (Johannesburg, 1978); P. Frankel, 'The dynamics of a political renaissance: the Soweto Students' Representative Council', *Journal of African Studies*, 7, 3 (1980), 167–79; and B. Hirson, *Year of Fire, Year of Ash* (London, 1979).

76   E. Webster and J. Kuzwayo, 'A research note on consciousness and the problem of organisation', in L. Schlemmer and E. Webster (eds), *Change, Reform and Growth in South Africa* (Johannesburg, 1978), p. 226.

77   These figures are cited in Kane-Berman, *Soweto*, p. 186.

78   Frankel, 'Dynamics of a political renaissance', pp. 173–9.

79   Cf. M. Swilling and T. Lodge, 'From protest to people's power: the United Democratic Front and the revolt in the townships' (forthcoming).

Bibliography

Official papers
Native Land, U.G. 19-1916, 22-1916, 25-1916 (Beaumont)
Local Government, T.P. 1-1922 (Stallard)
Pass Laws, 1920, Ann. 104-1923 (Godley Committee)
Native Economic Commission, U.G. 22-1932 (Holloway)
Johannesburg Public Health and Native Affairs Departments, 1935 (Murray and Thornton)
Native Laws, U.G. 28-1948 (Fagan)
Socio-Economic Development of the Bantu Areas, U.G. 61-1955 (Tomlinson)
Agriculture, R.P. 61-1968, R.P. 84-1970 (Marais), R.P. 19-1972 (Du Plessis)
Legislation Affecting the Utilisation of Manpower, R.P. 32-1976 (Riekert)
Labour Legislation, R.P. 47-1979 (Wiehahn)
Legislation Concerning Black Community Development (Grosskopf Committee, 1982)
Select Committee on the Constitution, S.C. 10-1982
Joint Report of the Committee for Economic Affairs and the Constitutional Committee . . . on Local and Regional Management Systems, P.C. 2-1982

Secondary sources
Adam, H. *Modernizing Racial Domination.* Berkeley, 1971
Bekker, S. and R. Humphries. *From Control to Confusion: The Changing Role of Administration Boards in South Africa, 1971–1983.* Pietermaritzburg and Grahamstown, 1985
Bhana, S. and B. Pachai (eds). *A Documentary History of Indian South Africans.* Cape Town, 1984
Bonner, P. (ed). *Working Papers in Southern African Studies,* vol. 2. Johannesburg, 1981
Bozzoli, B. *The Political Nature of a Ruling Class: Capital and Ideology in South Africa, 1890-1930.* Boston, 1980
Bundy, C. *The Rise and Fall of the South African Peasantry.* London, 1979
Carter, G. and P. O'Meara (eds). *Southern Africa: The Continuing Crisis.* London, 1979

Clarke, S. 'Capital, fractions of capital and the state: neo-Marxist analyses of South Africa', *Capital and Class*, 5 (1978), 32-77

Coker, C. 'Retreat into the future: the United States, South Africa, and human rights, 1976-8', *Journal of Modern African Studies*, 18, 3 (1980), 509-24

Cox, B. A. and C. M. Rogerson. 'The corporate power elite in South Africa', *Political Geography Quarterly*, 4, 3 (1985), 219-34

Dugard, J. R. 'South Africa's "independent" homelands: an exercise in denationalisation', *Denver Journal of International Law and Policy*, 10, 1 (1980), 11-36

Fine, R., F. de Clerq and D. Innes. 'Trade unions and the state: the question of legality', *South African Labour Bulletin*, 7 (1981), 39-68

Frankel, P. F. 'The dynamics of a political renaissance: the Soweto Students' Representative Council', *Journal of African Studies*, 7, 3 (1980), 167-79

Greenberg, S. *Race and State in Capitalist Development.* Johannesburg, 1980

Hirson, B. *Year of Fire, Year of Ash.* London, 1979

Hammond-Tooke, W. D. *Command or Consensus: The Development of Transkeian Local Government.* Cape Town, 1975

Hindson, D. (ed). *Working Papers in Southern African Studies.* Johannesburg, 1983

Johnstone, F. A. *Class, Race and Gold.* London, 1976

Kane-Berman, J. *Soweto: Black Revolt, White Reaction.* Johannesburg, 1978

Keenan, J. 'Migrants awake – the 1980 Johannesburg municipality strike', *South African Labour Bulletin*, 6, 7 (1981), 4-60

Kotze, D. A. *African Politics in South Africa, 1964-1974.* London, 1975

Kraayenbrink, E. A. (ed). *Studies on Urbanisation in South Africa.* Johannesburg, 1984

Lodge, T. *Black Politics in South Africa since 1945.* London, 1983

Lombard, J. A. *The Role of Mining in the South African Economy.* Pretoria, 1980

Manganyi, N. C. *Being-Black-in-the-World.* Johannesburg, 1973

Marks, S. *The Ambiguities of Dependence in South Africa: Class, Nationalism, and the State in Twentieth-Century Natal.* Johannesburg, 1986

Marks, S. *Reluctant Rebellion: The 1906-1908 Disturbances in Natal.* Oxford, 1970

Monama, R. *Is This Justice? A Study of the Johannesburg Commissioners' ('Pass') Courts.* Centre of Applied Legal Studies occasional papers, 4, Witwatersrand, 1983

Morris, M. 'The development of capitalism in South African agriculture: class struggle in the countryside', *Economy and Society*, 3, 3 (1976) 292-343

Nolutshungu, S. *Changing South Africa.* Manchester, 1982, and Cape Town, 1983

O'Meara, D. 'The 1946 African mineworkers' strike in the political economy of South Africa', *Journal of Commonwealth and Comparative Politics*, 13, 2 (1976), 146-73

O'Meara, D. *Volkskapitalisme: Class, Capital and Ideology in the Development of Afrikaner Nationalism, 1934-1948.* Johannesburg, 1983

Plaatje, S. T. *Native Life in South Africa.* London, 1916

Randall, P. *A Taste of Power.* Johannesburg, 1973

Randall, P. *Towards Social Change.* Johannesburg, 1971

Rich, P. B. 'Administrative ideology, urban social control and the origins of apartheid theory', *Journal of African Studies*, 7, 2 (1980), 70-82

Schlemmer, L. and E. Webster (eds). *Change, Reform and Growth in South Africa.* Johannesburg, 1978

Southall, R. 'Buthelezi, Inkatha and the politics of compromise', *African Affairs*, 80 (1981), 443-81

Southall, R. *South Africa's Transkei: The Political Economy of an 'Independent' Bantustan.* London, 1982

Southall, R. 'Review Article: South African labour studies', *South African Labour Bulletin*, 9 (1984), 88-114

Stadler, A. W. 'Anxious radicals: Spro-cas and the apartheid society', *Journal of Southern African Studies*, 2, 1 (1975), 102-108

Stadler, A. W. 'Birds in the cornfield: squatter movements in Johannesburg, 1944-1947', *Journal of Southern African Studies*, 6, 1 (1979), 93-123

Stadler, A. W. (ed). *The Creation and Distribution of Wealth.* The 1984 Senate Special Lectures, University of the Witwatersrand, Johannesburg, 1985

Stadler, A. W. 'The 1974 general election in South Africa', *African Affairs*, 74 (1974), 209-18

Trapido, S. 'South Africa in a comparative study of industrialisation', *Journal of Development Studies*, 3 (1971), 311-20

Van Onselen, C. *Studies in the Social and Economic History of the Witwatersrand, 1886-1914*, 2 vols. Johannesburg, 1982

Wolpe, H. 'Capitalism and cheap labour power: from segregation to apartheid', *Economy and Society*, 6, 4 (1972)

Yudelman, D. *The Emergence of Modern South Africa.* Westport, 1983 and Cape Town, 1984

Unpublished papers and theses

Bradford, H. 'Lynch law and labourers: the ICU in Umvoti, 1927-1928', African Studies Institute, University of the Witwatersrand, n.d.

Hindson, D. *The Pass System and the Formation of an Urban African Proletariat in South Africa: A Critique of the Cheap Labour-Power Thesis.* D. Phil. thesis, University of Sussex, 1983 (publication forthcoming)

Lodge, T. *Insurrectionism in South Africa: The Pan-Africanist Congress and the Poqo Movement, 1959-1965.* D.Phil. thesis, University of York, 1984

Roth, M. 'Domination by consent: elections under the Representation of

Natives Act, 1937-1948'. African Studies Institute, University of the Witwatersrand, 1983

Saunders, C. 'The creation of Ndabeni: urban segregation, social control and African resistance', History Workshop, University of the Witwatersrand, 1978

Sitas, A. *African Worker Responses on the East Rand to Changes in the Metal Industry, 1960-1980*. Ph.D. thesis, University of the Witwatersrand, 1983

Swilling, M. and T. Lodge. 'From protest to people's power: the United Democratic Front and the revolt in the townships' (forthcoming)

Swilling, M. *The Politics of Working Class Strategies in Germiston*. B.A. Hons dissertation, University of the Witwatersrand, 1983

Webster, E. 'Organisational trends, achievements and potential of the labour movement in the post-Wiehahn period' (publication forthcoming)

Index

De la Rey, General J. H., 69, 71
Democratic Party (Transkei), 133, 136
Diederichs, Dr Nico, 85
District Six (Cape Town), 61, 119
Dominion Party, 73, 74
Dube, J. L., 143
Durban, 49, 50, 68, 118, 120, 121, 173
East London, 49
East Rand, 174
English-speaking South Africans, 65, 77
Extension of University Education Act (1959), 178
Fagan Commission (1946–8), 91, 92, 93, 94, 97, 99, 100
farmworkers, 55, 56, 57, 60
Farrar, Sir George, 44, 70
Federasie van Afrikaanse Kultuurvereniginge (FAK), 49
Federation of South African Trade Unions (FOSATU), 176, 177
Fingo Village (Grahamstown), 118
First World War, 52, 55, 57, 58, 77, 86, 87, 88, 119, 122, 143
FitzPatrick, Sir Percy, 44
Ford Motor Company, 176
Fordsburg (Johannesburg), 119, 120, 122
Fourie, Jopie, 71
Freedom Charter (1955), 17, 18, 121, 149, 152, 153, 182
Frelimo, 172
Garvey, Marcus, 145
Gesuiwerde Nasionale Party, 73
Glen Grey Act (1894), 39, 41, 42, 87, 129
Godley Committee (1920–3), 90, 91, 92, 99, 100
Good Hope Conference, 166
Goodwill, King, 136, 137
Great Depression, 52, 110
Grosskopf Committee (1980–1), 96, 97, 100
Group Areas, 75, 77, 78
Group Areas Act (1950), 4, 120, 121, 122, 123, 124
Gumede, Josiah, 132, 145
Havenga, N. C., 74
Helpmekaar movement, 58
Herstigte Nasionale Party (HNP), 81
Hertzog, Dr Albert, 81
Hertzog, General J. B. M., 69, 71, 72, 73, 74, 145
Het Volk, 69, 70
High Court of Parliament Act (1951), 75
Hitler, Adolf, 73
Hofmeyr, J. H., 73
Hofmeyr, J. H. ('Onze Jan'), 67
Home Rule Party, 73

Human Sciences Research Council, 166, 167
Ikongo movement, 135
Immorality Act (1950), 118
inboek system, 37
Industrial and Commercial Workers' Union (ICU), 143, 144, 145, 151
Industrial Conciliation Act (1924), 48
influenza epidemic (1918), 109
influx controls, 87, 88, 90–100, 107, 113, 141, 151, 158
Inkatha, 136, 137, 177, 182
Intaba, 135
Internal Security Act (1976), 2
International Court of Justice, 19
Iron and Steel Corporation (Iscor), 77
Jabavu, D. D. T., 144
Jameson, Dr L. S., 42, 43, 44, 68
Jameson Raid, 68, 69
Johannesburg, 46, 48, 49, 50, 61, 104, 106, 107, 116, 119, 121, 123, 124, 125, 126
Joint Council movement, 144, 145, 164, 165
Kadalie, Clements, 144, 145
Kenya, 18
Khoi, 37
Kissinger, Dr Henry, 28, 29
Kruger, President Paul, 43, 69, 118
KwaZulu, 136, 137, 175, 177
Labour Party, 45, 48, 72, 76
Labour Relations Amendment Act (1981), 176
labour tenancy, 53, 54, 55, 63
Langa (Cape Town), 152, 155
Lembede, Anton, 149
Lesotho, 14, 23, 37, 40
Lewis, Ethelreda, 145
liaison committees, 176
Liberal Party, 12, 77, 79, 126, 127, 150, 152, 157, 171
Liberal Party (Britain), 44
liquor, 104, 105, 106, 107, 113, 114
local authorities, 102, 103, 104, 105, 106, 112, 113, 114, 115
Mabude, Saul, 135
mahau, 104, 105, 151
Malan, Dr D. F., 72, 74
Malawi, 23, 40, 144
Malay Quarter (Cape Town), 118, 119
Mandela, Nelson, 150, 151, 156, 157, 159, 177
Mangope, Lucas, 134, 136
Maputo, 84
Maseloane, Chief H., 136
Matanzima, George, 136, 138, 139
Matanzima, Kaiser, 134, 135, 136, 138, 139